MAKE AMAZING GAMES
IN MINUTES

MAKE AMAZING GAMES
IN MINUTES

JASON DARBY

CHARLES RIVER MEDIA, INC.
Hingham, Massachusetts

Publisher: David Pallai
Cover Design: The Printed Image

CHARLES RIVER MEDIA, INC.
10 Downer Avenue
Hingham, Massachusetts 02043
781-740-0400
781-740-8816 (FAX)
info@charlesriver.com
www.charlesriver.com

This book is printed on acid-free paper.

Jason Darby.
Make Amazing Games in Minutes.
ISBN: 1-58450-407-2

Library of Congress Cataloging-in-Publication Data
Darby, Jason, 1972-
  Make amazing games in minutes / Jason Darby.
      p. cm.
  Includes index.
  ISBN 1-58450-407-2 (alk. paper)
  1.   Computer games–Design–Amateurs' manuals. 2.   Computer games–Programming–Amateurs' manuals. 3. Computer graphics. I. Title.
  QA76.76.C672D35 2005
  794.8'1536--dc22
                           2005022085

Printed in the United States of America
05 7 6 5 4 3 2 First Edition

CHARLES RIVER MEDIA titles are available for site license or bulk purchase by institutions, user groups, corporations, etc. For additional information, please contact the Special Sales Department at 781-740-0400.

To my wife Alicia and children Jared, Kimberley, and Lucas,
the most understanding and wonderful family anyone can have.

Contents

Acknowledgments

I would like to thank a number of people who helped me write this book and make it interesting for you, the reader. First, my wife Alicia, for being very understanding of all the time I've spent on my computer over the years, and for doing the initial review of this text to make it as accurate as possible.

Many thanks must go to David Pallai, President and Founder of Charles River Media, who was so positive about the project, provided a great deal of support, and gave me the chance to write this book.

To my good friends Jeff Vance, DT Holder, and Rhon Schlick from Clickteam who gave advice and encouragement along the way.

Christian Burfelt, who has always been a great help with any project I've chosen to do. He has always been there to help, and his graphics work for some of the games included on the CD-ROM accompanying this book are first class. Thanks! A big "thank you" also goes out to Raymond Emonnot, who came to my rescue at the last minute to provide some advanced game concepts for the book and CD-ROM.

I also want to thank Francois Lionet and Yves Lamoureux, the creators of The Games Factory 2 (and many other games-making programs over the years), who have made such great products that allow me and thousands of like-minded others to enjoy games creation. Their constant help and advice helped this book become what it is.

Finally, to my beautiful children, Jared, Kimberley, and Lucas, who are wonderful, and provided me the inspiration I needed to write this book.

Foreword

I first met Jason Darby at the very first Clickteam convention in England in 2001. I knew him previously from discussions on the Clickteam support and chat forums, and always found him very capable. At the 2001 convention, he spoke about "What not to do when trying to publish a game," and was hilarious. With a wicked sense of humor, he described step by step all the things he had done to create a game and sell it, and at each step, described what he did wrong... and it did go wrong, because he found himself at the end with a few hundred CD-ROMs he couldn't sell.

So, believe me when say that he is the perfect author for this type of book: he has the creativity, the talent, and most of all, the experience. Follow his explanations, and in no time, you will have created your very first computer game. Then, you'll be able to create original games with your own ideas. Who knows, this book may be the beginning of a lifetime passion for game making!

—*Francois Lionet*

Introduction

Welcome to *Make Amazing Games in Minutes*, a book aimed at anyone who wants to make games. This book will show you the latest tools available on the market today, how to create your game from inception to completion, and what you might want to do with your game once you've finished writing it.

AUDIENCE

So, who are you, and who should you be? First, let's assume that you either purchased this book or are reading it in the bookstore because you're interested in making or designing games.

Perhaps you've been dreaming of creating your own games, or never found the right tools to do so. You may even be looking for a career in the games industry, or thinking of doing a games design course at a college or university. Perhaps you want to make and sell your own budget games to a publisher, or sell them yourself on an e-commerce Web site. You may even be a teacher or educator looking at running a games class at school. If any of the aforementioned are true, you're reading the right book.

AIM OF THE BOOK

This book takes you from your original idea to the final stage of writing, testing, and distributing your game.

Some of the topics covered in this book include:

■ Thinking about your ideas and developing them further

■ Learning about programming terms and concepts

■ Storyboarding your game idea

■ Installation and use of The Games Factory 2, the latest game creation program on the market

■ Paper testing your idea before committing to the work involved

■ Learning how to write pseudocode to make your programming easier

■ How and where to gather your resources for the project

■ Quality testing and making sure your games work

■ Making a number of game ideas, from simple bat and ball games to side-scrolling shoot-'em-ups

■ More advanced games

■ How to sell your own games

■ Retro game making

■ Creating an installation program so you can distribute your programs to friends, family, and potential buyers

We've tried to include everything we feel would be useful to anyone wanting to make his or her own games from beginning to end.

Use this book and the concepts in it as a starting point for making your games. You may not be comfortable with some of the things presented here, which is fine. This book is intended to be a guide to methods you should at least look at when making a game, so choose the bits you feel are necessary and amend them to your way of working.

This book does not:

■ Teach complex programming languages such as C++, C#, or Java, and isn't meant to. This book is aimed at those who want to make games easily without having to learn those more complex languages. If you are interested in C++, consider *C++ Programming Fundamentals* by Chuck Easttom.

■ Teach you how to be a graphic artist or music creator. We refer you to *3D GraphicsTutorial Collection* by Shamms Mortier.

■ Show you how to become an indie developer or build a team (if you want more information on being an indie developer, read *The Indie Game Development Survival Guide* by David Michael).

■ Assume you are an expert at game creation. This book is aimed at those with little or no knowledge of game creation, and those who might have an idea of how things are put together but need more information.

CHAPTER OVERVIEW

This book runs in a simple yet effective order to allow you to get the most out of reading it. It is possible to skip certain chapters, but it is recommended to read every chapter in order.

Chapter 1—Game, Games, and More Games: Why make games? Seems like a simple question, but there may be many reasons why you might start on the road to games creation. We will look at the reasons to create games, and the types of games people make. We also answer the question, "what is retro?" and talk about why retro gaming is becoming ever more popular. We complete the chapter by discussing what tools we will use to make our products, and a little history of games creation tools.

Chapter 2—Game Design Methods: Before you commit time, effort, and perhaps money to a game idea, you must first write down your ideas and expand on what will be created. This might include story creation and paper designs; this is an essential chapter to ensure that the game idea is completed within your expected timeframe and budget (if you have one).

Chapter 3—Programming Concepts: The good thing about The Games Factory 2 and other drag-and-drop tools is that although you are not using traditional programming (which some people find difficult), you are still learning concepts that are used in the real world. In this section, we discuss the main programming terms so you understand them when we come across them in the application.

Chapter 4—TGF Creation Basics: Before getting into a lot of terminology that is used throughout this book, this chapter gives you an overview of how a game is put together in TGF2 (its structure), and the general order in which you would complete it.

Chapter 5—Finding Your Way Around: It's now time to install TGF2 and take a look around so you can get used to the look and feel of the program. Soon you will be creating your own games, amazing but true!

Chapter 6—Objects, The Cornerstone of Creation: Objects are the cornerstone of game creation, and we discuss how to use them and what's available to TGF users.

Chapter 7—Configuring Properties: In this chapter, we look at the important aspects of frames and object properties.

Chapter 8—TGF Coding Basics: Now that you have a good understanding of all of the various editors involved in making your games, it's now time to explore basic programming techniques and concepts. It will become apparent this early on how powerful TGF2 is and how easy it is to make games.

Chapter 9—Backup and Game Recovery: Before we get too deep into making games, we take an in-depth and serious look at backing up our projects. Many users have lost games through tiredness or forgetfulness; either way, it can stop you in your tracks. We look at backing up via the program, and what you can do to make sure you are safe from viruses, hard disk failure, and errors.

Chapter 10—Movement: Movement is used a lot in TGF2 to make things more interesting, and all games have some form of movement in them. In this chapter, we look at the different movement options available with the built-in movement engine.

Chapter 11—Graphics and Animation: This chapter looks at the very important aspect of importing or drawing your own graphics, and how to animate them.

Chapter 12—Creating a Bat and Ball Game: You first real game is a bat and ball game, a common 2D type of game, but very useful for learning some key aspects of TGF2.

Chapter 13—Scrolling Game Concepts: Moving on to some more complex game effects, we look at how to create scrolling scenery and movement.

Chapter 14—Creating a Side-scrolling Shoot-'em-up Game: Using what we learned from the previous chapter, we now take on our first scrolling game.

Chapter 15—Robin Hood, the Rescue of Lady Marian: We move on to our third game, a platform game with ladders, traps, and enemy guards.

Chapter 16—Alien Invaders: Time to make our fourth and last game in the book, based on a retro classic, and learn some common techniques to make an exciting old-style game.

ON THE CD

Chapter 17—Additional Concepts: Now we take our games to the next level and look at additional ways to make our games more interesting, by including menus, uploading to a Web site, and finally introducing two more games that are included on the companion CD-ROM for you to try.

Chapter 18—Bug Finding and Fixing: What's the point of making all of these exciting games if as soon as someone starts to play them, they crash or don't work correctly? Q&A testing is an essential part of creation, and not very interesting, especially when you just want to publish and let people play your game. If your intention is for people to continue to download and play your games in the future, Q&A testing must be done. We go through the built-in debugger and try an example to see how you should go about it.

Chapter 19—Product Creation Afterthoughts: So, you have made your game, now what? In this chapter, we discuss how you will market, distribute, and sell it (if that's your intention).

Chapter 20—Getting Help: At some point in your creations, you will need to seek help. So, where can you go and find the answers you need to ensure a fast and efficient design time? This chapter deals with where you can get product and design help.

ABOUT THE AUTHOR

Jason Darby has been working in the IT industry for the last decade, writing user and systems documentation for users with little or no knowledge of the programs they are using. For a number of years, he has been working in the games and application creation market, making games, applications, and CD-ROM demos. Jason has also had a number of articles published in the UK press, including a number in *Retro Gamer* and *PC Format*, both leading magazines in their field.

1 Games, Games, and More Games

In This Chapter

- Why Make Games?
- 2D or 3D Games
- Game Types
- Why Retro?
- Software Tools Used

Games have been one of the most interesting aspects of computers since they began appearing in the home over 20 years ago. Nothing is more satisfying than loading up your favorite game and being transported to a world that no longer exists, perhaps to the future, flying a spaceship, or even taking part in a sport you could never conceive of doing in real life.

Today's games bear no resemblance to the first simple games of the late 1970s and 1980s. They now have high-quality graphics and sound, complex stories, and, in some cases, million-dollar budgets, making the games industry more like the movie industry. Games are big business, and one of the leading industries in which to work.

Unfortunately, making games is considered a black art in which you have to spend years learning how to program in complex machine languages before you can even get a simple graphic moving across the screen! Doesn't sound like much fun if you're just starting out, does it? Most of us want some immediate response from the computer, not spending a week just to get "Hello World" written on the screen (the first thing most programming books try to teach, and not very exciting).

Many game programming books are aimed at the professional user market; for example *Writing Games Using DirectX*, *Games Programming with C++*, and so forth. Typical game-loving people don't fit into the professional category, but would love to fulfill their dreams of making a game. In fact, many aspire to make games, but don't know if it's possible, and don't know where to start.

This book shows you how it is much easier than you may have thought to make fun and exciting games. It also allows you to progress quickly and take an idea from concept into a fully playable game by the end of the book. In the later chapters, we look at adding more complexity to games with additional things like scoreboards, putting them on the Web, and installation script building.

Whether you are looking at games creation for fun or for business, we cover aspects of both, so if you decide to move from a hobby to trying to sell a shareware product, the information is right here and ready to use. Don't think you have to create games just to make money or get a job in the games industry; it can be a lot of fun as well. In fact, many game creators are actually just doing it for the excitement of people trying the programs they create!

Finally, we look at the increasingly popular *retro games* creation market, which is fast becoming a favorite of the hobbyist programmer. Retro games are remakes of old games from the 1980s and early 1990s (although some people say that "retro" can mean anything that is old).

So, let's begin our journey in learning how to make and design games the easy way!

WHY MAKE GAMES?

You may have many reasons why you want to make games, and using The Games Factory 2 (TGF2) is a great way to achieve many of them. Some reasons why you want to make games include:

- You want a job in the games industry.
- You wish to sell your own games.
- You want to get your game published and sold by someone else.
- You wish to make games as a hobby.
- Perhaps you are bored of playing games and you want to make your own, as you feel you might be able to do better.
- You want to make games for your friends and family.

■ You are a teacher looking at getting the students to learn useful skills such as story telling, mathematics, art, and design while keeping them interested in the lesson.

As you can see, there are many reasons why you might want to make games (this list isn't definitive), but whatever your choice, it is important to ensure you enjoy the experience.

2D OR 3D GAMES

This book is all about making 2D (two-dimensional) games and does not touch on 3D game creation aspects. At the time of writing, TGF2 and its older brother Multimedia Fusion 2®(MMF2) do not currently support 3D natively. Work is currently underway to include a 3D aspect as an additional extension object (extension objects are discussed later in this book), but as it has not been released, this book only deals with 2D (go to *www.clickteam.com* for more details on the 3D object).

If you are interested in learning more about 3D programming or development, you can read the Charles River Media books Elementary Game Programming & Simulators Using Jamagic by Sergio Perez, or Awesome 3D Game Development: No Programming Required by Clayton E Crooks II.

GAME TYPES

Before looking at how to develop and design our own games, let's take a quick look at the various game types that you as a developer might want to make, and what people would like to play.

This is always a good place to start, as each game can be categorized, and you will then find it easier to think about which type you would enjoy making (enjoying the game-making process is very important for your overall sanity and making sure your enthusiasm is kept high for a project). Again, this list isn't definitive, but includes most of the game types you might be considering for your next project.

Platform

Most game players at some point have probably played a 2D platform game (see Figure 1.1). They disappeared from the game stores as premium titles some time ago, although they are still very popular as a children's or a budget game. They were replaced by 3D platform games, which as a game type is more popular on console machines than on the PC. From a retro gaming point of view, they are still as popular as ever (if not more so), as many games from that period were 2D due to the restraints on the hardware.

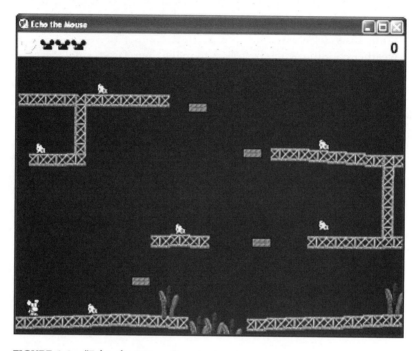

FIGURE 1.1   "Echo the Mouse" ©Ovine by Design—reprinted with permission.

You can still find 2D platform games as popular free downloads or games available to play directly from a Web site (as a marketing or sales tool)—therefore, a great type of game to pick, but certainly not the easiest to make. With this type of game, you have to take into account ladders, drops/falls, escalators, and elevators. Although this isn't a beginner's subject matter, it is not too difficult to do once you understand some basic concepts. We look at how to make platform games later in the book.

Racing Car

One favorite type of game on the Commodore Amiga® was the top-down view racing car game (see Figure 1.2). Various tracks, bonuses, and great computer AI (artificial intelligence) would make for an exciting and increasingly difficult set of racing tracks. The great thing about racing car games is that you can add so much to the game, and it's easy to think of new and interesting ideas for it. When considering what type of game you are going to make, consider a type of game from which ideas flow easily. If you are struggling for ideas early in your game creation, it may be better to pick another game type—you can always come back to your original game idea later if you have some more ideas to add to it. Car racing games are not the easiest to create from a graphics generation point of view, but you certainly won't be stuck for ideas. Car games could have weapons to destroy other cars, weather conditions, car upgrades to make them faster, single races, or tournaments. The main things you will need to consider when making this type of game are the graphics and the computer AI.

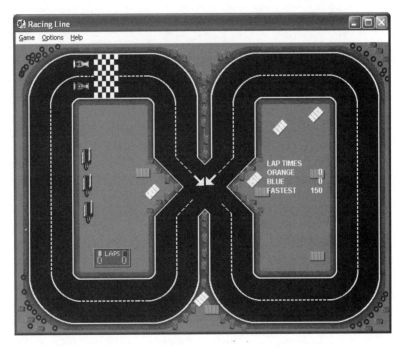

FIGURE 1.2 *Racing Line* ©Clickteam.com—reprinted with permission.

Bat and Ball

A very popular type of game on the early 8-bit and 16-bit computers was the Bat and Ball style of games (see Figure 1.3). You usually control a paddle and have to destroy blocks using a bouncing ball. There have been various variations of this type of game over the years in which several things have changed: the direction of the paddle/balls, various positive and negative effects when destroying certain blocks, and even 3D versions. As a game type, there many options for improving and adding new features, and you shouldn't have too many problems thinking up new ideas. As a starting point for making games, it's one of the easier game types to come to grips with, and one of the first games we will explore in our game called "The Lab."

FIGURE 1.3   *Choco Break* ©Olivier Behr 2004—reprinted with permission.

Side-Scrolling Shoot-'em-ups

This was a favorite type of game in the 1980s and it's still a popular format of game for retro game makers. Shoot-'em-up games would normally have the gamer playing a space fighter pilot defending the Earth against wave after wave of alien invaders (see Figure 1.4). The game could scroll from left to right or bottom to top and could include bonuses for destroying a wave of enemy fighters, including shield and weapons upgrades—very predictable stuff, but entertaining all the same. These types of games are relatively easy to create; in fact, once you have done the scrolling, most of the hard work is done (except for having some original graphics, of course).

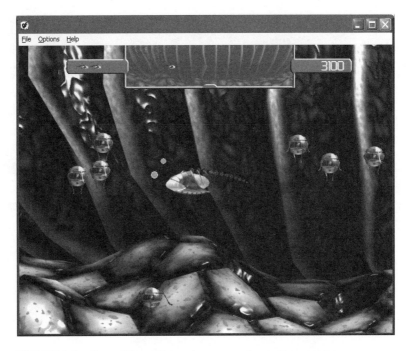

FIGURE 1.4 *Nano War* ©Olivier Behr 2004—reprinted with permission.

Board Games

Chess and solitaire are just two examples of traditional board games that have been converted to the computer game format (see Figure 1.5). It has a niche following with a specific part of the market, and this type of game seems to appear in large numbers on many budget labels. Board games are certainly not difficult to make with regard to the graphics side; the challenge you will face is with the computer AI responding to the player's moves. Computer AI is more complex and certainly more difficult to design/program, so you shouldn't attempt board games when just starting out. It is recommended that you move on to board games once you have a better understanding of TGF2 and have more experience programming in the Event Editor.

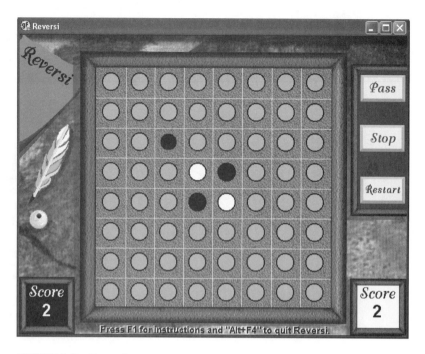

FIGURE 1.5   *Reversi* ©Clickteam.com—reprinted with permission.

Card Games

Another popular format on budget labels is card games (see Figure 1.6). A card game is a great time filler, so when you have a few minutes to spare, usually it's one of the first games to be loaded up. A very good reason for wanting to make card games is that they don't normally need a powerful computer to run or complex graphics.

Another plus of picking a card game as the type of game you would like to make is that there are many types from which to choose. You could also make memory games using your card graphics set, as this is another simple, straightforward concept.

Therefore, you won't have difficulty finding something you would be comfortable attempting to make; all you need is one set of card graphics, your game idea, and you are set!

FIGURE 1.6   *Card Game* ©Christian Burfelt—reprinted with permission.

WHY RETRO?

Retro, what does it mean? Unfortunately, whom you ask will depend on the answer you receive. Retro usually signifies something old or something from the past that forms a specific group of items such as retro clothes, music, or, in this case, games. If you are currently in your thirties or so, you would probably consider the 1980s and early 1990s as retro; if younger, you would start to think late 1990s. This isn't a given, but where computers are concerned, the Spectrum 48k®, Commodore 64®, Amiga®, and Atari ST® computers would be considered retro for the later age group, while the Sega® consoles might be looked at as retro by the younger generation.

There is no right or wrong answer, but for the sake of this book, we will be using the term *retro* as the early 8-bit and 16-bit computer platforms, although you can take inspiration from any source you like. This is the major benefit of being a game designer; you get to choose what you want to make.

Early computers had many restrictions because of the power of the actual machines; for example, the Spectrum 48k (an early successful European computer) had only 48 K of memory, limited colors, sound that consisted of beeps, and everything loaded by tape. People love making retro games because of the restrictions the programs had, and games were played more for the story than the graphics and sound contained within them. Therefore, retro games are considered by some to be more fun than the current blockbuster games of today; that's debatable, but they are certainly enjoyable for short periods of time. The other main reason why people love to make retro games is that because of the restrictions mentioned, they are easier to make. You are not going to be recreating anything that requires complex graphics or lots of time and effort, so the challenge is reachable. Many retro makers are also updating the games to look more modern with fancier graphics and complex sound/music rather than bleeps.

If you are looking to make your own retro games, you are in luck, as there is a massive back catalogue for you from which to choose. The other great thing is that even if you are only remotely interested in computer games, you will probably have played some arcade machines. If you are too young to remember the 1980s game scene, that's not a problem either. If you don't know where to look, use today's search engine technology to find what you're looking for. We've listed some retro sites in Chapter 20, "Getting Help," but there are many of them, so just search for the term *retro games* or *Spectrum/Commodore.*

Most of the game types just mentioned fit well into the retro genre, specifically platform games and side-scrolling shoot-'em-ups. These were basically the two most-used type of game on the early platforms, as the computers couldn't really make much else. Therefore, once you have figured out how to write your game engine for those types of games, it will be relatively easy to transfer this knowledge to your retro game idea.

We discuss the issues of copyright and permissions in Chapter 19, "Product Creation Afterthoughts," but it is something to be aware of before you start making your retro game remakes.

SOFTWARE TOOLS USED

A number of tools used in this book are essential to being able to design, create, and distribute games. Without a complete toolset, it would be harder to take your project idea from concept to completion.

The products used here have common themes:

■   They are cheap to use (or free in some cases).
■   They are relatively easy to use (especially for the beginner game makers who are reading this book).

- The results they give look professional, which is very important if you are to be taken seriously.
- Development time is much quicker using the tools mentioned here than others available on the market.

Obviously, there are many tools on the Web that you might choose in creating your games, but the tools on the companion CD-ROM and detailed in the book were selected because they meet the requirements: cheap to make, quick to create, and professional-looking products. The software products are from the same company, and so share a common interface and a single support contact point, which makes it much easier to get support for the products. You will need to consider why you are making games, as this will have a direct bearing on whether you should spend money on the tools needed to make, create, and distribute your programs. Finally, you will need to purchase *TGF2* if you intend to take your game making further than the demo included with this book (which is a trial version).

The Games Factory 2

We will be using Clickteam's The Games Factory 2 (an example game loaded into TGF2 is shown in Figure 1.7) to create our games. This product is the follow-up to the hugely successful and award-winning Games Factory product released around 1996. In fact, Games Factory is so popular that it is still in use today, and many Web sites are dedicated to games that were made with the program. Version 2 has many new features and much more power than the original version, including layers and parallax scrolling, and contains many features and removal of limitations that were put into TGF's bigger brother, Multimedia Fusion. Consequently, there's nothing to stop you from creating some fantastic games with this product.

The trial (demo) version is included on the companion CD-ROM for you to use when following the examples in this book. You will find TGF2, Install Creator®, and Patch Maker® on the CD-ROM in the demo's folder.

The trial version has a number of restrictions; for example, you won't be able to save .exe files or Internet-capable games, and there is a time restriction to prevent you from using it for an unlimited time period. If you wish to continue using TGF2 after the trial has ended, you will have to purchase the full version. You can, however, use the TGF2 trial to make your games, and once you have purchased the full version, you can load those games into it, so you won't lose anything you worked on.

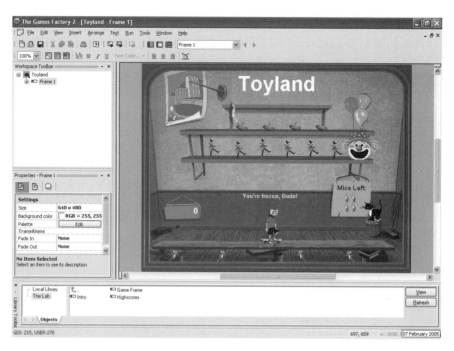

FIGURE 1.7   TGF2 in Action ©Clickteam.com—Printed with Permission.

Install Creator

Another product from the Clickteam stable is the installer product Install Creator, a powerful, feature-rich, and very easy to use product. Once we have our games, we want to make our own installer to package it and distribute it to our friends. Install Creator provides us with a professional-looking installation, which means that more people are likely to try our game rather than if we simply provide a zip file on a Web server. The Install Creator we will be using is the freeware version. There is a restriction to using this version, which is that there is a little Web link to Click-team's Web site at the end of the installation. This isn't a problem if you are using it just to distribute your game to your friends, but if you are looking to make a game for the shareware, budget, or professional markets, you can inexpensively upgrade the product to the registered or professional versions.

Patch Maker

So, you've made your game, it's now on Web sites ready to be downloaded by users, and you're feeling pretty good about yourself. Until, that is, you receive an e-mail from someone who downloaded your game and discovered that when he does something on a certain level, the game crashes. You review your program and are shocked to find that you have a bug in your code, and although it's easy to fix, you don't want people to have to download the entire game again just to get past this one issue (in theory, it might be more than one issue, but you get the idea). This is where Patch Maker comes in; rather than downloading the entire game installer again, it creates a difference file. This *difference file* contains only the difference between the files and then compresses it. The major benefit of using Patch Maker is that the user won't need to download your 20 MB game again. In addition, if someone hacks the patch, it is impossible to steal your software, as most of your data isn't stored in that patch.

ON THE CD   Using a similar licensing rule to Install Creator, we have provided a freeware version of this product on the companion CD-ROM. You are allowed to use it for both commercial and noncommercial projects, and in return, it displays a link to Clickteam's Web site at the end of the patch installation. As mentioned before, if you want to remove the message, you can upgrade quite cheaply to the registered version.

About Clickteam

Clickteam is the development group behind The Games Factory, Multimedia Fusion, and Jamagic (as well as many other programs). Having used Clickteam's games creation programs for many years, it was an easy decision to write about *TGF2*, as it's a combination of approximately 10 years of development work over different programs using the same "event" driven programming concept. TGF2 is one of the most powerful 2D games creation tools available, and one that certainly opens many doors for the game creator. If you want the most powerful and easy to use program on the market today, you have found it.

The two developers of TGF2 are Francois Lionet and Yves Lamoureux, who have been called "pioneers of personal computing." If you have been interested in games creation over the years, you may have heard of these two talented guys, as Francois created some of the most popular game-making programs on the Amiga and Atari ST computers in the form of Amos® and Stos®. Amos sold over 300,000 copies in its various versions, and is another of those retro type programs that still has a strong following on the Internet today.

Francois and Yves joined forces to create Klik and Play® in 1994 for the PC platform, and it was an instant success around the world. After K&P came the original version of The Games Factory released in 1996, and again it became an overnight success. For many of the developers, magazine editors, and game creators, it seems that TGF is the one program they have all used and have fond memories about. After 1996, more advanced versions of TGF were released that took into account multimedia and application development, but were published under different names, including Click & Create® and Multimedia Fusion. Each release of the product has become more powerful to meet the needs of the technology of the time, and more features have been added with each version. You can find more information about Clickteam and its products on its Web site at *www.clickteam.com*.

SUMMARY

Now that we have touched on game types and the tools we are going to use to create our games, hopefully the creative juices are starting to flow, and you have some idea of what you would like to make and why you want to make it. Don't rush off just yet to begin making your game, as in the next chapter we will be looking at how to grow those simple ideas into full-blown games. Most people have more than one idea, so we will also look at getting you to make a decision on the type of game you want to make based on set criteria.

2 Game Design Methods

In This Chapter

- Why Design?
- Product Design and Planning

I n this chapter, we look at why you might want to spend a little more time think- ing about the reasons for making your games, and what you will get out of it.

WHY DESIGN?

You're probably itching to make your first game and just get on with it. That's not all bad, as it's good to be enthusiastic about a subject you are involved in (it will be a major benefit later). However, before you decide to skip the games design meth- ods section, let's ask a simple question: "How many people do you think buy a new game and then proceed to read the enclosed instruction manual?" Many people who play games usually just install them and start playing. The problem with not reading the manual is that while you do learn when you're playing, you are likely to lose the first few games you play because you don't understand all the underlying things you need to do. It all seems easy enough when you first start playing the game, but you soon get out of your depth and have to start looking through the manual to find the answers. If we take this approach to making games, the same theory applies, but there are obvious pitfalls. Why design a game (which could take some time) when you can just come up with the idea quickly, make it, and then send it to friends? To some extent, there is no problem with just going off and developing a game idea, especially if it's just for fun. However, many game makers might spend a year or more making a game and then distribute it for free. Therefore, if you are going to take up the challenge of a larger project, you will find that if you consider making a change to the underlying game (or it doesn't work quite as you imagined), you may have to rewrite large portions of the program. Without some form of planning, you could be wasting a lot of time and effort, and increasing the overall development time of your game. On many game-making forums (ones using Clickteam's products), this problem occurs quite often and has even been given its own name, the "Click Curse." Many games made with these types of programs are dropped because:

- The ideas were too complex for the skills of the programmers at that time; they became stuck, couldn't get past the current issues, and so gave up.
- The code was badly written, which means the programmers probably took the long route to making their game. Early in the development cycle, they noticed that it could have been easier to write, decided to make the game easier by replacing their old code with the new superefficient program, and then realized it was large a task.
- Programmers found that the game didn't work as well with the original story after they began making it, and decided to make a new game.
- The programmers were too ambitious. Someone with no design and game experience who tries to make an online role-playing game first is likely to run into problems.

No matter what type of game you are going to make, be it for friends, family, shareware, or any other reason, you can pick and choose which ideas to use in this chapter to help you design your game. Use what you are comfortable with, and which areas will help you make the game as easily as possible; there are no right and wrong answers to best method of game development in tools like TGF2.

PRODUCT DESIGN AND PLANNING

What do you need to do, and in what order, to make sure your idea is a success? There are no right or wrong answers to that question, so this book simply points you in the right direction and gives you some ideas to try.

Figure 2.1 shows the order in which you should consider approaching your game design.

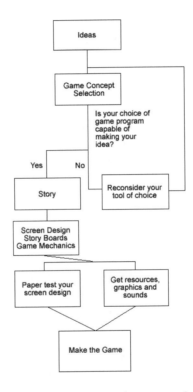

FIGURE 2.1   Approach to game design.

The Ideas

So, you have an idea; in fact, you are likely to have more than one. Therefore, which one would you choose, and start to put a lot of time and effort into? Even a small project will require you to invest some time and effort in the game design, even the tiny games you might make for the Internet or free download.

You may have many good ideas, but you have to be a bit more objective and realize that you cannot implement them all at once.

The best way to do this is to complete a simple table of game ideas, as shown in Table 2.1.

TABLE 2.1 Organizing Your Game Ideas

Game Type	Idea	Technology Concept	Rating	Difficulty
Car Racing	You are a budding race-car driver wanting to become race champion. Before you can compete in the world championship, you need to win the regional heats.	Top-down scrollling	High	Medium
Flight SIM	You are a WW1 pilot who has just joined your squadron and must take to the skies as soon as you arrive.	Story-driven 3-D flight SIM	Medium	High Impossible?
Scrolling	Aliens have invaded a small town in your local area. A band of citizens cannot simply stand by and watch the impending disaster. A small team armed with weapons goes in search of the alien menace.	Isometric scrolling	Low	Medium

Using Table 2.1, set out all your current game ideas; even if it's a silly or half-thought-out concept, write it down. Ideas shouldn't be judged at this point, so it's a good idea to keep notes of all game ideas in one place. The reason we make this table is to begin to reduce our ideas to a select few; that way, we can really make inroads into what we really want to make.

The table is then split it into five columns. Although the table is simplistic, we don't want to get into any detail at this stage. In fact, we want to keep it simple and not write too much; later, we will expand on the ideas of those games that deserve more time and effort.

The columns are separated as follows:

Game type: Categorize the game type into one of the standard gaming groups; for example, RPG, war game, flight simulation, isometric, fist-person shooter (FPS) etc.

Idea: A brief overview of what the game is about; at this stage, we are keeping it simple. Just a quick overview of the story and the aim of the game.

Technology concept: What game technology will the game use? This could be top-down scrolling, side scrolling, 3D FPS, etc. This is to give you an idea of what might be required from the tool you intend to use to make your game. It's not a good idea to make a 3D FPS if the product you're choosing can only make 2D games.

Rating: How high do you rate your idea? How excited are you at the prospect of making this game? If it's a low rating, it's not worth spending time and effort to make, as you will probably get bored and give up. We want you to get to the end of your game happy in the knowledge that you saw it through to the end!

Difficulty: It's time to be honest about your skills in your chosen game-making product. Many people on the game-making forums have never used a game-making product and want to make an online role-playing game or something similar that is just too complex. If you really think the game idea is too difficult, put that aside, as you don't want to start a project and then struggle with the concepts. This is meant to make your life easier, not for you to deceive yourself into thinking you can make anything you want. There is no shame in admitting that an idea at this stage is too difficult, because later it might not be, and you'll have the idea on paper.

After you have reviewed at the table and found the highest rating game that strikes you as the most interesting (there may be more than one), you are ready to continue. However, before you get all excited and start making the game, you need to make sure that the game-making tool is capable of carrying out your idea!

Remember to use the "difficulty" column to decide between multiple high-rating game ideas.

Tool Choice

You have the game you want to make reduced to a few choice game ideas, or perhaps just one. Before you rush off and start it, take a few minutes to check that your ideas are compatible with the game-making tool you are using. In this book, we are going to be using Games Factory 2, which is specifically for 2D games; therefore, if you selected a 3D FPS, this wouldn't be the right tool for the job. It is very important that you understand both your own capabilities and those of the tools you are going to use.

Investigate your product choice thoroughly before starting any project. This includes making sure what any compiled program created with it runs on, and any other specifications that might affect your decision, including what machines the final program will run on, and any licensing rules regarding distribution.

The Story

It is very difficult to be unique with regard to stories these days, as many things have already been tried. Your story doesn't have to be unique or new; as long as the idea is well presented, you should be fine. Spend some time writing your story, as this is the key to what will be included in your game. Make sure you spell check your story, and any material that other people will see. If users see anything that looks amateurish within the story (which would probably be detailed on a page where they click to download the product), they will probably decide not to download the demo/product. The Internet is full of buggy software, viruses, and spyware, so users are hesitant to download anything that might contain dubious content, and may think that your software might contain one of the aforementioned if there are many spelling mistakes. It is amazing how you can influence the quality of your product by checking some of the simplest things.

You now need to pad out your story to get a fuller picture of what it's about, and then need to make some notes of what is going to be contained in the game. This is called the *story plan*, which is a simple document detailing some of the main key elements of the story and what it will contain (it doesn't go into too much detail, as it's just trying to bring out the flavor of the story/content).

At this point, don't go into major detail, as it's just a scoping exercise to make sure you have an idea you ultimately like. You might find that once you have done this, you no longer like the idea and don't want to make it. If that's the case, you have succeeded, because no one should make games he or she doesn't want to make.

From the list of game ideas, let's pick "car racing" as an example. The story plan goes something like that shown in Table 2.2.

So, even at this stage, you have an idea of what your game is all about and what is contained in it.

- Six regional heats in various locations
- One final track once you have progressed through the heats
- Car upgrades
- Track obstacles
- Prizes
- Car repairs
- Computer-controlled drivers
- It is a dangerous sport

TABLE 2.2 Story Plan

Game Name	Car Racing
Story	After working seven years at the local carting center (where you practiced your driving skills during your lunch hour), you are now convinced you can compete in the world's deadliest and dangerous racing event, "Death Racer." Unfortunately, entry to the event is very competitive, and people have to compete in the regional heats for a chance to be in the ultimate racing event and win the ultimate prize
Initial Game Details	You will need to complete six regional heats (tracks) and be in the top 10 drivers to be promoted to the Death Racer event.
	You will get points if you appear in the top three of each regional heat. Additionally, you will be awarded cash prizes, which you can then spend on car upgrades, or a new vehicle.
	If you come last in any regional heat, the game will end.
	The Death Racer event is one track that contains some of the most dangerous obstacles you come across in the entire game.
	There are 50 drivers competing in the heats. The top 10 drivers with the most points get promoted to the Death Race. There are computer-controlled heats in which you will not compete, but the computer generates the results.

Now you have your initial story and basic game details. This isn't going to be enough for you to start making your game, as you will need to break the game down further so you know what needs to be included and written. Using the list of items generated from your story plan, you need to get into some more detail by creating a game list. This list will then be our starting point for creating our game; once you have created it, you will need to review it, and you may decide to remove or add extra items.

So, brainstorm. Write every little bit of game idea down, regardless of whether the idea is far from good or ideal. The list is very useful for confirming all the things you want in the game.

Let's take a look at your game list:

```
Dangerous Racing
   Weapons
               Forward Firing Missile
               Rear Firing Missile
               Laser
               Mine
      Obstacles
               Oil Slick
               Water
   Fall off Track
   Weather
               Snow
               Rain
               Sunny

Car Improvements

   Engine
   Speed (Turbo)
   Power
Bodywork
   Durability
   Damage
   Other Cars Bounce off
Tires
   Breaking
   Cornering
   Affected by Oil, Water and Track Conditions
```

This is just a small example of a game list, which could in theory run into many pages. "Why so many pages," you might ask? It is best to know all of the options that might be in the game up front, rather than deciding two or three months into development that you want extra items that will require additional programming or even recoding sections of code. Making your list as complete as possible now will save you lots of time later. If some of the items are too difficult to code or perhaps just too much work, you can always mark them as version 2.

The whole point of this exercise is to structure what is going to be in the game, and what is not going to be in it. Once you move from this stage, the list will generally not change, so where possible, set it in stone from that point forward. This isn't to say that you cannot make changes in your game, but you should only be looking at gameplay rather than new features.

Changes to the way the game plays are considered acceptable as it makes the game more enjoyable, once some initial user feedback has been received. However, it isn't a good idea to add new features when the game is close to being released, as this is a sure-fire way to delay it further.

Game Mechanics

The final stage of generating the story and game mechanics is to take your final list of items into the game and begin to make them computer specific; in other words, to write down the boundaries of each object that will be in the game. Some examples of this might be the normal maximum speeds of the cars, the cost of items from the garage, and how many levels can be upgraded to.

This part of the documentation is quite detailed and in-depth, so you do need to have some patience when creating the list. It will speed up your game programming greatly and reduce the amount of time needed to think about how the game works.

So, let's look at a couple of examples of detailing the mechanics of the game.

```
Car Types

At various stages of the game you will be able to purchase a new car or
upgrade your current one.

Cars will have various starting stats, which can then be upgraded, but
each car will have limits on how far it can be improved.
```

Table 2.3 is an example of the breakdown from the description.

TABLE 2.3   Car Levels

Car Type	Engine Start	Tire Start	Speed Start	Bodywork Start	Cost
X1	Lvl – 1	Lvl – 1	Lvl – 1	Lvl – 1	Default
Speeder	Lvl – 1	Lvl – 2	Lvl – 1	Lvl – 1	$15,000
Hoffe-E1	Lvl – 2	Lvl – 2	Lvl – 1	Lvl – 1	$20,000
Panther	Lvl – 1	Lvl – 2	Lvl – 2	Lvl – 2	$35,000
Turbo-x	Lvl – 2	Lvl – 2	Lvl – 3	Lvl – 2	$55,000
Win Fusion	Lvl – 2	Lvl – 3	Lvl – 3	Lvl – 2	$70,000
Etc.					

You can then break down even further to detail each specific level of component so it is easy to program when you get to that point.

An example of the further breakdown is shown in Table 2.4.

TABLE 2.4   Car Speeds

Engine Levels	
Speed Level	**Top Speed**
Lvl – 1	8 Mph
Lvl – 2	12 Mph
Lvl – 3	15 Mph
Lvl – 4	17 Mph
Lvl – 5	19 Mph
Lvl – 6	22 Mph
Lvl – 7	24 Mph
Lvl – 8	27 Mph
Lvl – 9	30 Mph
Lvl – 10	35 Mph

This probably seems like a lot of work, but for simple games, it might only take you 20 minutes. For a bigger game, it might take a few hours or even days to document the features of what's going to be in the game. Without detailed game mechanics and story information, you're going to spend much more time programming the game to try to get it to function correctly.

Screen Design

Now that you've completed the story and game mechanics, you need to understand how the game is going to look, which will give you an idea of how each screen (frame in TGF2) or level will appear. This allows you to cast a designer's eye over the recommended structure and ensures that everything works correctly from a usability and layout point of view. If someone else will be making your graphics (this isn't uncommon), the screen design is also for his benefit, so you should create the designs how you want them to look and then send them off to the graphic artist to generate.

Game Map

The game map is a simple yet effective way to break your game into sections, levels, or areas of the game. This will also include main menus, level menus, end-of-game screens, or high-score tables. Using a single letter-sized piece of paper (you may need to stick more together), map out the main parts of your game and where they link (see Figure 2.2).

FIGURE 2.2   Game map showing connections between screens.

You can see in Figure 2.2 how each screen connects and how it relates to other screens around it. On each box within the game map should be a number that signifies which picture it is on the screen map (we will talk about screen maps next).

Screen Map

The screen map takes the process to the next level whereby you start to draw each screen. This is the detail part of the drawing process, and it could take a while to complete. It is very important, though, as this makes you think about what each screen will look like and what components of the game will appear and where (see Figure 2.3).

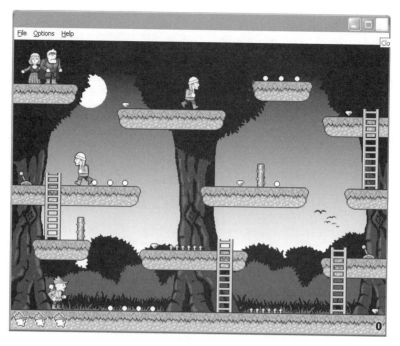

FIGURE 2.3   A screen map details everything on each screen.

You may find that when you do this, you will suddenly realize that there isn't any room left to put other graphics, or it just doesn't work on paper. This is another step that clarifies what you are trying to do and gets your approval before approaching the programmers or beginning to write the code.

Paper Testing

This might sound a little strange at first, and you might not want to do it. As with everything mentioned so far, it's a very useful process to follow and will help reduce errors later. Most people understand that testing is done at the stage at which the code has been written and the game is ready for its beta testers, so this may seem alien as a concept. Paper testing is very easy to do and not very time consuming, but again it's something that could save you time and effort in the long run, so why not just try it? Taking what you drew in the screen map and game map sections mentioned previously, we now play the game on paper. Starting at the first box on the game map, imagine you are playing your game, and follow the process through. You will need to do this a few times to take into account different routes that the user might take while running your game.

For example, you might want to look at:

- Is it easy to navigate to the start of the game?
- Is it easy to get to the options (keyboard redefine, sound options)? Are all of the options on a single screen or on multiple screens? If they are on more than one, do the screens connect well, and is it easy for the player to navigate back to the main options screen?
- What happens when the game is over, if the game player loses all his lives, or decides to quit? Make sure your game allows the player to exit at any time. Does trying to exit go to another screen?
- Are there any screens in between the game levels to announce "Next Level?"

Once you have done this, you may have to go back and amend your game and screen maps. If you do, make sure you go through the paper testing once more to ensure that the changes do not adversely affect the game. Paper testing is very effective for making sure you have the right screens at the right place, and that you have designed your navigation between screens correctly. It will soon show up if you have made any major mistakes anywhere in the entire design process.

Graphics

Only a small percentage of people can make good-looking graphics and animation. If you are one of the few, that's great, and it will be very helpful when you design your game layout and graphics to be used in the game. If you are not, you will run into some issues, so here are some ideas of where you might be able to get some material for your programs.

You can choose from a number of options when looking for graphics:

TGF2: The full version of TGF2 comes with a large collection of graphics that you can use within your games. Please read the license agreement concerning releasing the products as a commercial venture.

Graphics libraries: There are a few graphics libraries available on the Internet, some of which are free to use while others have options to purchase. Again, make sure you read the small print on the Web sites, as some sites say that if you sell/distribute over 10,000 items of any one product, you will need a different license agreement. You may not want to worry about this right now, but you still should consider it, as you don't want to pull your product off the Internet or a CD because you cannot afford the licensing fees. Make sure you know what costs are involved before you start; that way, nothing will be a shock to you when and if you get past those levels. There are a few graphics CD-ROMs available on the market, but most of them are either clip art (which is no good for what we want to do) or very specialized.

Make your own: You may be a good enough artist and have the right tools for the job. If you decide to make your own graphics, consider the impact this might have on the time scales for making your game. This will definitely have a bearing on if you have the time, effort, and patience to complete the project, as making graphics can be very time consuming.

Get someone else to make them: One of the challenges of making a game is to get help from other people, especially people you have never met. If you can find a graphic artist to help, make sure you understand how he works, and come to an agreement on time scales. Most graphic artists won't accept work unless there is some form of demo or game in existence. Don't try to get help when you have only written the story, as many artists won't bother to reply to the requests for help at that point. They need to know that you are serious about the project before putting their own time and effort into the work.

Sound and Music

Very much a secondary thought in game creation, but still an important aspect to consider is the sound and music you are going to have in your games. Although not as important as the graphics or gameplay of your game, think about watching a movie without sound, and your overall opinion of the film would definitely go down. Sound and music give a game atmosphere and make it appear more professional, if done correctly. The problem with sound and music is that they have the same problems that come with graphic creation: most people can't make their own, and need to find someone or something to supply them.

TGF2: In the full version of TGF2 are many music tracks and sounds that you could use in your game. Music is more specialized, as you want to match a certain sound to a particular time in the game. Definitely take the time to browse the CD-ROM to see if there is anything you could use, as this is definitely easier than some of the other options available to you. Please read the TGF2 license agreement concerning releasing the products as a commercial venture.

Sound libraries: Do not to rush out to the local computer store and buy a sound CD-ROM. These CD-ROMs are usually very poor quality and not very useful, even if they are cheap to buy. There are a number of excellent professional Web sites that you can listen to, and purchase and download a range of sounds and songs. Although you are going to have to spend money, you will be able to pick the exact sounds you want in your game. Conversely, if you purchase a cheap-sounding CD-ROM, you will have to browse the entire program looking for something that fits your needs. Moreover, you may find there is nothing you would want to use, and the quality isn't high enough for what you want. Always read any licensing text off the Web site concerning using sounds commercially; most are okay, but read the small print to make sure.

Make your own: A few years ago, this would not have been practical unless you had some form of sound equipment (MIDI) and a talent in music creation. Today, however, a number of products are available that can help you make music and sounds relatively easily. See Chapter 20, "Getting Help," for a few suggestions.

Get someone else to make them: The same issues exist as with outsourcing graphics; make sure you have a specific time scale for completing the work.

SUMMARY

As presented in this chapter, take some time when planning the design of your program, be it games, applications, or even screensavers (yes, even for the smallest of projects). This ensures that you keep to a good development time and stay within budget (if any). If you are creating a small game, the process doesn't have to be as intense or in-depth as some of the suggestions written here. These are only recommendations, and you can amend them to suit your way of working. By doing so, you might not make millions or be an instant success, but it will certainly make your life easier and make sure you are focused on what you are trying to do.

Remember, we all have different success levels; for example, if your plan is to make your game fun and enjoyable for friends and family, that's your success criteria. These concepts will help you even if you are creating for a small audience, so don't think you need a big plan to put some structure into what you are making. You don't need to be making the next *Doom*© or *Half-Life*© to use a common sense approach to game design and game making.

3 Programming Concepts

You now know how to design your game, and soon you will be shown how to make your own games using The Games Factory 2 program. Before you begin, this chapter discusses some of the programming concepts used within TGF2. Although TGF2 doesn't use traditional programming like C++ (or other languages), you are still going to be exposed to some concepts used in everyday programming languages. Finally, we discuss how to write your programs in pseudocode, so you can easily convert it to any other language you might learn in the future.

TRADITIONAL PROGRAMMING LANGUAGES

Programming languages have been widely available to the general public since the beginning of the 1980s (before this, the hardware and software would have not been cost effective unless you were a medium-sized business). Today, there are many different programming languages you can choose from to make a program, game, or application. Not all programming languages can be used efficiently for game creation; for example, you might consider using C++ to make your games engine, but you wouldn't use COBOL or Pascal. Nearly all programming languages on the market require some form of text/code entry to make "your" program.

An example of the more traditional-based programming languages is shown in Figure 3.1; the code displays the text "hello" on the screen, using Clickteam's 2D- and 3D-creation program Jamagic.

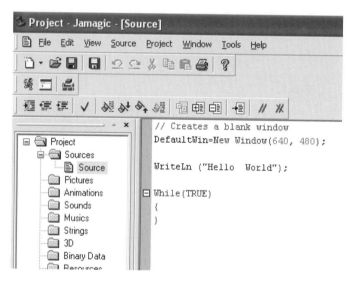

FIGURE 3.1   Jamagic code example.

Once the code has been entered, the programmer would generate a file that would run on the operating system they are developing on (normally, this is an executable file, but other languages and programs do have other types). What you will notice from the basic "hello" code is that it seems straightforward to put text to screen. As programs get more complex and are expected to do more, coding becomes much more complicated.

TRADITIONAL PROGRAMMING VERSUS TGF2

The major benefit of using TGF2 over the traditional languages is that the actual programming is hidden behind a GUI (graphic user interface) front-end, which makes it easier to program, and much easier to understand and manage your code (using code comments and groups).

Some of the benefits of using TGF2 over traditional code include:

- Traditional code and concepts hidden behind an easy-to-use GUI front-end.
- Results from creating programs are seen much quicker than using traditional coding. Therefore, you will stay more focused and will be more excited, as you will have something on screen very quickly.
- Creating games in TGF2 means you are still being exposed to programming techniques and concepts. For example, you will still learn about sprites, loops, arrays, INIs, and more.
- Although not as powerful as some traditional-based languages, TGF2 is specifically designed for making games. Thus, you get the power of its drag and drop programming system, which will allow you to make games with animation, hotspots, destruction, and movement (also many more functions) without the need to write your own engine using another programming language. The major benefit of this is that the code has already been written for you, and all you need to do is write your game idea!
- TGF2 helps break the game into manageable chunks so you can concentrate on different aspects at different times.

Over the last few years, there have been many successful TGF and MMF developers (MMF is TGF's bigger brother), and programmers have stated that the game player hasn't realized what tool was used to make the games. Who cares what makes your game, as long as it does what you want it to do. Just because it only take a few minutes to get a graphic on screen and move it about, compared to perhaps many minutes or hours with traditional coding (obviously, this wouldn't be the case if you were an experienced C++ programmer), does it really matter? If you have a time restraint, and TGF2 can do what you need to do, why make life more difficult for yourself?

PROGRAMMING TERMS AND CONCEPTS

Before we begin making our programs, it will be very beneficial for you to understand some of the terms and concepts we will be dealing with in this book and within TGF2, so you won't have to struggle with terms when moving "full steam" on your project.

Variables

A *variable* is a piece of data the computer will store that will change (or more specifically, can contain something different from when the program started). This could be either a string (text) or a numeric (number) variable. At the start of a program, you would normally set these to blank so you don't have to worry about incorrect data being passed to your program. This is normally called *initialization*, and is a process in which you set all variables and other data to specific data.

What can a variable hold? Basically anything. If we had a program that asked a user two questions:

- What is your favorite number over 10?
- What is your favorite number under 10?

we would need two numeric variables to store the response from the user input. As a group of people queues up to enter the details, each user could enter a different number. The reason for a variable is that the number entered could be different each time. We could also store string variables (where it stores text in the variable rather than a number):

- What is your name?
- How old are you?

This is a simplistic view of a variable, but in theory, the data inside it could change all the way through a program's execution. An example of a variable in actual use within TGF2 is the counter object (there is no need to go into too much detail at this point), which is used when you want to put a changing number into a game. This could be used to count down the time or the number of lives the player still has left. TGF2 has an object for this type of thing, and all you need to do it set the starting number and then keep amending it when you need to (e.g., when the player has lost a life).

Loops

You will often need to instruct the program/game to do the same thing several times in a row. This is called a *loop* and is very useful when you want to draw some items on screen or do something repetitive. It is also much easier to write a loop to do this rather than write the lines of code separately without a loop. As an example, perhaps you are trying to make a crossword game and have to display a 17x17 grid of pictures on screen to represent the crossword puzzle boxes. There are two ways you could achieve this: you could write 17 lines of code to represent each row of boxes, or you could use a loop, which would achieve the same result in two lines of code. Hopefully, from that example, you will understand what the power of a loop can do for your programming; it will simplify your code, and you won't have to write as much to achieve the same result. You will also find that reducing your code makes your program more efficient, which means in the long run, it might actually take up less space and run faster. However, more importantly, the less code you have to write, the easier and quicker it is to debug your program.

Arrays

Arrays are a way of storing and retrieving large amounts of data in an organized format. They are very efficient for storing data for many different reasons, but can only contain text or numbers in each array file (in TGF2's point of view). There are typically three types of array dimensions: one-, two-, and three-dimensional. Each piece of data is stored in a location within an array file and called upon when needed. The array can also be written when the program is running, which means it can be used to save real-time data. You could effectively class an array as a less sophisticated database, or in some respects similar to a spreadsheet that stores data.

The most basic type of array is a single (one-dimensional) array, which is just like having a row of boxes one on top of each other that contain data (be it text or numbers). To access the relevant data, you would specify its location within the array, which in the case of Figure 3.2 would be [2].

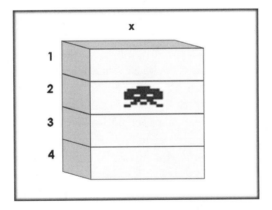

FIGURE 3.2 An example of an array.

NOTE *The image of the invader is being used to signify data and would not contain a graphic, but could contain a pointer to a graphic file (this would be the folder location and filename). Remember, the array can store either numbers or text, but not both (when using TGF2's default array options).*

A 2D array is slightly more complex and allows you to have a typical gridlike data structure very much like a spreadsheet, and is usually called the [X,Y] axis as shown in Figure 3.3.

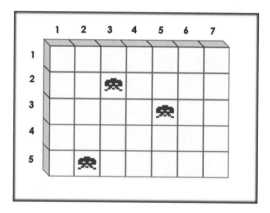

FIGURE 3.3 A 2D-array example structure.

As most people are familiar with programs similar to Microsoft® Excel, a 2D array is not a difficult concept to understand; you are basically placing your data in a structure that has rows and columns (the X,Y axis).

Finally, we have a 3D array, which is again a more complex type of array, and one you will find very useful for your game making. Think of a cube shape, and that will help you understand the basic structure (see Figure 3.4). With a 3D array, you need to specify three numbers, an [X,Y,Z] axis to locate the data.

The main considerations between a 2D and a 3D array are that with 2D, you are dealing with a flat sheet of paper with rows and columns of data. A 3D array is shaped more like a cube, and each block (rather than cell or face) contains the data. Although arrays are quite efficient and a basic 3D array doesn't use much hard disk space, it is a good idea to only pick the one you need and not move up to the next type unless necessary. Arrays can get quite complex, so keeping with a 2D array where possible will also help make your program understandable if you were to stop programming and come back to it after an extended period of time. We need to discuss one more concept concerning arrays that you will come across, 1-based index. As you know, each array item is numbered by its axis (e.g., x and y) but the 1-based index would state whether the numbering begins with a 1 or a 0.

Figure 3.5 shows how the 1-based index works; in the first example, the first item in that array is [1] and then [2]. In the second illustration, you would be accessing [0] and [1] instead. It is very important to remember which index you have selected, because if you try to read and write to a 0-based index and have selected a 1-based index, it will not work (you will not get any error messages to suggest otherwise).

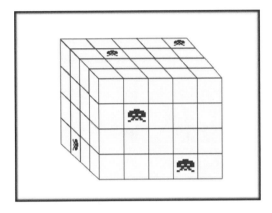

FIGURE 3.4   A 3D array, which looks like a cube.

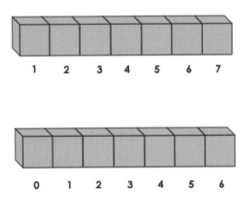

FIGURE 3.5   An example of a 0- or 1-based index.

With TGF2, you have the benefit of putting multiple array files into your game, so you can break your game down into smaller and easier-to-manage files. This allows you to create a small array file and make sure it works, and that your game is reading/writing the data correctly—then, you can move on to the next section. If you create a single massive array file, you might find that it doesn't work, and the more data you are dealing with, the harder the testing becomes. When you start to break your program down, ensure that you make many comments in the program so you know what you did. This will help you when you go back to a project after a break.

INI Files

INI files are basically text-formatted files that computer programs can read. These were used quite extensively in older versions of Windows, but less so these days as they were replaced by the registry. Most traditional programming languages do not use INI files anymore, but for simple data information, it is still a useful format to use in TGF2. It is very common to store information relating to configuration and program settings in an INI file (see Figure 3.6).

FIGURE 3.6   An INI file showing the program configuration.

Flags

Flags signify on and off states. They are very useful for many simple situations, and shouldn't be overlooked. For example, do you want to check if a door is open or a light switch is on? If so, a flag can show you the state of that item very simply and allow you to check its state. You could say that a flag is a "state" compare; it allows you to compare the current state of an in-game object and then react to it. There is no restriction to the type of game a flag is used in, and they can be very useful in many different situations. For example, you might want some flags to signify when the adventurers have triggered a trap. Therefore, once it had been triggered, you could then specify that the trap was now *off* so it doesn't happen again. In one of the games you will be making later, a flag is used to see when a certain event has happened so it can initiate some alternative code.

Local and Global

In the programming world, *local* and *global* refer to variables and how they are defined within the program, whether available to the entire program or just a certain section of the code. TGF2 is not much different in concept from using a text entry -based coding tool; in fact, the ideas are the same. Local means using an object or code to a single frame, and global means that the information is available to the entire program. TGF2 has a number of global options, including global events and global values.

PSEUDOCODE–PROGRAMMING IN ENGLISH

At many colleges and universities, taking a computer science course could mean learning a number of programming languages, including Pascal, Visual Basic, and COBOL. These languages aren't particularly difficult to learn, but when asked to make more complex programs, it does begin to get very difficult and time consuming to complete those projects. This is when pseudoprogramming makes its appearance, as it can really help you understand what you need to do within your program with regard to coding. If you have never programmed before or don't think you are good at it, this is a great way to become a better programmer. The main problem with programming is that it can be a bit daunting until you've had enough practice.

Now, of course, TGF2 doesn't use text programming, and although pseudocode is most useful for those types of languages, we can still put it to good use to understand what we need to do in our program. Pseudocode is also very good for giving you an idea of how you should structure your program, and will help you with what areas you will need to put into it to get it to work. Let's take a simple example of what you want a program to do and then rewrite it in pseudocode. First, we want to make a program that displays a message on screen, and when you press a key (any key), it will disappear. Sounds easy enough, doesn't it? Well, not if you're not sure where to start, so let's break it down into what needs to happen.

```
1. Start of the Program
2. Text message appears on screen
3. Another message stating "click any key."
4. User presses any key
5. End of program
```

So, you have now written your first pseudocoded program and it's practical in any language—Pascal, C#, or even TGF2. Each language has its own rules for what you would need to do in each section, but you can understand what you will need to look for within the product documentation or help file. We will now go through each of the options and see what it means to our program. The start and end of the program should always appear in your pseudocode, as these will always happen. The options in between are what you want to happen in your program, so in this example we are putting text to the screen, showing another message, and responding to a key press. Once the key press has been completed, the program ends.

This is pseudocode at its most basic; for it to be more useful, we need to be a little more descriptive in what we are trying to achieve and how we will do it within our programs.

```
1. Start of the Program
2. Setup Screen, initial objects, variables and initialization.
3. Text message appears on screen
      Put text to screen at specific location on screen.
4. Place another message stating "click any key."
      Specify location on the screen.
5. User presses any key
      Await User Input
6. End of program
7. Close and remove objects and close window/screen
```

The great thing about pseudocode is that it can make quite complex code much easier to write and create. You will notice that some pseudocode is indented; you can do this to separate groups of code that work together, making it easier to read. Once you have converted your program to pseudocode, you can then go to each line and transfer it into TGF or another language.

SUMMARY

Understanding the concepts in TGF2 is very useful if you decide to learn another programming language. A number of TGF users have gone on to become prolific C++ programmers, and the catalyst for that was these types of programs. Sometimes, it can just be a case of understanding a concept, so once you know what it is all about you can then apply it in the real world. Do not underestimate the benefit of learning the basics, as it will definitely come in handy later if this is something that you wish to pursue.

4 TGF Creation Basics

In This Chapter

- Structure of a Game
- Game Creation Process in TGF2

I n this chapter, we discuss basic game creation concepts and what you are likely to see in any game you might download or play. We also cover some of the concepts and terminology you will be exposed to later in this book.

STRUCTURE OF A GAME

In game development, a number of configurations are available to programmers to make their games look more professional, and give the players more control over the way the game behaves in their operating system environment from a Windows GUI point of view. An example of this could be games running in a window, full-screen games, menu bars, and minimize and maximize options. In this section of the book, we go through the options available in games today, so when you start to program them yourself, you will know if these options would be useful to use. These are issues you should consider before beginning development of your games, as you might have to rework your program at a later stage if you decide to do things differently.

Some of the areas that you will come across in your development time include:

Full screen: The majority of modern full-priced games use full screen to display their game. With full screen enabled, you will not be able to see any part of the Windows operating system screen (e.g., the desktop or task bar).

Application window: Certain types of games prefer to use an application window to display their game rather than full screen. This allows game players to continue to use the Windows desktop and any programs they might be running (e.g., email). Card games and board games (chess, solitaire) are common games that run in an application window (see Figure 4.1).

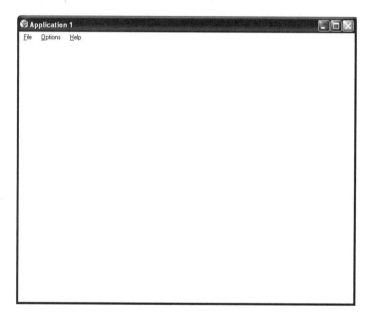

FIGURE 4.1   A game running in an application window rather than full screen.

Headings: If you are running your game in an application window, you can include a heading bar, where the name of the game (or application) is displayed (see Figure 4.2).

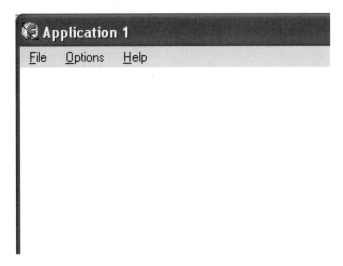

FIGURE 4.2 The heading bar is at the top, and the menu is directly below it.

Menu bar: When running your game in an application window, you can include a menu bar. You might be familiar with this concept, as they are included in many applications within the Windows environment. A menu bar allows the player to click on different bits of text and select options from a menu system (see Figure 4.2).

Minimize button: In the top right corner of an application window is the minimize button, and clicking on it can reduce a game to a small bar on the task bar. Clicking on the button (it will be an icon with the product's name on it) again will then restore the game to the desktop area (see in Figure 4.3).

Maximize button: In the top right corner of an application window is another button that allows you to maximize the game to the whole area of the desktop (this is not the same as full screen, as you can still access applications and the task bar using this option). The maximize button can be seen in Figure 4.3.

FIGURE 4.3 The three buttons signify minimize, maximize, and close.

Close button: Another option when using an application is the ability to close it. The close button is in the top right corner of the application window, and appears as a cross icon with a red background (see Figure 4.3).

Thick frame: If an application window has a thick frame, it means that it can be made larger or smaller using the mouse.

GAME CREATION PROCESS IN TGF2

Games created in TGF2 are comprised of a series of frames. These frames can be defined as a particular aspect of the game you are creating, perhaps the main menu, the game itself, or a frame for the high scores. The frame system provides a simple and easy way to break your game into sections; for example, you could create a frame for every level in your game, so each could be different (it also makes it faster to code). Frames make it easier for you to get other people involved in the development of your game, as you can get them to create the different sections and you can then import them into your final game structure. If you are working on your own, the frames system allows you to pick any area of the game, program it, make sure it works, and then move on to another area. If a particular aspect (frame) is causing a problem, you can still continue to program and leave the difficult frame for another time. The frame system provides an easy way to visualize the structure of your creation much more than using traditional programming languages. When you first open TGF2, no frames are present, and when you create a new game, it creates a single frame for you to get started with. If you have already designed the structure of your game, you can add new frames immediately to the program, and rename them appropriately (by default, they are "Frame 1," "Frame 2," etc.). Each of these newly created frames will be blank, as you will need to put graphics on them. To move between frames, double-click on the frame name in the workspace toolbar, or use the next frame option in the navigate menu toolbar (this will be covered shortly).

Each game created in this book contains three frames: one for the main menu, one of the actual game, and one for all the high scores.

Graphics and Objects

Once you have created your frame structure, you can then move on to the next stage of game development with TGF2, which is placing your graphics and objects on the play area. You may want to use the built-in graphic libraries that come with TGF2. If this is the case, you will need to drag the specific item from the graphics library (from the Library toolbar) on to the play area. A number of objects can be placed within TGF2 that can display images (objects are discussed later in the book), two of which are the Active object and the Backdrop object. If you want to use graphics that will be moving on the screen (e.g., a spaceship or a bullet), you would use Active, and if you want to have an image that is not going to interact in the game (e.g., a background image), you would select Backdrop. You may have already created your images in a third-party graphics tool, which is fine, because you can import a wide range of formats into TGF2 to use in your games. After inserting the object, you can double-click on it to open the Picture Editor, where you can then import any images you have created. As discussed in the next few chapters, a number of different objects can be added to a frame to add extra functionality. Each object has its advantages and uses within a game, and you will need to try them to see how you can use them (many of them are self-explanatory). There are some functions built into TGF2, and you don't have to insert an object onto the play area to use them; for example, input (keyboard and mouse), sound, and movement between frames are just some of the built-in functions you can access via the Event Editor using code. When playing a game, you may find that a graphic image looks like it is on fire or explodes. These are animation frames, and you can assign different animation effects to any active object you insert into your game.

The Event Editor

Once all of your graphics and game objects are in place, you need to do one more thing to get your game working: you need to tell TGF2 what to do with these objects, and what happens when the player does something specific (clicks with the left mouse button, uses the arrow keys, etc.). This requires you to create a number of actions for each event that can happen from within the Event Editor using TGF2's point-and-click programming language. Coding in the Event Editor is straightforward, and powerful. The programming language provided with TGF2 is very powerful and optimized for making many different game types. Each object has its own set of actions and conditions that can be accessed through the Event Editor, giving game developers a large number of possibilities in their creations.

SUMMARY

In this chapter, you were given a brief summary of the three main areas of game creation within TGF2. First, the creation of frames, which are the building blocks of your screens or levels. Then, we discussed objects, which are placed on each of the frames, and provide functionality within your games, using joysticks, graphic objects, video, and sounds. Finally, once you have placed your objects on your frames, you would then begin to code your games using the Event Editor.

5 Finding Your Way Around

In This Chapter

- System Requirements
- Program Installation
- Starting TGF2 for the First Time
- Toolbars
- The Editors
- Making More Space

In this chapter, we will be installing the TGF2 program and learning the interface. This is very important if you want to quickly start making games, and understand where to click when making the example games included with the book. By the end of the chapter, you will understand how to access each of the screens and why you might want to use them.

SYSTEM REQUIREMENTS

You need to consider two areas of system requirements when using TGF2: the system requirements for installing the product on your machine, and the requirements for the machine on which your completed game is going to be installed. This isn't a concern with the demo version on the companion CD-ROM, because you

47

can only make games for your own machine and cannot create executable games that can be distributed. We have included details on this for completeness in the event you purchase the full version of TGF2.

Installation Requirements

Table 5.1 lists the general system requirements for installing TGF2. Although these are the minimum required to install and run the product, a faster and better machine will improve the overall performance and speed of the product. The recommended installation requirements are listed in Table 5.2, and if your computer meets or exceeds these settings, you should have a much better game creation experience.

TABLE 5.1   System Requirements for Installation

Minimum Requirements

Operating system: Windows 95 with IE 4.0, Windows 98, Windows NT4 with Service Pack 3 or above, Windows 2000, Windows XP

Pentium processor

32 MB with Windows 9x, 64 MB with Windows NT, 128 MB with 2000 and Windows XP

CD-ROM drive

Graphics card with 8 MB or more

Sound card (optional but recommended)

50–100 MB free hard disk space

TABLE 5.2   Recommended System Requirements

Recommended Requirements

Operating system: Windows 98, Windows 2000, Windows XP

Pentium 4 processor

64 MB RAM with Windows 98, 256 MB RAM with Windows 2000 or XP

CD-ROM drive

Graphics card with 32 MB RAM

Sound card

100–200 MB free hard disk space

Runtime Requirements

Runtime requirements correspond to the developer giving a completed executable file to a user (it could be just the .exe or part of an install program), and the user installing it and running it on his PC. Runtime requirements are much more complicated to work out compared to installation and running requirements, because they are based on the size and complexity of the game. For example, a simple game with a single graphic that moves across the screen would have different runtime requirements than a game with hundreds of graphics and sound. To know what specifications you should put on your product, you will need to test it on a variety of hardware platforms. Many of the specifications for running your game on other people's machines can be found out easily. For example, CD-ROM, memory, and hard disk space can all be measured, while processor power required is much harder and would probably reveal the limits from your testing group. Finally, whenever you are specifying runtime system requirements, make sure your minimum settings match at least the operating system minimum requirements.

PROGRAM INSTALLATION

ON THE CD

The installation of the demo version of TGF2 is straightforward and requires following the on-screen prompts, accepting the license agreement, and accepting (or changing) the install path. The demo version of TGF2 is on the CD-ROM that accompanies this book. The TGF2 installation file, TGF2Setup.exe, is in the Demos folder. Double-click on this file to begin the installation.

NOTE

At the time of writing, TGF2 was not released, and a special demo version has been provided for users of this book. Please check for updates to the demo installer on www.clickteam.com or www.makeamazing.com before running the included installer; newer versions will include bug fixes and new features.

STARTING TGF2 FOR THE FIRST TIME

To start TGF2, double-click on the TGF2 icon on the desktop, or click Start, Programs, Clickteam, and then TGF2 Demo. TGF2 will now load and appear on screen, as shown in Figure 5.1.

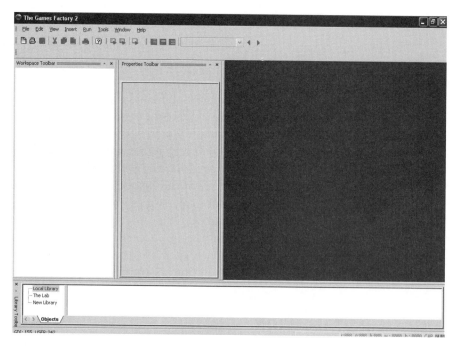

FIGURE 5.1   The TGF2 main screen.

The TGF2 program can be broken into a number of separate sections (see Figure 5.2):

Menu bar: Item one in Figure 5.2 is the menu bar, which is where you can access all of TGF2's creation, configuration, and display options. To reveal the options, click on the menu text and select a word from the drop-down menu. Some items will be grayed out, which means they are disabled, because you cannot set an option while in the current screen. Items will become enabled when you are in the correct screen.

Menu toolbars: Item two in Figure 5.2 is the Toolbar, which is a graphical icon used to move to another screen, to another editor, or to change an option. There are a number of toolbars that will appear or disappear depending on the screen you are currently in.

Workspace toolbar: Item three in Figure 5.2 is the Workspace toolbar, which contains the building blocks for each level.

Properties toolbar: Many items within TGF2 have property settings, allowing you to configure the look and the way they interact within your game. Every time you click on anything that has configurable properties, it will appear in item four in Figure 5.2.

Editor area: You will use a number of editors within TGF2; for example, the Storyboard, Frame, and Event Editors all appear in item five in Figure 5.2

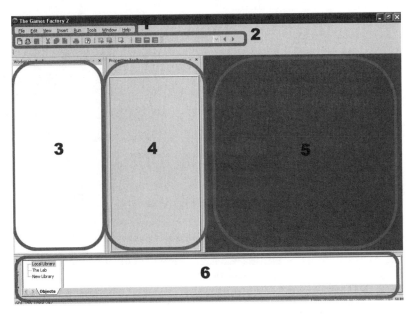

FIGURE 5.2   Breakdown of the main sections in TGF2.

Library toolbar: The Library toolbar contains images and objects that you can use within your game. By simply using drag and drop, you can move an item from the library into your game. The Library toolbar is shown in item six in Figure 5.2.

Menu Bars

The menu bar is at the top of TGF's application window, and looks like a row of text. Clicking on any of these words will reveal a pop-up menu, an example of which is shown in Figure 5.3. The menu bar contains a number of configuration and display settings for you to choose. Some of the items have an underlined first letter (e.g., the "F" in File), which means that you can access the menu option using a shortcut key. The shortcut key can be enabled by holding down the ALT key and then selecting the underlined letter you want to access. For example, if you wanted to access the File menu, you could use the shortcut ALT and then "F" to make the pop-up menu appear.

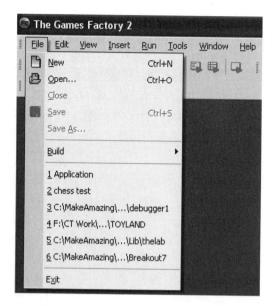

FIGURE 5.3   An example of what happens when clicking on the menu.

   Consult TGF2's help documentation on any specific option in the menu bar for more information.

TOOLBARS

Toolbars can be broken up into two distinct areas: graphic icons that can be clicked to create, enable, or configure something within TGF2, and toolbars for specific purposes; for example, gathering all your graphic resources or looking at multiple layers (a number of toolbars can be switched on or off by right-clicking on the toolbar area). The toolbars available in TGF2 include:

- Standard
- Navigate
- Run
- Editor—Storyboard and Frame
- Workspace
- Properties
- Library
- Layers

The Standard Toolbar

The Standard toolbar exists on all screens that you will navigate to within TGF2 (see Figure 5.4). There are eight buttons, and are basic file and print operations. The icons from left to right are:

FIGURE 5.4 The Standard toolbar.

New: Create a new game.

Open: Open a previously saved game or example. A dialog box will appear and you will need to browse to where the programs are located. TGF2 can open a range of file types, including TGF2 files, previous versions, and library files created with CT's older software.

Save: You have to have a document open to be able to save it. When you first open TGF2, this option will be disabled.

Cut: Allows you to cut (remove and place in the clipboard) an object or event, ready for pasting back into the TGF2 application.

Copy: Makes a copy (doesn't remove the object or event, but places an exact copy on the clipboard) ready for pasting back.

Undo: If you make a mistake or decide the change you just made was incorrect, you can revert to the previous version by using the Undo option.

Redo: If you use the Undo option and then decide that you didn't want to, you can reapply the changes.

Paste: Paste the object or event back into the TGF2 application.

About: The About box contains information on the makers of TGF2, and the version number of the product you are using.

The Navigate Toolbar

The Navigate toolbar is used to move between the Storyboard, Frame, and Event Editors, and to move between game levels (known as frames) (see Figure 5.5).

Back and Forward: If you move from one frame to another and want to quickly go back or forward between screens, press the red arrowed buttons. Think of this as a Web browser, where you can move between Web pages, except in TGF2, you are moving between screens.

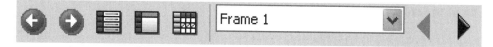

FIGURE 5.5   The Navigate toolbar.

Storyboard: Clicking on the Storyboard icon will display the Storyboard Editor, which is a high-level view of all of the levels within your game.

Frame Editor: The Frame Editor allows you place all of your images and game objects within each of your levels.

Event Editor: The Event Editor is the area in which to code your game. You will use actions, events, and conditions in a simple mouse-clicking environment to build your games.

Frame Navigator: Using a drop-down box, you can select a specific level of your game to go to, which is identified by its frame name.

Previous Frame: Go back to the previous frame, if one is available.

Next Frame: Go to the next frame, if one is available.

The Run Toolbar

When you want to test your games, you use the Run toolbar. Three options are available, as shown in Figure 5.6.

FIGURE 5.6   The Run toolbar.

Run Application: This option will start the game and run it from the beginning as if the end user was running the final executable on his PC, so you can test each part of your game as a final running program.

Run Frame: The Run frame will run only the frame you are currently editing. Use this to test a particular frame; any exits to other frames will automatically close the running game.

Stop: This option will be grayed out until you select either Run Application or Run Frame, after which you can stop the game from running by pressing this button.

The Editor Toolbar—Storyboard Editor

When working in the Storyboard Editor, there are a number of buttons in the toolbar you can choose from (as shown in Figure 5.7).

FIGURE 5.7 The Editor toolbar for the Storyboard.

Zoom Bar: The zoom option is a small bar that you can drag either left or right to increase or decrease the amount of zooming. This will make the Storyboard Editor increase or decrease in size.

Zoom Entry: You can enter a specific amount you wish to zoom the Storyboard Editor. The default is set at 100; anything below 100 will make the Storyboard area smaller, and anything above 100 will make it larger.

Show Headers: By default, this is turned on, and clicking it will turn the column headers off (the headers detail what is shown below them). You can turn them back on by clicking the button again.

Show Comments: The comments column in the Storyboard Editor can be turned on and off by clicking on this button (comments are turned on by default). To turn them back on, click on the button again.

The Editor Toolbar—Frame Editor

When doing any work within the Frame Editor (as shown in Figure 5.8), you will have a number of options to choose from, but not all will be available at all times. You will only have access to certain features when using specific options (e.g., editing text).

FIGURE 5.8 The Editor toolbar.

Zoom: You can zoom the Frame Editor in or out using a drop-down box to select the percentage you need. You can choose from 25%, 50%, 100% (normal size), 200%, and 400%.

Grid Setup: Clicking on the Grid Setup button will display a dialog box to allow you to configure a grid. This grid can then be placed on the Frame Editor to help you place your game objects and images using the Show Grid button.

Show Grid: Once you are happy with the grid configuration, you can display it on the Frame Editor by clicking this button. You can turn off the grid by clicking the Show Grid button a second time. The grid appears as a set of dots across the playfield.

Snap to Grid: By clicking the Snap to Grid button, you can precisely position any objects on the playfield using the grid dots.

Font: If editing text, you can select the font you want to use by clicking on this button.

Bold: As with the Font button, if you are editing text, you can apply the bold option.

Italic: You can apply the italic option to any text you are currently editing.

Underline: A line will appear under any text you are editing.

Text Color: If you are not happy with the default text color (black), you can select a different color. As with the other text options, you must be editing a text object to have these options available.

Align Left: Moves the text to the left in the edit box.

Center: Centers the text in the edit box.

Align Right: Moves the text to the right in the edit box.

Center Frame: This will force the display to center the current frame you are editing, which is very useful if you are editing a very large playfield and want to go back to its center.

The Workspace Toolbar

The Workspace toolbar shows the application and the frame (levels) that make up the game. This is a high-level view and is used to navigate between the levels of your game quickly. It is also used in conjunction with the Properties toolbar, so clicking on the application name or a frame will reveal its properties. An example of the Workspace toolbar in use is shown in Figure 5.9.

Within the Workspace toolbar, you can also see all of the game objects involved in the creation of your game (which you can see by clicking on the plus icon to expand the text). You can also create folders to contain a selection of the game objects, so you can place similar objects together for ease of use.

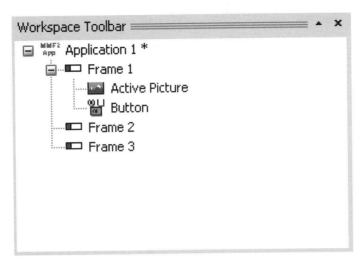

FIGURE 5.9 The Workspace toolbar, high-level game view.

The Properties Toolbar

When clicking on an application or frame within the Workspace toolbar, or clicking on an object in the Frame Editor, its associated properties will appear in the Properties toolbar. Properties of these items allow you to configure them for your game, which can change the look and the way they behave in your final executable. An example of the properties toolbar can be seen in Figure 5.10.

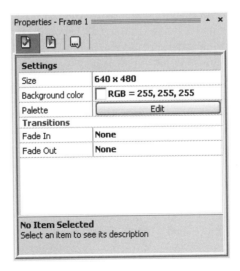

FIGURE 5.10 Application, Frame, and Object properties.

The Library Toolbar

With the full version of TGF2, you receive a number of graphic images and animations, which can be accessed via the Library toolbar. When creating the games in this book, you will use this toolbar. The Library toolbar allows you quick access to a folder on your hard drive that contains images, animations, or library files from previous versions of your product. The Library toolbar can be seen in Figure 5.11.

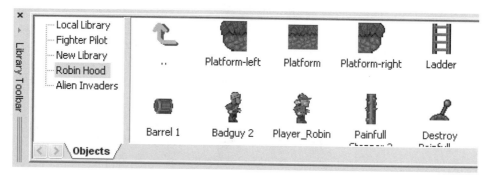

FIGURE 5.11   An example library loaded and ready to use.

The Layers Toolbar

Layer is a term usually used in graphics packages to describe various layers an image or color might be positioned in (think of a stack of books, and each book is a layer). You can position forward or backward, display, and hide each layer if need be. Layers are a great way to make images disappear behind other images or produce a scrolling technique called *parallax scrolling*. Parallax scrolling was a popular type of scrolling used on many older game creations. The Layers toolbar allows you to create your various game layers, turn them on or off, and configure the scrolling settings. The Layers toolbar can be seen in Figure 5.12.

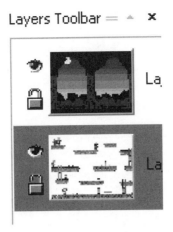

FIGURE 5.12 The Layers toolbar with two layers configured.

THE EDITORS

When making games within TGF2, you will use a number of editors. These editors are the core components for putting all of the various aspects of your game together or for viewing its current state.

The Storyboard Editor

To understand what the Storyboard Editor is, you need to understand how games are created. Each game can be made with a number of frames that generally relate to a level or story within your game. Consider a frame as a blank piece of paper on which you will design your game, and then place a number of other pages under it to create your levels. The Storyboard Editor can be described as the top-level layout of your game creation. From here, you will be able to see all of your game's levels and screens, and be able to select a specific frame to go into more detail. Figure 5.13 is an example of what the Storyboard Editor looks like.

Within the Storyboard Editor, you have a number of options that you can configure:

- Each game frame is represented by a picture. This is a zoomed-out picture and is not meant to show the full game screen, just a representation so you know what the frame is about.
- Each frame can also be identified by the frame title, which is the name you give to each frame; by default, it takes the form of frame 1, frame 2, and so on.

- You can assign a password to each frame, by entering a combination of letters and numbers.
- A transition can be applied to the start and end of a frame. Transitions are very common in multimedia and films, and can be put to good use in your games.
- Each frame will have a screen size. There can be different screen sizes for each frame and for the application.

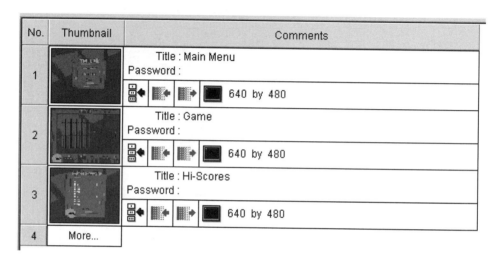

FIGURE 5.13   An example of a game seen in the Storyboard Editor.

The Frame Editor

The Frame Editor is where you place all of your game objects on screen to create your levels. You can have multiple frames, but can only work on one frame at a time. Frames can contain many types of objects, which are the building blocks of your game creation. The Frame Editor is very visual, and you can use drag and drop to move and place items on the screen. An example of the Frame Editor can be seen in Figure 5.14.

On the left side of the Frame Editor is the object list bar, which displays all of the objects that are placed on the play area. You can display the items as small or large icons, or sort them by name or object type. It is possible to reduce or increase the size of the object bar list by holding down the left mouse button on the edge of the window and moving it smaller or bigger.

The right side of the Frame Editor is called the play area, which is where the game will be shown when the program is run. By default, the area that will be displayed is shown as a white box, but this can be configured to another color if required. Any objects within the white box will appear in the game. If you are making complex games, you will place a number of objects out of view (outside the white box) and introduce them when they are needed.

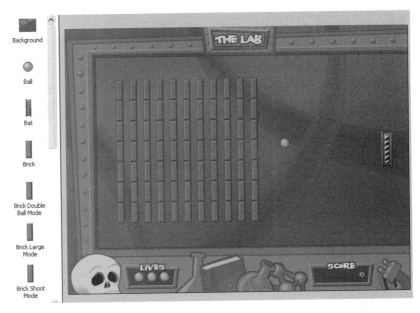

FIGURE 5.14   The Frame Editor. ©Jason Darby 2005. Reprinted with permission.

The Event Editor

Once all game graphics and objects have been placed on the frame, it is time to make them interact, and you do this by coding in the Event Editor. The coding in TGF2 is not the same as a traditional scripting program, but consists of creating events, conditions, and actions using the right mouse button. An example of the Event Editor with some code programmed into it can be seen in Figure 5.15.

- Each number represents an event line.
- Text on a white background (in this example) are comment lines.
- The first six icons across the top are called System objects and are always present.
- All objects after the initial six are objects that have been added to the program by the developer.
- Each event is made up of conditions.
- A tick indicates that an action has been applied to the condition on the left to the object directly above it.

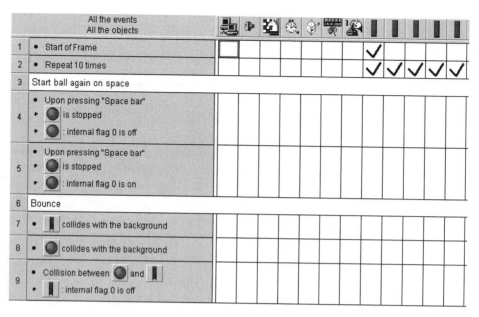

FIGURE 5.15 The Event Editor in use.

The Picture Editor

The Picture Editor is used when you are making changes to the appearance of any image or creating a new image. This image might be an active object or another object that has graphic properties. It is also used to edit the Application icon (the icon that is displayed when the game is run in an Application window). An example of the Picture Editor in use can be seen in Figure 5.16.

The Picture Editor contains many options that you might find in a graphics package. The benefit of using the one included in TGF2 is that you can save some time, as you are making changes directly within TGF2 rather than in another program and then importing them. Some of the options you can find in the Editor are (starting from the top line and working to the right):

Clear: This will remove any images that are currently being displayed.

Import: You can import a number of precreated graphic formats into TGF2, including TGA, PNG, JPEG, GIF, BMP, and PCX. Browse for the image, highlight it, and then click Open to complete the import.

Export: If you have created or amended an image, you may want to export it to a file. The same image file formats are available for import that you can use when saving for export. When exporting, you will need to specify a format and its name.

FIGURE 5.16 The Picture Editor. Game developed by Teddysday Ltd–Reprinted with permission.

Grab: If you want to obtain an image from another program that is currently running, or perhaps on the desktop, you can do this by clicking the Grab icon.

Cut: Takes the selected area of the image and places it on the clipboard ready for pasting into this or any other package.

Copy: Copy the selected area and place it on the clipboard for pasting.

Paste: Take the contents of the clipboard and paste it into the Picture Editor.

Delete: This will take the selected area on the graphic and delete it.

Undo: Undo what you just did. For example, you may have deleted something or drew on a part of the picture that you didn't mean to; selecting Undo allows you to go back a step and start again.

Redo: If you have just pressed Undo and feel that the change you made was actually okay, you can put that change back by clicking on the Redo button.

Flip Horizontally: This will flip the image horizontally (left to right).

Flip Vertically: This will flip the image vertically (top to bottom).

Crop: If you have an image that has a lot of white space, and you want to resize the canvas to the size of the graphic image, you can use Crop. Select the area of the image you want to keep, and then click on Crop to remove the rest of the graphic area. The canvas will automatically be resized.

Options: The Options button allows you to configure how the right mouse button is used in the Picture Editor. The default setting when pressing the right mouse button in the Picture Editor is set to draw the selected background color. If this option is amended, it will pick the color under the mouse cursor when pressing the mouse button.

Zoom: Zoom out is only available if you zoomed in (making the image bigger).

Zoom x1: This will reset the zoom so the image returns to its original size.

Zoom +: Zoom in, which will make the image larger.

Alpha Channels: The Alpha channel button allows you to assign varying levels of transparency to an image.

Selection Tool: Using the Selection tool, you can pick an area of the image ready for cropping, deleting, copying, and so forth. The selected area will be shown as a dotted box.

Color Picker: The Color Picker allows you to click anywhere on an image and get a specific color, which can then be applied to the drawing tools.

Brush Tool: If you want to draw freely (like a brush on a painting), you can use the Brush tool. Keeping your finger on the left mouse button will activate the drawing effect.

Line Tool: If you want to draw straight lines on the images, you can use the Line tool.

Rectangle Tool: If you need a Rectangle shape within your image, you can use the Rectangle tool rather than trying to draw it with individual lines.

Ellipse Tool: If you want to apply an ellipse shape (circular-based shapes), you can quickly create one using this button.

Polygon Tool: You can quickly and easily create a polygon shape by using this icon. When using it, you will have a line-type object where you will draw a line, and then continue to draw another line from the last point of the previous line.

Shape Tool: Using the Shape tool, anything you draw will become an enclosed shape. You can then apply fill and line size options to this.

Fill Tool: If you want to apply a specific color to an area of an image, you can use the Fill tool to do this.

Spray Tool: Exactly like a spray can, you can draw color to your image in various sizes.

Text Tool: If you want to write some text on your image, you would select the Text tool and then apply the font, size, and color properties.

Eraser Tool: The Eraser tool allows you to delete parts of your image using a small square. You can change the size of the Eraser by increasing the size number.

Size: If you want to increase or decrease the size of an image, you can use the Size tool. You also have the option to redraw proportionally, stretch, or re-sample the image.

Rotate: You can rotate an image on its axis to change its orientation.

View Hot Spot: A hot spot is an invisible location on your images that is used as an image reference point. You can reference this hot spot within the Event Editor.

View Action Points: An action point is the location at which something can happen. For example, if you have a spaceship that will fire bullets, you could state the location of the action point so the bullets appear from a certain location. You can move the action point by clicking on the View button and then left clicking on the image to relocate it.

On the right side of the Picture Editor is the color grid, which is where you would select the specific color with which you want to draw. You can use the left and right mouse buttons to apply a different color to the clicking of each button. The bottom half of the Picture Editor includes the ability to create animation frames. You could create an image of a space ship, and then create an animation frame for it moving upward, being destroyed, and appearing on screen. You would then access these animation frames from code within the Event Editor.

You can find out what an icon is called using the Tools Tip. Keep the mouse over the icon, and a text name will appear.

The Expression Evaluator

The Expression Evaluator looks very much like a large scientific calculator (see Figure 5.17). The Expression Evaluator's appearance will change, depending on where you use it. The Evaluator is used to create mathematic calculations, text and number comparisons, text manipulation, and a number of other things.

The Expression Evaluator may look complicated at first, but once you have used it a few times, you will find it an extremely powerful tool. Some areas of the Expression Evaluator include:

Number Keypad: Here you can press a number or mathematical sign (plus, minus, etc.) to insert it into the expression. Alternatively, you can use the number pad on your keyboard, as this is much quicker method.

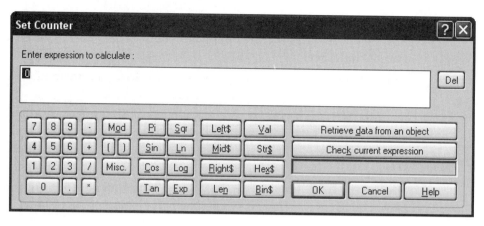

FIGURE 5.17   The Expression Evaluator.

Mod: Mod is used to find the remainder of an integer that's been divided from two numbers. For example, if you typed "100 mod 15," the answer would be 10. If you find how much 15 can go into 100 the amount would be 90. Therefore, from this calculation the answer is 10.

((Left Bracket): When creating some expressions, you will need to separate certain items (usually numeric calculations) with a set of brackets. This inserts a left bracket. You can also use the keyboard to enter this.

) (Right Bracket): When you want to close an expression that uses a left bracket, you must use a right closing bracket.

Misc: When you click on the Misc button, you will be given four options: Power, Bit-wise AND, Bit-wise OR, and Bit-wise XOR. It is a way to compare bit-wise operators and find if they are true. Power takes the form of "Number Pow Number"; for example, "2 Pow 5 = 32," which is the first number times itself up to the second number. Therefore, the number 2 is multiplied by 2 five times, to make the calculation look like "$2 \times 2 \times 2 \times 2 \times 2$." Consult the program's help file if you require more information on this subject.

Pi: Pi is a word that is used to represent a mathematical equation, which is displayed in TGF2 as 3.141592654.

Sin: Sin (also known as sine) is a basic mathematical function used in trigonometry.

Cos: Cos (also known as cosine) is a basic mathematical function used in trigonometry.

Tan: Tan (also known as tangent) is a basic mathematical function used in trigonometry.

Sqr: Sqr stands for Square Root; the result is the reverse if squaring a number. The number that gives the square root is when the result is multiplied by itself; for example, the square root of 9 is 3, as $3 \times 3 = 9$, and the sqr of $100 = 10$, because $10 \times 10 = 100$.

Left$: Takes a number of characters from a piece of text from the left-hand side. For example, Left$("Hello this is a piece of text",5) would return the word "Hello."

Mid$: Allows you to remove a number of letters from the left and right of a string. For example, Mid$ ("Hello again",7,5) would return "again." The first number (in this example, 7) tells TGF2 how many characters to remove from the left, and the second number (5) tells TGF2 how many characters to keep.

Right$: Removes a number of characters from the left side of a string. For example, Right$("Hello",1) would return "ello."

Len: This returns the number of characters in a string. For example, Len("Hello") would return the number 5.

Val: Converts a string to a number. An example of this would be Val("5").

Str$: Converts a number to a text. For example, Str$ (5) will convert the number 5 to a string so it can be displayed in a text object.

Hex$: Converts a decimal number to a hexadecimal number.

Bin$: Converts an integer number to a binary number.

Retrieve Data From an Object: You can obtain data from another object, compare it, and read it into the Expression Evaluator. You could, for example, read the number of lives from the lives object and display it in a string object.

Check Current Expression: This checks the expression that has been typed in and confirms that it is correct. It will display a message of valid or invalid expression depending on the situation.

You cannot mix numbers with text when doing calculations; they can only contain one or the other. You can, however, convert a number or a string to another format using the Val( ) and Str$( ) commands. You will use these a lot when programming in TGF2.

MAKING MORE SPACE

With all of the Properties toolbars in use, the TGF2 screen can get very busy, especially if you are running a screen resolution equal to or less than 1024 x 768. You can create more space by minimizing areas of the screen that you are currently not using, or alternatively hide them from view until you need them. There are a couple of ways to make more space:

- Right-click anywhere on the button toolbar area to bring up the "Toolbar" pop-up menu. Click on any of the ticked options to hide them from the screen; additionally, if you want to bring an option back, you can click on an unticked option.
- Move the mouse cursor to the edge of a toolbar window; a double pointed arrow will appear. Hold down the left mouse button and then drag in the direction you desire to increase or decrease the size.
- On the corner of each toolbar is a small "x"; click on this to remove the toolbar from the screen. Use the Toolbar pop-up menu to bring it back.
- Drag the Toolbar buttons, so some are on the same line.

SUMMARY

You should now have installed TGF2 and have a basic understanding of its screens and editors. In the rest of the book, we will start drilling down into the editors and programs of TGF2 in more detail, so you can make amazing games. The program is extremely powerful and can feel a little complicated initially; however, once you have made a couple of games, you will find it straightforward. In the following chapters, you will begin to learn about objects and properties, a very important aspect of configuring how your graphics and screens react.

6 Objects, the Cornerstone of Creation

In This Chapter

- What Are Objects?
- Objects in TGF2

In this chapter, we discuss what objects are and how they are used within TGF2 to make your games even more powerful. Within your game you will use a group of objects, which, as the chapter title suggests, are the cornerstone to your creation, and you cannot create a game without them. We will look at what you can do with them and what specific objects are available in TGF2.

WHAT ARE OBJECTS?

Objects are the building blocks to your games. A game is comprised of various components—for example, a simple alien spaceship graphic, a noise sample when bullets are fired, background graphics, and in-game video—all of which will be put into your game using objects. TGF2 comes with a number of built-in objects that will help you generate many different game types.

Adding an Object

To view the objects, you must be in the process of adding an object. To add an object, you must be at the Frame Editor screen (where you can see the playfield of where you will make your game).

1. Start TGF2. Select File | New from the menu.
2. Double-click on the text "Frame 1" in the Workspace toolbar (this will load the Frame Editor and display the play area).
3. From the menu, select Insert | New Object. You will now see a list of all the objects you can use in your game (see Figure 6.1).

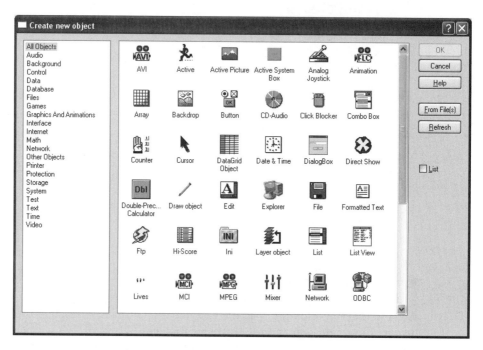

FIGURE 6.1 The Create New Object dialog box.

Browse through the list and select the object you want to use by clicking on the object image once and then clicking the OK button, or you can double-click on the icon. Your mouse cursor will then change to a crosshair over the playfield frame; click the left mouse button anywhere on the playfield to place the object. Once you have placed the object, you will be able to configure its properties and use it within your game.

OBJECTS IN TGF2

It is very useful to understand how each of the default objects included with TGF2 can be used within your game, and more importantly when you need to use them. Each object has its advantages, and some may seem similar but are used for different reasons. Some objects can only play a single role within your game creation; for example, the "High Score" object.

The following objects are included in TGF2:

AVI: AVI is a popular video format that allows you to play Windows movie files in TGF2. You can use video clips to enhance your games by making them more exciting, or as a way to separate levels. You have standard video controls available to you so you can pause, play, stop, and move forward and back any AVI file you have within your program.

Active: Any object that will move and interact within TGF2; a perfect example of this would be a player's ship or a set of planes. The object may also have animation assigned to it.

Active Picture: Allows the import of various picture file formats including BMP, GIF, JPG, and PCX onto the playfield. You can then move, rotate, and resize the object in real time. You can import the image when configuring the object properties, or when using the Event Editor.

Active System Box: If you want to create a button or background that can use the local computer's system colors, you can use the Active Box. The Active Box also allows it to be used as a checkbox or hyperlink.

ActiveX: Allows TGF2 to access and make use of ActiveX controls installed on the computer, thereby increasing the functionality of the program. It is possible to write ActiveX programs within other languages such as C++, or use those that are installed locally. A popular ActiveX program that TGF2 can use is Internet Explorer, which would allow the programmer to put a Web browser within TGF2.

Analog Joystick: Although many users these days are used to playing games via the keyboard, there is a joystick option where you can configure the buttons to specific actions within the game.

Animation: Using file formats such as FLI, FLC, and JPEG you can import a number of still images and play them as a single animation, which will create the illusion of smooth, animated movies.

Array: We discussed the concepts behind arrays in Chapter 3, "Programming Concepts." If you want to store game data or configuration information, the Array object is a great way to do so. You have the option of selecting a one-, two-, or three-dimensional array, which allows more power and flexibility in storing data.

Backdrop: A backdrop is a static image, and is perfect for background images and pictures that do not need to move.

Background System Box: Used as a background object that can have a tooltip (text appears when the mouse is over it) or an image.

Button: You will see buttons in use in standard Windows dialog boxes and programs. Within TGF2, you have the ability to apply a number of button types to your games, including pushbuttons, bitmap buttons, checkboxes, and radio buttons.

CD Audio: If you want to play audio tracks from within your program off a CD, the CD Audio object is the way to do it. It will allow you to play, pause, skip, and stop tracks. This is a very useful object if you want to make your game play high-quality CD music tracks off your CD-ROMs.

Combo Box: The Combo Box is another standard Window control, and allows you to create simple lists and drop-down menus.

Counter: Used as a counting mechanism, and provides it as a graphical representation.

Date & Time: The Clock object allows you to put a clock in your productions. You can insert either an analog- or digital-looking clock onto the playfield. The Clock object is also useful for setting a time, or creating a countdown or stopwatch effect (you may want to limit the amount of time a player has to complete a task on a specific level).

Draw: Using the Draw object, you can paint directly onto the playfield while the game is running. You can do this passively (where you set the shape in the code), or you can do it interactively (where you use the mouse or other control to draw directly to the screen).

Edit: The Edit object is another standard Windows control that allows simple text editing features such as data entry, and cutting and pasting of text.

File: The File object allows you to create standard disk operations such as creating a file, appending to a file, and allows you to run external files or applications.

Formatted Text: If you want to insert text onto the screen and apply formatting to it (font, size, bold, color, etc.), you would use this object.

Hi-Score: Many games have the capability for users to enter a high score if they beat a specific score. TGF2 allows you to set up a hi-score table to record the score and the name of the player. You can specify the number of scores the game will display and some default names.

INI: An INI file is a specially formatted text file contained on the end user's hard disk. The file contents can be written to and read from.

List: A simple yet effective way of creating lists in TGF2 using the standard list box, with configurable options.

Lives: A special object that can be used to track, add, and reduce player lives.

MCI: MCI stands for Media Control Interface, and is a format for controlling multimedia devices that are connected to your computer. It is useful for playing sound and video files.

MPEG: MPEG stands for Motion Picture Expert Group, and the object allows movies saved in this format to be played with TGF2. You will need to have a software MPEG driver already installed to use this within your games (so will the client computers that you want to distribute your programs to).

Mixer: If you want to control the volume of samples and music files, you would use the Mixer object. The Mixer object also allows you to specify which speaker you want sound to be played in (so you could configure certain sounds to go through the left or right speaker only).

Picture: The Picture object is very similar to the Active Picture object in that you can import a picture in various formats (BMP, PCX, JPG, GIF, and others) for showing in your game. You cannot rotate and resize the object in real time, though; this is for simply showing a picture as a background. You can get the user to select an image or import one before the game starts.

Print: If you want to allow the player to print a specific part of the screen or perhaps the in-game instructions, you will need to use the Print object.

Question & Answer: This object allows you to set up simple question and answer commands. For example, you could ask the users if they like a certain color, and then make the program react to the answer.

Quick Backdrop: Creates a simple yet effective background picture, which can also be a gradient (selection of colors).

Score: An object to keep track of the player's score.

Screen Capture: Allows you to capture parts of the screen and save them to the hard disk.

Search: Allows searches to be completed of text-based files on the user's hard disk.

Shared Data: Ability to share data between two TGF2 programs.

String: Simple text-based object.

Sub Application: Allows you to insert another TGF2 file into an area on the current loaded file.

Vitalize Plug-in: The Plug-in object allows you to connect to an external URL (Web page), and download a file.

Window Control: The Window Control object allows you to change the visibility, size, and location of your game window on the screen, which is very useful if you want to display multiple windows in specific positions on the screen.

Additional objects may be included in the latest version of TGF2. Visit www.clickteam.com for the latest information.

SUMMARY

Objects are a key component in making games in TGF2, and allow you to create many possible game types (different game types were discussed in Chapter 1, "Games, Games, and More Games"). Take a good long look through the objects available in TGF2 before starting any major projects, and make a note of which ones you will use. This will make the process of creation much quicker, rather than trying to find an object to suit your needs when you are already in the process of making your game. With its previous product, Clickteam released bonus packs that contained a number of new and interesting objects that extended the product's power and functionality. Visit the Web site (*www.clickteam.com*) every so often to see if one has been released, as it may be an object that can make your game development much easier.

7 Configuring Properties

In this chapter, we look at how to configure our games. To do this, we use the Property window. We will be able to set up our programs at various levels, from the entire game, to each level, and each object added on the playfield. The properties will allow you to configure many different aspects that the end user will see when playing your game. We will also look at properties that only apply to objects, and some useful shortcuts that will allow you to set the same configuration for any number of objects.

PROPERTIES EXPLAINED

Within TGF2, each application, frame, and object you create will have its own set of properties, which in turn will affect its appearance and behavior. Properties for each of these items will appear in the Properties toolbar. An example of the properties sheet can be seen in Figure 7.1.

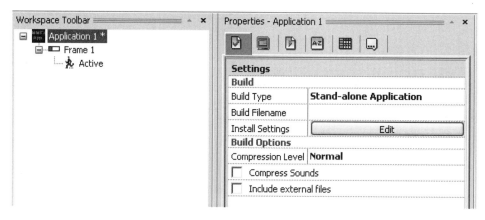

FIGURE 7.1   The Properties toolbar showing application properties.

 A frame can be thought of as a level within a game, and you can have multiple frames within a game, each representing different aspects. In the games we will be making, a frame will be configured as a main menu, the game itself, and the area to add high scores. We discuss frames in more detail in the next chapter.

Every time you select a different frame, application, or object, the Properties toolbar will display the relevant options that can be configured. Three property sheets will appear when using the product:

Application Properties: The Application properties apply to the entire game. The configuration of these properties are generally high-level settings for the game you are making, which include properties such as the filename, or the type of program it will be exported as (e.g., screensaver or executable).

Frame Properties: Within each game you create, you can have multiple frames, and each frame has its own configurable properties, allowing you to tailor each section of your game to your specific needs.

Object Properties: Each object you place on the frame can have its own set of properties. The individual object properties can be quite in-depth and allow configuration of things such as text type and size, movement and position, and many other options. You can also set object behavior and qualifiers using the property sheet (discussed later in this chapter).

Property Tabs

Each property sheet (Application, Frame, and Object) has all of its properties categorized and grouped into tabs, which allow you to easily find a specific set of properties you want to change (see Figure 7.2). The tabs for both the application and the frame level are static and do not change. However, for the object properties level, each object you can add onto the frame may have a different set of tabs depending on what type of object it is. For example, a text-based object will have text formatting configurable options, whereas an active object would not.

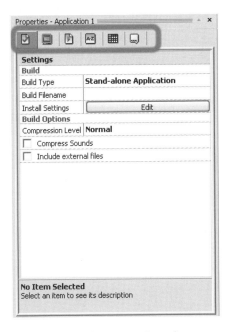

FIGURE 7.2 The Properties tabs.

You can find out what a tab is supposed to do by highlighting the tab image with your mouse cursor; a text description of the tab will then appear.

Application Properties

To see what properties are available at the application level, you will need to click on the Application icon within the Workspace toolbar (the topmost icon within the workspace area). Upon clicking it, the configuration details for the entire application will appear in the Properties window. The tabs within the Application properties are shown in Figure 7.3.

FIGURE 7.3   The Application Properties tabs.

The tabs are from left to right as follows:

Settings: Options for building the game and how much compression should be used.

Window: Details what size the game should be, and options for how the window should behave once the program has been built.

Runtime Options: Options for when the game is running, including graphics and sound options.

Values: The application's global options that allow you to set up global values and global strings.

Events: The setting up of any events that will apply to the entire application (global events).

About: All about the application; this includes information that will appear once the game has been built, and the option of including help files and documentation.

Frame Properties

The Frame properties can be accessed by clicking on the Frame icon, which is located below the Application icon in the Workspace toolbar. As there can be multiple frames within each game, you will need to select the relevant frame for which you want to change the properties. Any changes you make on one frame will not change the properties on any of the others. The tabs within the Application Properties are shown in Figure 7.4.

The tabs are from left to right as follows:

Settings: Basic screen settings for each frame.

Runtime Options: Configuration of each frame when the game is running; includes options for background colors and frame size.

About: Contains just the name of the frame and no other settings.

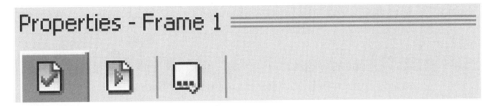

FIGURE 7.4 The Frame Properties tabs.

Object Properties

The Object properties can be accessed by clicking on any object on the frame. Once you have left-clicked on any object, the Properties sheet will then appear in the Workspace toolbar. An example of the Object Properties tabs can be seen in Figure 7.5.

FIGURE 7.5 The Object Properties tabs.

Remember that different objects may have different property tabs, unlike an application that only has one set of tabs, and frames that can have multiple properties but have the same set of tabs for each.

Tabs that might appear include:

Settings: These are object settings that will be different on each object, as they are the configuration of that particular object.

Display Options: Will the object be visible on the playfield, and will it use any transparency or ink effects?

Alterable Values: You can assign up to 26 alterable values against each object. This allows you to store numerical data against a particular object rather than using other objects to achieve the same effect.

Size/Position: The size of the object and where will it be placed on the screen (using screen coordinates).

Text Options: Setting the text display object, font types, sizes, and color.

Movement: Will the objects move, and if so, which type of movement, in what direction, and at what speed?

Runtime Options: Allow the object to follow the frame, or be destroyed if it goes off the playfield. Options that will allow you to reduce memory allocation to your program by tidying up the use of the objects.

Events: The setting up of behaviors and qualifiers in an event(s) that will apply to the object when running the program.

About: This will contain the name of the object and display the object's icon (which you can modify).

Now that you understand how the Properties tabs work, we will now look at them in more depth, so you will know when to use them when putting together your game, and be able to use this book as a reference for finding the right options to amend.

APPLICATION PROPERTIES IN-DEPTH

As mentioned previously, amending the Application properties affects the entire game, so it is important to understand that any changes here might override any set in each frame. If your game is not displaying the way you want it to, there might be a conflict between these two groups of properties.

The Settings Tab

An example of the options in the Settings tab can be seen in Figure 7.6.

Build Type: This will be the final outputted file format, and you have three choices: a standalone application (an executable), a screensaver (a "Scr" file), or an Internet application (can be played within a Web browser such as Internet Explorer).

Build Filename: The filename of the final build type.

Install Settings: The settings for the built-in installer, and how will it be packaged and configured when being installed on the end user's desktop. You can configure in the preferences to use the built-in installer or another product (if you have the full version of Install Creator, you can use that instead and ignore these settings).

Compression Level: Using the compression level, you can try to reduce the overall size of your game. You have the option of normal or maximum. Unless you feel your game is too big, you wouldn't normally consider compressing it. Many users have DSL connections these days, so they will not be concerned about downloading file sizes in the order of 20–30 MB. Unless your game is quite large, you can leave the compression level at normal. If you do select maximum compression and your game is quite large, it may take a while to build the final executable (using maximum compression will take longer to build than standard will).

FIGURE 7.6 The Settings tab with its properties displayed.

Compress Sounds: You also have the option of compressing any sounds you have included within your game. It will only compress WAV formatted sound files, and compressing them does reduce the quality (although it may not be that noticeable to the end user). Always test any settings to make sure you are happy with the results before distributing your game.

Include external files: If you have links to external files within your game (e.g., pictures), tick the box to compress them also.

Command line: If you want to force your TGF2-created program to use a certain system resource, typing in a specific command achieves this.

Enable debugger keyboard shortcuts This is used to avoid conflicts between the game keyboard shortcuts and the debugger shortcuts.

The Window Tab

Figure 7.7 shows the configuration options available in the Window tab.

FIGURE 7.7   The Window tab settings sheet.

Size: This is the size of the application window, which is the area the user can see when running the game.

Background color: If you want to change the color of the area around all of the frames, you can use the Color Picker, which is located in the Background Color option. You would only see the background color if you maximize the size of your application (using the maximize button on the game) to a resolution that is larger than the frame size. This happens when your game is smaller than the resolution of your computer display and you have the default No Maximize Box option switched off.

Heading: The heading is switched on by default, displays the name of the program, and presents the user with a text menu for selecting options within the game (which can be configured).

Heading when maximized: If you click this option, the heading bar will still be on screen if you maximize the game. If it is unticked and you maximize the game, the heading bar will disappear.

Disable Close button: If you don't want the user to close the program using the x button in the top right corner of the Application window, select this option. You will need to give the user an alternate method of closing the game window if you do this (either through a key combination or through a menu system).

No Minimize box: If you don't want users to minimize your game (put the game on the task bar and hide it from the Windows desktop), tick this option. They will be able to expand it again by clicking on the item on the task bar.

No Maximize box: If you want to prevent the user from maximizing the game, tick this option. This is a good option to select if you want to restrict the user to a certain window size.

No Thick frame: In many games and applications, you can put your mouse cursor on the edge of a window and drag it to make it bigger. Clicking this option removes the dragging/resizing option. Again, this is a very useful option if you are keeping the game screen to a specific size.

Maximized on boot-up: This option will expand the Application window size to the size of the monitor's resolution when the game is started.

Hidden at start: This will hide the application when it is started (so it will look like nothing is running). You can make it reappear again using code in the Event Editor.

Menu bar: You can include a menu bar on your game by leaving the option ticked (it's on by default). This will allow you to include the standard menu system of File, Options Help, which is already configured as standard. You can click on the Edit button to change the menu system more to your liking.

Menu displayed on boot-up: By default, when a game is started, the menu is displayed; if you wish to remove it, untick this option. You can, however, re-show it later by entering some code into the Event Editor.

Change Resolution Mode: Change the resolution of the monitor to the resolution in the game. Once you have quit the game, it returns the monitor to the original settings.

Allow user to switch to/from full screen: If you use the key combination Alt-Enter, you can change the size of the game window to full screen or back to its original size.

Resize display to fill window size: This option stretches the playfield of the frame to fit the application screen size. The screen will appear zoomed, but has been stretched to fit the screen.

Do not center frame area in window: Each frame can be bigger than the application size. With this option ticked, it will not center in the middle of the frame, but at the top left instead.

The Runtime Options Tab

An example of the runtime options can be seen in Figure 7.8.

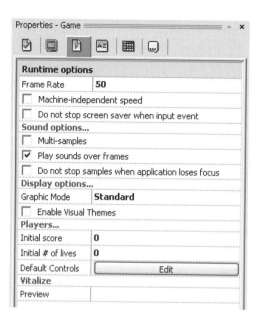

FIGURE 7.8 Default settings of the Runtime tab.

Frame Rate: The default setting for TGF2 is 50, you have the option to increase or decrease this amount to increase the speed of your game. Increasing the frame rate will cause TGF2 to use more processor power (CPU) to make the game faster.

Machine-independent speed: If you want the game to run at the same speed regardless of the type of machine the user has, tick this option. This is very useful for ensuring that a game doesn't run too fast on the latest leading-edge equipment.

Do not stop screen saver when input event: Screensavers usually will continue to run until the user moves the mouse or presses a key. Using this option, you can prevent that and configure a different way to exit from it (setting up the Escape key, for example). It is very important to let the user know how to exit the screensaver; otherwise, you may have some unhappy customers contacting you.

Multi-samples: If you wish to play a number of samples (sounds) at the same time, you will need to tick the Multi-samples check box.

Play sounds over frames: Sometimes, you may want to play the same music across multiple frames; if so, you will need to tick this item. The main reason for selecting this is when you want continuity within your games sound wise from one frame to another.

Do not stop samples when application loses focus: Losing focus means clicking away from the game on to another application or the desktop. This will allow the sound to continue uninterrupted while you are doing other things.

Graphic Mode: You have three possible choices when changing the graphics mode: Standard, DirectX, and DirectX + V RAM. Using the DirectX driver from Microsoft, you can get better graphics performance in your games. By selecting video RAM and DirectX, you will improve scrolling games, but this has a negative effect on applications that use transitions.

Enable Visual Themes: If you want your game to support Windows XP visual themes, tick this option to enable it. If the user was to change his Windows desktop settings, the games application and menu bar you have created will also change.

Initial score: You can set an initial score using this entry box. Most games start from zero and don't require you to change this, but you may decide that your game starts from another number and counts down.

Initial # of lives: The number of lives with which the player starts. This is an easy way to set the default number of lives whenever a user starts the game.

Default Controls: You can configure the game to be controlled by a joystick or via the keyboard. You can configure up to four players by pressing the Edit button. The default options can be changed at runtime by the player if you wish.

Preview (Vitalize): This will allow you to specify a bitmap image. When you export to the build option Internet Application, and then put the file on the Internet, it will use the BMP as a temporary image while it is loading your game on the user's browser.

The Values Tab

Next is the Values tab, which can be seen in Figure 7.9

Global Values: If you want to transfer values between frames, you can create a global value. You can define a large number of global values by clicking the New button. Using global values is a fast way to move values between frames, and takes up less memory space than using a specific object to do the same thing.

Global Strings: If you want to transfer text between frames, you can create a global string. You can define a large number of global strings by clicking the New button. Using global strings is a fast way to move text between frames, and takes up less memory space than using a specific object to do the same thing.

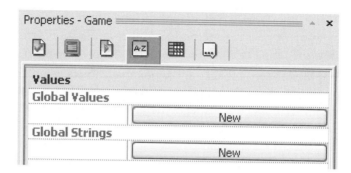

FIGURE 7.9   The Values tab in the Properties sheet window.

The Events Tab

The second from last tab is the Events tab, and can be seen in Figure 7.10.

FIGURE 7.10   The Events tab default options.

Global Events: Global events look like normal events configured in the Event Editor, but will run from when the application is started to when it is closed, regardless of what frame the game is on. This makes them independent of any frame and useful for code that needs to run through the life of the program. Click the Edit button to enter the Global Events screen.

The About Tab

The last tab for the Application Properties sheet is the About Properties sheet. The settings within that tab can be seen in Figure 7.11.

Name: This is the name of the game you have created and it will appear on any menu bars or in the About box (the About box is an informational dialog, which can be seen by running your game and then selecting Help/About).

FIGURE 7.11   The About tab Properties sheet.

Icon: Icons appear at various stages when your game is running. You will see an icon in the top left corner when you are running your game, you will see one if you click on the Help/About menu option and the icon for the actual executable. If you click on the Edit box, you can amend the different icons in your game to a picture more suited to their function.

Filename: Filename displays the folder path to where the TGF2 game has been saved, and its saved filename.

Help file: With your games, you can have a help file that the user can open by pressing the F1 key. The help file can contain product information, where to get help, and perhaps hints and tips on playing. Create your help file in Hlp, Txt, Doc, or Wri format and then select it using the file Browser button. If you are not sure how to create certain help formats, start with Txt (using Notepad), and then move to a more complex format if necessary.

Author: Who created the game; put your name in here (or your company or team name).

Copyright: If you want to enter a copyright to your game, enter your name in the copyright box.

AboutBox text: When the user clicks on the File menu Help | About, the text entered here will be placed in an About box.

FRAME PROPERTIES IN-DEPTH

You can have multiple frames within one game; in fact, it is generally assumed you will have more than one. Each frame can be configured with its own properties, which means you can have different frames taking different roles within your program. Any configuration you do on one frame does not pass over to any other frames, so if you want something to be global (available to the entire application), you will need to configure it in the Application properties.

The Settings Tab

Figure 7.12 shows the Settings tab of the frame properties.

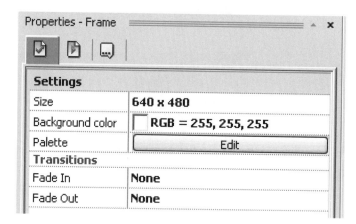

FIGURE 7.12   The Settings tab.

Size: Enter the size of the frame; remember, frame size can be different from the application size. To make scrolling games, you would make the frame size bigger than the application settings size.

Background color: Select the background color you wish to use for the frame. You can have different background colors for each frame, but you would in most instances create a graphic image that covers the frame background.

Palette: Using this option, you will be able to select an image and use the colors contained within it as the game palette. Perhaps you have a certain image you want to keep at the same range of colors throughout the frame or game. Clicking Edit will show you the different colors used in the palette, and from there, you can import an image.

Fade In: When the frame starts, you can insert a fade-in transition, which is a special wiping effect that moves across the screen to reveal your game.

Fade Out: At the end of the frame, you can insert a fade-out transition, which is a special wiping effect that moves across your screen to make your game (frame) disappear.

The Runtime Options Tab

Figure 7.13 shows the Runtime options tab.

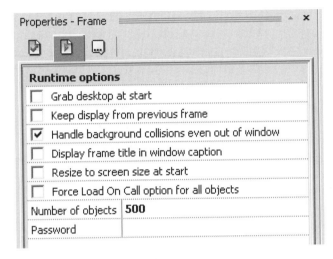

FIGURE 7.13 The Runtime Options tab.

Grab desktop at start: Grabbing a user's desktop at the start of the frame will paste the contents of the current screen into your game. If a user has other programs open on the desktop that overlap the frame area, they will be copied and then pasted into the game. If you want to create a game or screensaver that would take advantage of the user's desktop, tick this option.

Keep display from previous frame: If, when changing frames, you would like to keep the graphics from the previous frame, you will need to select this option.

Handle background collisions even when out of window: If objects collide outside of the window area, selecting this option will mean that any code written to deal with any collisions will still be handled. With this selection enabled, TGF2 will still test to see if collisions are happening.

Display frame title in window caption: The name of the frame (each frame has its own name to distinguish it) will be displayed in the window caption (also known as the title bar).

Resize to screen size at start: This option will maximize your game window to the same size as the screen resolution.

Force Load On Call option for all objects: This will only load the objects into memory when they are required. This will reduce the overall memory utilization of your game, but may slow your program if many objects need to be loaded into memory per frame.

Number of objects: The number of objects option lets you define how many objects each frame will contain. TGF2 uses this figure to generate the memory space to run the program. The default setting is 500, but if you have more than this in a frame, increase this figure or you may get strange results (certain objects may not work). Setting this number too high will have a negative effect and reduce the performance of your game.

Password: A password will allow users to navigate to a specific frame within your game if they know the password. You can set a separate password for each different frame, and the user will then enter it using the menu—File/Password option. A pop-up dialog box will appear asking the user for a password. A password is very useful if you want the player to be able to come back to a specific level in the game at another time.

The About Tab

The About tab has only one configurable bit of information, as shown in Figure 7.14.

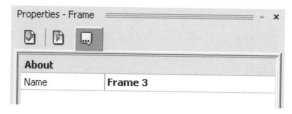

FIGURE 7.14   The About tab Properties sheet.

Name: You can change the current frame name to something more appropriate by clicking on the text area. The default names are frame1, frame2, frame3, and so on, but it is useful to change these to something more descriptive; for example, main screen, high-scores, game frame, and so forth.

OBJECT PROPERTIES IN-DEPTH

A number of different objects come standard with TGF2, and each object you place within a frame may have a different set of properties. This will depend on the type of object you select; for example, the Hi-Score object is different from the Active object. Some objects will have Settings or Properties tabs, and others will not. The wide range of object configurations available makes it impossible to list them all here. Some tabs and properties are common to all or most objects and are discussed next. If you need to see an object's properties, click on the object in the Frame Editor.

The Settings Properties Tab

The Settings Properties tab is different for each object and defines how that object can be configured and used within your game. For example, if you are using the Date and Time object, you will be able to specify if you will use a digital or analog clock to display the time. If you were using an array, it would allow configuration on the size, and whether it's one, two, or three dimensions. It is very important to check the Settings tab of every object you place within your game, as there may be some important configuration you will need to amend. An example of the Settings tab for the Animation object can be seen in Figure 7.15.

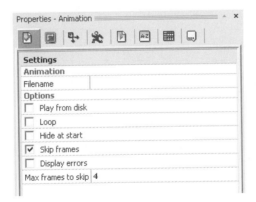

FIGURE 7.15 An example of the Settings tab for objects.

The Size/Position Tab

Using the Size/Position tab on the object's Properties sheet, you can specify the screen location, the object's actual size, and if it should be rotated. An example of the Properties tab for this is shown in Figure 7.16.

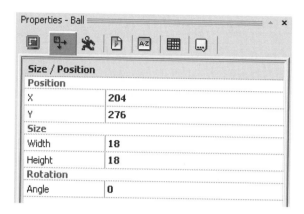

FIGURE 7.16   Size and position of the objects.

X (Position): The X position on the screen (left to right).

Y (Position): The Y position on the screen (its location top to bottom).

Width: The width of the object.

Height: The height of the object.

Angle: The angle the object is displayed at (zero is the default where there is no rotation).

The Display Options Tab

The Display Options configuration is for setting up how the object will appear on the playfield when the game is running. An example set of options is shown in Figure 7.17.

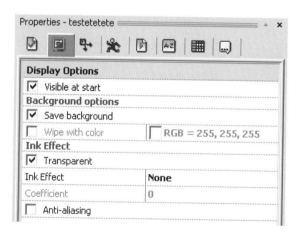

FIGURE 7.17   The Display Options tab for an object.

Remember that not all objects will contain the same set of display (or any other tab) options. Each will be different depending on the role of the object.

Some common options for the Display Options tab include:

Visible at start: Is the object visible when the frame starts? You can make it invisible (by not ticking the checkbox) and then show it using code at an appropriate time.

Save background: This option is enabled by default, and for most games should be left ticked. This option saves the background, so once the object has moved away from it, it will then paste the original image back so you get a smooth-scrolling object. If you untick this option, the object image will be pasted across the screen, as it doesn't have information on what other image should be stored on screen. If you want to make some interesting screensavers, this is an option worth trying.

Wipe with Color: If you untick Save Background, you will be able to select Wipe with Color and select and choose an RGB color (this is a number that represents a color). You do not have to enter its RGB number, because when you click on it, you will be able to pick the color you want from a drop-down box. If you do this rather than just untick Save Background, it will paste the selected color over the background where the object has been.

Transparent: All images when created are drawn in a square. When you create any images, you can "paint" a transparency around the image that creates a perfect shape. Without transparency, your image (e.g., a ball) will have a square around it. With transparency, the area around the ball will be transparent, which means it will be invisible to the user.

Ink Effect: You have six options when selecting ink effect: none, semitransparent, inverted, Xor, AND, and OR. Use the Coefficient option to state how much these effects will be implemented.

Anti-aliasing: Select anti-aliasing if you want your object's appearance to look smoother.

The Events Properties Tab

The Events tab for objects contains two very important options for your game creations: Qualifiers and Behaviors (see Figure 7.18). The Qualifier property allows you to place like-minded objects into named groups. A set of groups has already been defined by default (e.g., Good, Bad, Player, Friends, Bullets, Arms, Collectible, etc.). Once you have assigned an object to a particular Qualifier, you can then go into the Event Editor and program code for that particular group. This allows you to code efficiently (as you can assign code to multiple objects using just one object column in the Event Editor), and is very useful when you are making games because you can assign your object to game types. For example, you could create an enemy group or obstacle grouping and then create code specifically for how they will react within your game.

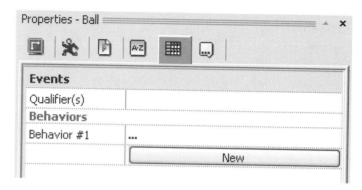

FIGURE 7.18   The Events Properties tab.

To assign an object to a Qualifier:

1. When you click on the Qualifiers button, you will be presented with an Edit box. Click on the Edit box to bring up the Object Qualifiers dialog box.
2. Click on the Add button to bring up a list of predefined types; these are just examples and are there to help you place the object. When you have chosen one, select it and then click OK.
3. Notice that the group you selected is now visible in the Object Qualifiers dialog box. You can click on Add again if you want to add it to other groups, or click OK to get back to the Properties sheet.
4. The Qualifier icon image now appears on the Properties tab.

Adding a qualifier to an object will not have any effect until you program code for it within the Event Editor. If you don't like the initial object types, you can select one of the others, which are numbered 1 to 99. The initial groups are only suggestions, so you do not have to use them if you do not want to.

The Behavior option within the Events Properties tab allows you to open the Event Editor and set up specific code events to each object. The benefit of this is that if you want a single object to work in a certain way, you can code it to so. The only downside is that you must remember that you have put events on the object. When testing the game, you may find it acting strangely. If you look at the main code and cannot find the reason why, it could be object assigned code. This problem aside, it is a very useful way to reduce your main code list size, and you can copy and paste code between objects, so you only need to code an event once.

The About Properties Tab

Figure 7.19 shows an example of the About Properties tab for an object. This tab details general information about each object (also called an *extension*), including creator and copyright text. You can also change the information here, which will amend its appearance on the Frame Editor and be easier to work with if you have many of the same objects on the screen.

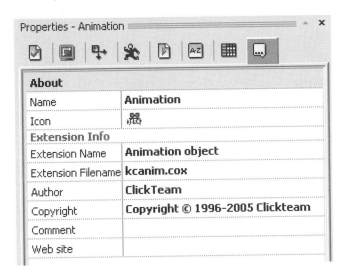

FIGURE 7.19 The About Properties tab.

Name: The name of the object, which you can amend to something more useful; for example, from animation to player1 animation. Click on the text to amend the name, which will then be updated on the Frame Editor and within the Event Editor.

Icon: The icon image that will appear on the Frame Editor and within the Event Editor. You can amend this to something more memorable if you wish, but it will not appear in the game; it is for programming identification only.

Extension Name: The name of the extension (object).

Extension Filename: The filename to the extension (object).

Author: The person who wrote the extension; the majority of the time this will be Clickteam, but it could be another author.

Copyright: Copyright text for the object.

Comment: Any comments about the object will appear here.

Web site: Any Web site of the object author will appear here.

SUMMARY

Properties are a very important aspect of configuring your games, and you need to know how to make them work to your benefit. It may seem a little daunting at first that so many properties can be changed. The defaults will be sufficient in many cases, and you only need to change them if you want an object to perform differently. Some of the properties will only need to be changed at the beginning of your game creation, and you can ignore them for the rest of that project's development. Take the time to look over each object's Properties sheet to see what you can do with each object, and the power TGF2 has. We cannot list every property of every object here (as that would be a book in itself), so make sure you review the help files that come with the product if you require more information on a specific object.

8 TGF Coding Basics

In This Chapter

- Introduction to the Event Editor Screen
- Coding Concepts
- Code Comments
- Code Groups

In this chapter, we discuss basic coding techniques and concepts that you will be using later in this book. Using the Event Editor, you can make your games extremely powerful using mouse clicks and selecting items from menu pop-ups.

INTRODUCTION TO THE EVENT EDITOR SCREEN

The Event Editor screen (as shown in Figure 8.1) is the primary screen for pulling all the game content together and creating the game's playability. Any coding (programming) that needs to be done will be done from this screen, so it is very important to understand how the Event Editor works; although easy to use, it can be slightly confusing at first. The Event Editor has a spreadsheet appearance (albeit with a graphical top row and first column) with a selection of blank rows. Using Figure 8.1 as an example, the naming of each of the items can be detailed as such:

■ The numbers down the left side represent the event line number.
■ Next to each event line number is an attached box, within which can be a single or many conditions.
■ Across the top of the Event Editor are a number of graphical icons. The first seven icons will always be present in every game you make, and are called System Objects. Any objects after the seventh will be ones you add manually to the game.
■ Within each of the blank boxes to the left of the Events and below the objects is where you can insert an action (these are called *action boxes*). Once you have added an action, it will then be represented by a large tick icon. If you hover the mouse over the tick, you can read the action in that location. You can have multiple actions in each box by right-clicking on the same action box a second (or third, etc.) time.

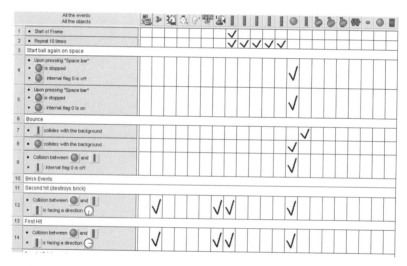

FIGURE 8.1   An example of game code in the Event Editor.

When you add a condition (a line will appear after a number) and then add an event (so a tick appears), you will end up with a system very much like a treasure map grid. The action will correspond to the relevant condition on the left, and the corresponding object above it.

A more detailed description of what each of these items means and how it can be used is discussed next.

CODING CONCEPTS

The Event Editor uses a simple yet powerful point-and-click programming language to allow anyone to program a game, even if that person has little or no previous programming experience. Clickteam came up with an ingenious way to achieve this simplicity using coding logic, and presenting it in an easily comprehendible manner. Within TGF2 are a number of elements that can be assigned to an object:

- Events
- Conditions
- Actions
- Functions

The great thing about TGF2 and previous versions of these products that use the Event Editor is that all of these elements can be explained and understood using simple logic. This makes programming a breeze, and means that you can complete games faster.

Events

An event is when TGF2 is waiting for something to happen in its lines of code. An event is only created in TGF2 once a condition or group of conditions has been added to it. Each event waits until any conditions placed within it are "true" before running any actions. Each event is given a line number, which is displayed down the left side of the Event Editor screen. Figure 8.2 shows a blank Event Editor where nothing has been programmed. The number 1 on the left side is the event, which is awaiting some conditions to be assigned to it before it creates a line numbered 2.

FIGURE 8.2   A blank event with no conditions programmed in.

Conditions

Conditions are the test criteria within your games to allow the program to understand when to do "something." Examples of conditions include:

- Left mouse button is clicked
- Ball hits bat
- Score reaches 200
- Player lives = 0
- Arrow key is pressed
- 15 seconds have passed

You could place one or all of these conditions within a single event. An example of single and multiple conditions in a number of events can be seen in Figure 8.3. By adding more conditions to the same event, you can create very complex programming logic that is easy to read and create.

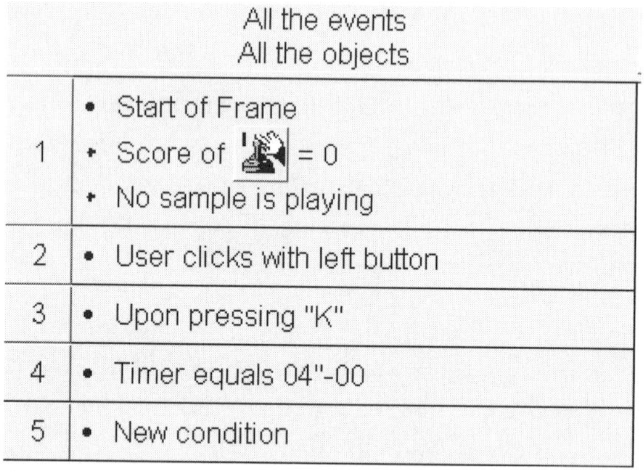

FIGURE 8.3 An example of conditions and events.

To create a single condition and event:

1. Click on the text "New Condition" in the Event Editor. If you have just started a brand new program in TGF2, it will be the first event line. If it's a program you have been working on, it will be the last event line.
2. A New Condition dialog box will appear; select the object you want to test. You can do this by double left-clicking or a single right-click on the icon of the chosen object.
3. A pop-up menu will appear with a list of conditions that TGF2 can test for that object. Choose one, and it will then appear in an event.

To create another condition in the same event line (make sure you have at least one condition in an event line before attempting to do this):

1. Right-click on the condition in the event line to which you want to add another condition.
2. A pop-up box will appear. Select Insert, and a New Condition dialog box will appear; select the object you want to test.
3. From the pop-up menu, choose one item, and it will then appear in the same event.

The Order of Conditions

It is very important to note that the order of conditions can impact the way your games react when running; the way the computer reads the code determines what happens. With regard to conditions (remember, you can have multiple conditions), it is read from the first to the last in each event. Using an example that is not computer related, perhaps you are posting a letter to a relative. You wouldn't walk all the way to the post office and then decide to write the letter; you would write the letter first, then put it in the envelope, write the address, and then go to the post office to post it. The same is true with TGF2 and programming languages generally. You must be very careful in ordering your conditions, as you will be creating actions based on this order. Once you have written many lines of code, it can be easy to place code in the wrong order. If you are experiencing strange results in your code, check the order of your conditions. Because your code will branch off to other parts of the code, putting the conditions in the wrong order may make the program do something it's not meant to do at that time. Another thing to note is that when creating multiple conditions, it is best to place a specific condition first before placing any other conditions below it. For example, if you have two conditions—the first being "when user presses left mouse button," the second being "when counter equals one"—it is best to put the more "nongeneral" condition first. In your game, the user might press the left mouse button many times, but the counter may only equal 1 at a specific time in your program. If the mouse button condition is first, TGF2 will begin to read that line of code and then see if the second condition is true every time the mouse button is clicked. You might be wondering why this is a problem, but the fewer events TGF2 has to read (check), the more processing power it has to put over to the game. Therefore, ensuring that your conditions are in the correct order will make the code run correctly, and make it more efficient, saving valuable processing time for more important things like graphic movements and animations.

Negating Conditions

You might want to create a condition that is the opposite of the one you just created. To do this, you can use the Negate option. For example, perhaps you created a condition to see if an object is visible, and you want to test to see when it isn't visible. The events would then be true if one or the other is correct, and then it would run the relevant action associated with it.

1. On the menu bar, click File | New; this will generate a brand new game for you to work on. Double-click on the words "Frame 1" in the Workspace toolbar.
2. Click on Insert | New Object and then select the Date & Time object from the list. When the dialog box appears, select Create a Clock Object.
3. Click on the Event Editor button in the toolbar.
4. You will now be in the Event Editor. Click on the number "1" or the "New Condition" text to begin creating your events. Double-click on the Date & Time object in the object list and then select Is Visible from the pop-up menu.
5. Create another event (by clicking on New Condition) and then select the same (Date & Time object, and Is Visible).
6. Now, two events are checking to see if the Date & Time object is visible. Perhaps in your code you wanted to check to see if it was invisible or visible and then run a specific set of code. Right-click on one of the Button Date & Time is Visible conditions. A pop-up box will appear, and you will see an option called "Negate." Select it, and it will now make one of the conditions have a red cross next to it. This means that it is the opposite of the statement (negated), and so would be checking when the object is not visible. An example of a negated condition is shown in Figure 8.4.

	All the events All the objects	
1	• Button 🕐 is visible	
2	• ✕ Button 🕐 is visible	
3	• New condition	

FIGURE 8.4   A normal and negated condition.

Not all objects can be negated. If it is not possible on a specific object, the negate option will be grayed out.

ON THE CD On the companion CD-ROM is a simple example of the negate option in use. Load and run the example file "negate" located in the CD-ROM\examples folder to see how you can use negate to test to see if the opposite is true.

Actions

An action is the result of a condition that has been found to be true. For example, you have a condition that tests if the player's score is greater than 100. Once this condition has been met, any actions on that event line will be run. Each object that is added onto the play area has its own actions that can be used once the condition has been met.

When an object you have never used before is added to your game, it is a good idea to read the help file or examine what actions are available.

Examples of actions that objects can make include:

- Execute an external program
- Play a sample or sound
- End the application
- Set the timer
- Set, add, or reduce the score

The Order of Actions

The order in which you add the actions will be the order in which they will be executed when that specific condition has been found to be true. It is important to understand that the order of the actions can have a positive or negative effect on your program; this is very similar to the order of conditions, the only difference being that this is the order in which things will happen on screen. If you get the order of actions in the wrong sequence, you can create a coding bug. It may also create unexpected results, making things happen on the screen that you do not expect.

Functions

Functions play a very important part when using the Event Editor. A function allows you to retrieve data from one object to use in another object. There may be information in one object that you want to display, for example, or you may want to read in some data from an array that points to an image, and then use this in the Picture object to display the image. Functions are classified in two groups:

- General functions
- Object functions

General functions retrieve data from the System objects, which are those you cannot add to the play area and always appear in the Event Editor. These functions are Special Conditions, Sound, Storyboard Controls, The Timer, Create New Objects, The Mouse Pointer and Keyboard, and Player 1. Object functions retrieve data from all objects other than those that are restricted (i.e., anything you can place on the play area using Insert | Object). To access these functions, you will need to use the Retrieve Data from Object in the Expression Evaluator (you can also type it in if you know what you need to retrieve). An example of the Expression Evaluator is shown in Figure 8.5.

FIGURE 8.5   The Retrieve data button on the Expression Evaluator.

CODE COMMENTS

In every programming language, you can comment your code. Comments within your programs are very important for a number of reasons. When you have created many games (even those that are not finished), you might decide to go back and restart or update them. When you created the game, you were familiar with what you were writing at the time, but later it is easy to forget why you coded something a certain way. Commenting your code is a great way to put notes in to remind you why you were doing something. You can also use code commenting to put copyright messages into your programs, so if you allow a program to be used in the "game community," you can stamp the code with the copyright message so other programmers understand what is required of them if they take that code and use it in their own games. An example of a code comment in a traditional programming language might look something like Listing 8.1.

LISTING 8.1   Traditional Coding Comments.

```
// Copyright Jason Darby
// Date Created : 10 February 2005
// Date Last Modified: 13 February 2005
// Program Name : The Lab
// If you wish to use this code email me at name@name.com
```

As you can see in Listing 8.1, traditional languages allow programmers to put in dates when the program was created and when it was last updated. It is also common to put in a date for the last change made (including a description to what has been changed), so if it stops working, you know exactly what was done, and you can check it to see if that was the cause. TGF2 allows you to make comments in the Event Editor between event lines; to do so:

1. If you have the Event Editor already open, you are ready to enter a comment line. If you are not in the Event Editor and TGF2 is not currently open, start TGF2, then click on the menu system, and select File | New. Double-click on the frame and then click on the Event Editor button in the toolbar.
2. Right-click on any number on the left of the events (if you have not added any previous events, this will be event 1) to bring up the pop-up menu. Select Insert Comment. An example of the pop-up is shown in Figure 8.6.

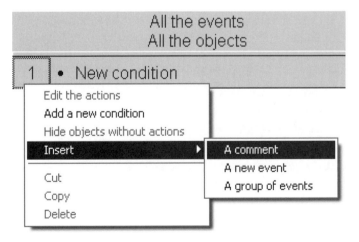

FIGURE 8.6   Example of the pop-up for adding a comment line.

3. The Edit Text dialog box appears (as shown in Figure 8.7). You can type text here to help you remember why you coded a specific part of your game, a copyright message, and so forth. You have the option of changing the text size, amending its alignment, or changing the background color. Type the words "My Game Copyright" in the text box and then click OK.

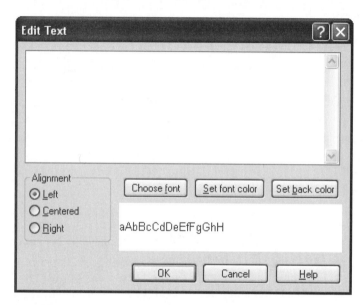

FIGURE 8.7 The Edit Text dialog box where you can put your comments.

4. You should now have a comment line in the Event Editor that looks like Figure 8.8.

FIGURE 8.8 Your event list with a single comment line.

CODE GROUPS

When programming, it is very easy to separate your game into logical steps and concepts. For example, a side-scrolling shoot-'em-up game might consist of ship movement, enemy ships appearing from the right side of the screen, scores, and explosions when a bullet hits an enemy. In a scripted programming language, you would create a selection of code to handle some of these items independently from the main code. Doing so makes your code more structured, and makes it very easy to make changes to a specific part of your game. It is also easier to find any bugs related to a specific issue, as it will be contained in a group. TGF2 uses groups as well, but the benefit of course is that it is graphical in its approach. There are two main reasons for using code groups in TGF2: first, to organize specific aspects of your code so you can keep it tidy, as you can store code within them and then hide the code until you need to see it. Second, with code groups you can enable and disable each group throughout the running of the game. This allows you to code specific events within your game that only happen at a certain point in time. To create a code group:

1. Start TGF2, and from the menu bar click on File and then New. This will load TGF2 with a blank game.
2. Double-click on the Frame 1 text in the Workspace toolbar to open the Frame Editor. Then, click on the Event Editor icon in the menu bar, which will take you to the coding screen, which is currently empty.
3. To insert a group, you need to right-click on an event line number (in this case, starting from a new program, you will only have line one available). From the pop-up menu, select Insert and then Group of Events. A New Group dialog box will appear; enter the group name "First Group" (it will now look like Figure 8.9).

FIGURE 8.9 Group dialog box.

4. Click OK. You will now have an entry in the Event Editor that will look like Figure 8.10.

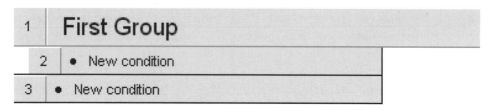

FIGURE 8.10 Group in the Event Editor.

The Group Events dialog also allows you to password protect a group, which allows you to distribute source code by only allowing users to open specific areas. When you create a group, by default it is active when the frame starts, which means that TGF2 will read the code within the group and run it. If you disable this option (by unticking it), the program will ignore it until you enable it again within the code. This is particularly useful when you only want the group to run at a specific time.

Groups within Groups

Groups within groups are a new feature within the Click range of products, which allows you to place multiple groups under another group, and enable and disable them when needed. You may be wondering why you might want to do this, and has a lot to do with code redirection. As mentioned previously, you can have a group disabled when the program is first run, which means you can go to a specific selection of code at a certain time and enable it (run it). If you have more groups under this, you can enable them when a specific condition is true. This allows you to make very powerful programs that only run code when you need it to, and makes your games easier to write. To make a number of groups within a group:

1. Start TGF2, and from the menu bar, click on File and then New. This will load TGF2 with a blank game.
2. Double-click on the Frame 1 text in the Workspace toolbar to open the Frame Editor. Then, click on the Event Editor icon in the menu bar, which will take you to the coding screen, which is currently empty.
3. Insert the first group by right-clicking on an event line number (in this case, starting from a new program you will only have line one available). From the pop-up menu, select Insert and then Group of Events. A New Group dialog box will appear.

4. Enter the group name "First Group" and then click OK. You will now have the first group entry within the Event Editor.

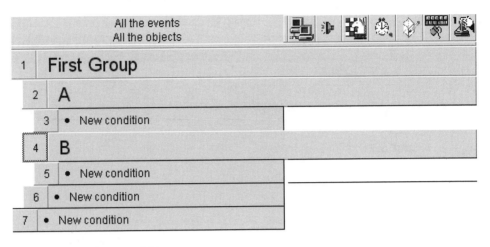

FIGURE 8.11 Groups within groups.

5. On the number 2, below the First Group, right-click again and insert another group, this time called "A."
6. On the number 4, right-click and insert another group, call this one "B."

You will now have two groups within a group as shown in Figure 8.11.
Although this example shows all three groups being enabled (disabled groups will not run and are shown as grayed out), it is best to disable them and use conditions to enable each group.

Loops

A loop is something that happens repeatedly a number of times. When programs begin to get more repetitive in nature (where you have to do something more than once), you can code it over a number of lines of code, or use a loop. Take as an example the drawing of a crossword puzzle. If you had a 17x17 grid, you could code each line of boxes, or write a loop that would generate the 17 lines of boxes for you. The obvious benefit of a loop is that you have less code to write, and it is a more efficient way to write your programs. To create the basic loop structure, you will require two lines of code. The first is the 'On Loop "Name" Start' where you put all of the code you want to run. Next, you will need a line of code to tell TGF2 that the loop has indeed been started and how many times it will need to be run. An example of a very basic loop is shown in Figure 8.12. This loop just adds 1 to the counter each loop, and runs five times, so the final counter number is 5. It runs too fast to see this happen, and will just display the number 5.

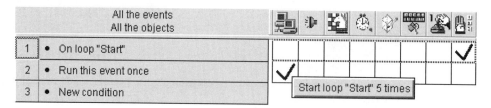

FIGURE 8.12   A loop example.

Runtime Order

When you run a game created with TGF2, it will read the events, conditions, and actions in a specific order. We have already detailed the order of conditions and actions, so you should have a good idea of how to structure your code to reduce any problems when you are bug finding. When a game is run, TGF2 reads the first event line; if the condition is true, it will then run the actions to the right of it. If it is not true, it will continue to the next event line, and so on. Additionally, if there is a comment line, it will also ignore that, as there is no code for it to run.

Qualifiers and Behaviors

Qualifiers and behaviors are two ways to improve how you code within TGF2, and can be configured in the Object Properties Workspace toolbar. Learning how to use both of these options well will allow you to write better code, and make it easier to read, so when you go back to a program at a later stage, you will understand it faster.

Qualifiers

When you want to logically group your objects, you can place them in a group. This qualifier group then allows you to code events and actions specifically for that group of objects, rather than one at a time. This makes it easy to put in specific logical types (e.g., enemy, bullets, doors, collectibles, etc.), but also means that you can significantly reduce the amount of coding needed in the Event Editor to do specific actions. A simple example of a qualifier in use can be seen as follows:

1. Start TGF2, and from the menu bar click on File and then New. This will load TGF2 with a blank game.

2. Double-click on the Frame 1 text in the Workspace toolbar to open the Frame Editor.
3. Insert three Active objects, by using the Insert | New Object menu option. Place them across the bottom of the frame all at the same height.
4. Click on one of the three Active objects (which will appear as green triangles) to reveal that object's properties. Click on the Events tab in the Properties toolbar. You will now see text that says "Qualifier(s)." Click on this to bring up an Edit box. Click on the Edit box to bring up the Object Qualifiers dialog box.
5. If you click the Add button, you will get a list of possible groupings to which this object can belong. TGF2 provides a list of default qualifier names; if they do not suit your purpose, you can always select one of the numbered group names. For this example, select the Good group (which looks like an apple). Then, in the dialog box, click the OK button to save the configuration. On the Qualifier(s) in the Properties toolbar, you will see a small red apple. Do the same for the other two Active objects.
6. Click on the Event Editor icon to begin to code your new Good group. In the Event Editor, you will now see a group called "Good" in the object listing.
7. Click on New Condition, select the Timer option (which looks like a stopwatch) by double-clicking on it, and then select Is the Time Equal to a Certain Value from the pop-up menu. Move the second bar until it is five seconds, and then click OK.
8. Move across to the right until you are directly under the Good group icon. Right-click and select Position, Set Y Coordinate. In the Expression Evaluator, type in the number 20.
9. If you now run this example, you will notice that the Active objects start at the bottom of the frame, and then after five seconds, all three move to the top end of the frame. If you were to do this coding without groups, you would have had to program in three actions to make the Active objects move. When your programs become more complex, you will save a lot of programming effort and time simply by using qualifiers.

Behavior

A behavior is a set of events that are applied to a specific object. If you have a set of code on how an object should behave within a game, you can then copy and paste this to another object. You might want to code the events in the main Event Editor, and that would be fine, but again, this is a time- and effort-saving method. If you have objects that behave a certain way, you can copy and paste the code between the objects and then make the necessary changes. The final thing that is great about behaviors is that you can copy them between games and they will still contain the code you originally made. Perhaps you made a side-scrolling game in the past and had a Bullet object with specific behaviors you would like to use in your latest creation. You can just import that object and use all of its code and properties. If, over time, you build a collection of game objects, you could put together a new game quickly and easily with this method.

1. To use object behaviors, click on the object in question and then select the Events tab in the Properties toolbar.
2. You will now see some text that says "Behaviors," and under this is a button labeled "New." Click on the New button to create a new event behavior.
3. A set of dotted lines will appear; click on them to bring up an Edit button, and click this button to go to the Event Editor for this object.
4. An example of a behavior applied to a single Active object can be found on the companion CD-ROM. The file is located in the CD-ROM\examples folder and is called "behavior." Open this file and you'll see three Actives from the qualifier example, but one of the Actives now has a behavior to flash separately.

ON THE CD

NOTE

It is important to remember that if your object references other objects that are not in the new game you move it to, that code will not work. You must ensure that any references are available in the new game. For example, if you reference a Counter object in the original game, you must have a Counter object (with the same name) in the new game.

SUMMARY

You should now have a good idea of how to use the Event Editor, and some of the terminology used throughout this book. Later in the book, we will be spending a lot of time entering code within this screen, so if you are unsure of any concepts, come back here and review the details.

9   Backup and Game Recovery

In This Chapter

- Why Back Up?
- What Systems Are Available?

One of the most important things you can do when making your programs is to ensure that you have a good set of backups. Many programmers use support forums when they have had a hard disk failure or been infected by a computer virus, and want to know if they can recover from it. You can understand their frustration when they are told that nothing can be done, and the program they have been working on for the last 12 months is lost. They relied too much on technology and became complacent about making sure their work was safe and secure. So, let's explore one of the most important areas you need to consider before taking on any major project.

WHY BACK UP?

Before we get into the details of what solutions and systems are available, let's take a step back for a moment and think about why we might need to backup. Let's ask a simple question:

"Do you want to lose any game you are in the middle of, or have completed?"

The answer to this is probably "no," you do not want to lose your game(s). Don't take anything for granted when it comes to backing up your programs. There are many reasons why you will lose data, some of which are detailed here:

Viruses: Viruses have become a serious problem for PC users over the last 5 to 10 years, with more appearing each month. The generic meaning of a computer virus is something that replicates itself. Generally, they are more than that; some are just irritating, and many will cause data loss or open your computer to hackers (who might steal your data). Many people will get a virus from downloading a program from the Internet or opening an email attachment. If you are careful about what you download from the Internet, you are generally safe, but remember, even what you consider safe could distribute a virus to you. Some computer magazines over the years have accidentally put a program infected with a virus onto their CD-ROMs. Therefore, you can never be too sure of any file, wherever you are downloading it from.

Power loss or spikes: These are much more common than people realize (even more so in older houses where power cables are old). Power spikes occur when the current of the electricity suddenly goes higher, which doesn't sound too serious, but can cause data loss and hardware failure. Power loss can cause the same problems as power spikes, increasing the risk of damaging opened files.

Hard disk failures: This is a very common reason for data loss; many people take disks for granted and think their data is okay because it is stored on disk. A total disk failure can happen very quickly with little or no warning.

Theft: This is something we hope will never happen, but in the world we live in today, it is a possibility. Not only is your data taken from you, which means others have access to it, but many people store multiple copies of their data on the same machine. Consequently, once their base unit is taken, they won't have any way to get their files back.

Accident: We are all prone to making mistakes, especially after long hours at work or just general tiredness. You may decide to clean up your hard disk or move some folders, and suddenly you've deleted all your work, and emptied the Recycle Bin.

Hackers: Hackers weren't such a problem a few years ago when 56 K modem connections were common, but now, most people are moving to DSL and cable, with connection speeds ranging from 256 K to 3 MB. Unfortunately, this makes it easier for hackers to copy files, run scripts, steal data, crash or delete data, and even take control of your machine. They are unlikely to want to steal your TGF2 files, but will probably try to delete much of your data indiscriminately.

Time and Money

It takes time and effort to make any program, and you certainly don't want to have to start from scratch. Most people would probably want to give up if six month's of work were lost (you would probably move on to something else if only a small amount of work was lost).

Many creators like to work on something and then go back to it either to continue it or to take some work (code) from it to put into their latest creation. Game creating with TGF2 is very much like any other form of programming; you can write your code and then import it into other games. Consequently, making sure that even your old code is backed up and stored somewhere safe is something to consider.

WHAT SYSTEMS ARE AVAILABLE?

A number of possible solutions are available to us that we need to explore:

- Backing up using TGF2
- Media backups—CD-R, DVD-/+R, thumb drives, web sites
- Other hardware considerations—UPS, spike-protected power unit

Unfortunately, like many things with computers or technology, the more secure and reliable you want your system to be, the more money you will have to spend. Each solution has a cost or reliability factor associated with it, so pick the one that you can afford that gives you the most security.

Backing Up Using TGF2

TGF2's system for game and application recovery is straightforward. First, you will need to configure it, as it is not turned on by default. Go to the menu options and select Tools/Preferences, which will bring up the Preferences dialog box mentioned in Chapter 4, "TGF Creation Basics." Click on the General tab; a number of options will appear. From here, you will see the General Options section, which is shown in Figure 9.1.

FIGURE 9.1   The Autobackup feature.

As you can see in Figure 9.1, the Autobackup option is unticked by default, so to enable it, tick it and then specify the number of backup copies to keep by using the up and down arrows. The number you specify in the Number of Backup Copies to Keep box represents how many times your file will be backed up. For example, if you put the number 5 in the box, every time you save your game it will save an additional copy up to the maximum number you entered (in this example, five more copies). You will be able to identify these versions, as the filename is followed by the save copy number. If your game is called game1, it will save copies called game1001, game1002, game1003, game1004, and game1005. Once it has reached the maximum number, it will then begin to overwrite those files starting from game1001. The system is not complex, but will allow you to rescue an earlier version of the program if you run into problems. It is recommended that you set the number of copies to no fewer than 20, as anything less could mean that you may have a problem but not notice it, and all five backups could, in theory, have the same issue, rendering all the files useless. This option is not the only method you can use to secure your files, and should only be used as an extra way of covering yourself. Always make regular backups to other media, or when you save the program, change the name of the file you are working on. You will then get a new set of backup files, and you can archive the others. The only downside to this is that you can end up with many very large files.

Media Backups

There are quite a few different options available to you if you want to back up to something other than just a folder on your hard drive. One benefit of using different media to back up is that you can store backups off-site, so if anything happens at the place your computer is located, you can go and retrieve the backup.

Let's go through a few of the options you have to ensure you have backups of your files:

CD-R: CD-R is the writable version of a standard CD. Media for these devices are relatively cheap to purchase (in 25s or 50s), and many new machines have a writer device by default when you purchase the PC. The great thing about CD-R is that you can back up quickly and onto multiple CDs. You must ensure that all disks are labeled correctly so you can identify them later (which can be a difficultly with this type of media after a period of time has passed). Also, make sure they are stored in jewel cases or paper sleeves to protect them from becoming scratched or collecting dust, which could make it difficult to retrieve the data at a later date. As the media is so cheap and you can store around 700 MB (or a little more, depending on the media type and manufacturer), this should be enough for most of your project needs. Try to get into a routine of backing up as often as you can, as the main problem with this media is that you might only do a small number of backups, and programs often change. Over-all, CD-R is an easy to use, cheap format that can help you store copies of your files away from your computer.

DVD+/–: DVD writers have been around for a shorter time than CD-R, but have enjoyed much success as a replacement format. While CD format can only hold around 700 MB, DVD can contain around 4.7 GB of data, the ad-vantage of which is that if you store multiple backups of the same program on your hard disk, you can save them all to a DVD rather than just a selected few. You can now purchase a DVD writer for less than a $150. DVDs come in more than one format, which makes it harder to choose the right format. More ver-sions of DVD writers are appearing on the market with different format speci-fications (dual layer), so it is important to choose a format that is popular, and the media is cheap.

USB thumb drives: One of the most exciting prospects for moving data be-tween machines is the USB thumb drive. Thumb drives are about the size of a key ring and can store 128 MB to 1 GB of data. USB is a common computer connection type, and all modern computers have at least one USB 2.0 port. If you have an older computer, you might have a USB 1.0 port, but any device that supports version 2 is backward compatible and can work with an older port. It is easy to upgrade your computer to support USB with a PCI card (they are relatively inexpensive). When you plug the USB thumb drive into your PC, it shows up as a removable hard disk, which allows you to copy, delete, and use it like a normal disk. It is not recommended to use the thumb drive as a long-term backup device, but it is handy for moving data between machines and storing short-term data copies. Thumb drives are very small and can be dam-aged if you are not careful; the other downside is that as they are easy to pick up and put in your pocket, so they can easily be lost or stolen.

Tape backups: Tape backups are still a good way to back up and recover large amounts of information, but for the hobbyist or home developer, DVD writers have replaced them as the device of choice. The main reason for this is that the media is still quite expensive, and it can take a while to find and recover a file off a tape device (even though tape backup devices are very much faster today than a few years ago). Therefore, unless you have to back up many GBs of data, tape devices are not really worth investing in.

USB hard disks: You can now purchase external (USB connected) hard disks, which you can use for extra storage or backup disks, with the ability to move them between machines. These are very useful if you want to store multiple copies on a separate disk that isn't stored internally in the PC.

Floppy disks: Floppy disk drives are still available to use for storing files, but are not recommended. We've mentioned them here for completeness, and because some developers may still consider floppies an acceptable format for saving files. Standard floppy disk drives can store around 1.4 MB of data, which probably won't be enough to store any games in development. There are direct replacements for the floppy drive, but none has taken off and become a standard. In fact, some PC manufacturers have started to remove them all together and use USB as the main copying device. Floppy disks are easily damaged and can corrupt any data on them if not stored correctly, so it is best to stay away from this format if possible.

Web sites: With the number of DSL and cable users increasing at a staggering rate, a new storage possibility has opened up for developers: the ability to store backup files on an Internet Web site or storage facility. Many people get a Web site with storage space when they join an ISP (Internet service provider). For some, it may only be 20–100 MB, but this should be enough to store a number of backup files for safekeeping. If you have the finances available, you may be able to purchase your own domain name and hosting package, which could give you a few GB of space. Unfortunately, there is a downside to this type of storage: many ISPs will not back up your data, so if they have a server problem, you could lose everything you uploaded. For temporary storage and as another way to store files, it is a very useful and easy option. However, do not use this as the only backup option, and password protect any files to prevent any unauthorized access.

Other Considerations

There are a few other areas to consider to help protect and secure your data, some of which require some investment, and others that are free.

UPS: A UPS (uninterruptible power supply) is used to prevent power surges and power loss so you can close your work and then shut down your computer safely (using the UPS's battery power). If you live in a house or an area in which there are power fluctuations, buying a UPS is a sound investment. UPSs were, in the past, used solely for businesses, but in the last couple of years have become a piece of hardware that is now cheap enough for hobbyists and semi-professional developers to invest in.

Surge protectors: If you feel a UPS is overkill with regard to protecting your files (you may be in a situation in which you have a system that is backed up regularly), investing in a surge protector might be the next best thing. The surge protector is a standard power block (where you can put in multiple power sockets from all your devices), but has built-in power spike/surge protection. They will not protect you from power loss, but they will regulate the power, so a surge doesn't damage your equipment or open files.

Bios password: When your PC boots up, it first has to run the motherboard's BIOS. You can create a password that needs to be entered before the operating system takes over and loads. The benefit of a BIOS password is that it can prevent unauthorized access to your PC. Of course, you need to ensure that the password is something you can remember so you can get into your own PC. The BIOS password is not a fully secure system, and can only be used to prevent people within the same location from accessing the machine. It isn't a secure method if your machine is stolen, as the BIOS password option can be reset by using jumpers located on the motherboard. Users who just want general access would not take your PC apart to get access, as it would be too much hassle.

ZIP® file password: With Windows XP, you can place a number of files and folders into a single file called a Zip file. You can then specify a password on that Zip file that has to be entered when the file is accessed. Any Zip file you upload or store on other media retains this information, meaning that it will ask for the password regardless of where you store it. This is a simple way to protect files from being accessed, with no cost to the developer. Make a note of any passwords you use and keep them somewhere safe so you can access the files again.

Laptops, PDAs, and desktops: Computers have become much cheaper over the last few years, leading to many households having more than one PC or PC-based device (e.g., a PDA). Using networking technology or CD-ROM/USB, it is very easy to transfer data between machines for backup purposes. It is a useful way of storing files away from your main machine so that you have a backup, which can be recovered in the event of hardware failure.

Firewall: With the advent of DSL and cable, it is much easier for hackers to try to gain access to your data files. Luckily, various companies came up with a technology called a *firewall*, which protects your computer from unauthorized access. There are two types of firewalls available to developers, hardware based and software based. You may find that the DSL/cable router that is connected to the Internet has a firewall built in. If you have upgraded your PC operating system to Windows XP Service Pack 2, you now have access to a software-based firewall. There are a number of software products on the market today (some are free and some are not) that can help protect your PC from hackers.

SUMMARY

Unfortunately, developers don't consider the consequences of data loss until it's too late. It doesn't have to cost a lot of money or effort to provide a reasonable level of protection, so there is no reason not to invest now rather than after disaster strikes. The only issue when making multiple backups on hard disks, CD-Rs, and Web sites is ensuring that you know what and where the latest revisions of your changes are so you can go back to an earlier version if necessary. Even larger game development companies with the equipment and investment can lose work to hardware failure or illegal activities.

10 Movement

In This Chapter

- Movement Basics
- Movement Type Examples

Before creating your first game, you need to understand how movement works within TGF2. In the games you are making in this book, all of the movements have been predefined, so it is essential to understand how these concepts work, as you may have to refer to them in your own game making.

MOVEMENT BASICS

A large number of games that you will create will need some form of movement applied to the Active objects you are using. For example, in a side-scrolling shoot-'em-up game, you would require movement for the Player object, the Enemy objects, and any bullets or missiles that are fired against them. TGF2 comes with a number of prebuilt movement engines that allow you to configure your game quickly without the need to program a large number of events. These movements are separated into the following groups:

Static: This is the default option for any Active object inserted onto the frame. This means the object will not move unless you specify it within the Event Editor.

Bouncing Ball: This gives the object ball-like movement. You can set options for speed, deceleration, number of angles, randomizer (how random the bounce), and security (to prevent getting stuck). Bouncing ball movement is very useful in bat-and-ball-type games, and is used in the first game example in this book called "The Lab."

Path Movement: If you want to make your game use path movements (whereby objects follow a specific route), you can use this option. You might consider using path movement in maze-type games.

Mouse Controlled: This allows an object to be directly controlled by the movement of the mouse. When creating this type of movement, a box will appear on screen that can be increased or decreased in size. You can also move it to a specific area to limit its use to a particular portion of the screen.

Eight Directions: You can configure an object to have eight possible directions using this movement type, and can set speed, acceleration, deceleration, direction of movement, and the initial direction in which it should move. This is a good option if you only want a basic movement type, as you can easily preconfigure a group of options quickly.

Race Car: This allows you to preconfigure speed, acceleration, deceleration, rotation angles, and initial speed. This is a useful movement configuration if you are trying to replicate a racing car game.

Platform: If you want to create a platform-based game, this movement type sets up the basic requirements for creating one, including speed, acceleration, deceleration, gravity, jump strength, jump control, and initial direction of the object.

NOTE

TGF2 allows you to create movement based on one of the preprogrammed options, but you can create your own movements using code if you feel you need to do something that is not a standard feature of the program.

The movement groups are labeled for a specific type of game; for example, bouncing ball movement. While you would expect to use this movement for bat-and-ball-type games such as "The Lab" in this book, you can also use it in many other types of games that are not of the bat-and-ball type. For example, we could have used bouncing ball movement in our second game "Amazing Fighter Pilot," for moving the enemy planes. Therefore, don't think that you have to use the race-car movement for racing cars or the platform movement for platform-only games;

each has a particular feature that you may be able to apply to the movement of an object within your games.

Applying Movement

The movement types previously mentioned are only applied to specific types of objects, so you will not find the Movement tab on all objects available within TGF2. You can apply movement as follows (in this example, we are using an Active object, but it could be any of the other objects that have the Movement tab properties assigned to them):

1. Start TGF2, click on the File menu option, and select New.
2. Double left-click on the frame labeled "Frame 1" in the Workspace toolbar.
3. Select New Object from the Insert menu option, and when the Create New Object dialog box appears, double-click on the Active object and then click anywhere on the play area. The Active object will now be visible on the play area; click on it with the left mouse button once to reveal the properties of the item within the Object Properties toolbar.
4. Click on the Movement tab in the Object Properties toolbar. You will see a screen as shown in Figure 10.1.

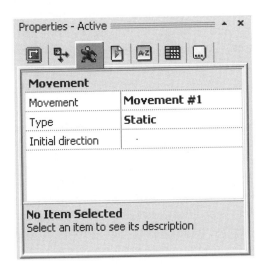

FIGURE 10.1 The Active object's Movement Properties.

5. Notice that within the Properties dialog is a movement number, and a movement type. You can apply multiple types of movement to the same object, which allows you to change the object's direction and movement response depending on a specific condition. The Type is a drop-down box containing the movement groups discussed earlier. Selecting any of the types from the drop-down box will reveal more properties specific to that movement type.

By default, there is always a single movement type already created called "Movement # 1" with the type of "Static" defined.

MOVEMENT TYPE EXAMPLES

Now that you know where to find the movement properties for an object, we will now go through a number of examples to show them working, and introduce you to any specific dialog they might have.

For each of the movement types, a basic TGF2 file was created and is on the companion CD-ROM. These files were created to speed up the process of going through the examples by having the objects already inserted onto the play area. No movement has been applied to any of the objects, and they only have the default settings configured (it would be exactly the same settings as inserting a new object onto the frame). All example files can be found in the folder \Movement on the CD-ROM.

Bouncing Ball

A good example of where you might use the Bouncing Ball movement is the game featured in this book called "The Lab." The Lab is a bat and ball game, where you try to keep the ball in play and destroy all of the blocks. The Ball object has been given a movement of Bouncing Ball, and is made to bounce off the walls around the screen, with the exception of the right side, where it will disappear and the player will lose a life. We will now make an object bounce around the screen, which will require us to apply the Bouncing Ball movement to the object and create one line of code to keep it on the screen at all times.

A final version of the example (called "bouncing ball final") can be found on the companion CD-ROM in the Movement folder.

1. Start TGF2, and then click on the File | Open option from the menu. When the Open dialog box appears, browse for your CD-ROM drive and locate the file "Bounce basic," which is stored in the Movement folder. Choose this file and then click OK to open the file.
2. Double-click on the text "Frame 1" in the Workspace toolbar to open the Frame Editor.
3. Click on the Active object that is located within the frame (it will look like a green diamond shape). The properties for the object will appear in the Properties toolbar.
4. Click on the Movement tab within the Properties toolbar.
5. You will now see three options: Movement, Type, and Initial Direction. Click on Type, and a drop-down list will appear; select Bouncing Ball. A set of new properties for this object will now be shown (as seen in Figure 10.2), allowing you to fine-tune the object to react in a specific way. Also notice the Try Movement button, which allows you to run the frame and see how the object reacts to its new movement.

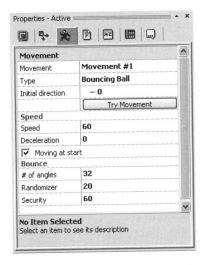

FIGURE 10.2 Object properties for Bouncing Ball movement.

6. If you click on the Try Movement button, you will notice that the object flies off to the right and then disappears. This is because the initial direction is set to go to the right, and there is no code to prevent it from leaving the frame.
7. Click on the Event Editor button in the toolbar, and then click on New Condition to create a new event.

8. When the New Condition dialog box appears, double left-click on the Active object (this will look like a character running), and then select Position, Test Position of Active from the pop-up menu.

9. A Test Position of Active dialog box will appear. Click on all of the outward pointing arrows on the edge of the white box (four in total), and then click OK.

10. Move to the right of the event until you are directly under the Active object. Right-click and add the action Movement, Bounce.

If you now run the program, you will see the Active object bouncing around the screen. From within the properties, you can vary the speed, number of angles it bounces, the Randomizer (how random is each bounce), and the security (to prevent it getting stuck).

Path Movement

Path Movement allows you to set a specified route of an object around the screen. You create this route by placing a number of markers for which you can set the speed or allow the object to be paused at each point.

ON THE CD   You will find the basic working file "path basic" for this walkthrough on the companion CD-ROM in the Movement folder.

1. Start TGF2, and click on the File | Open option from the menu. When the Open dialog box appears, browse to your CD-ROM drive, and locate the file "path basic," which is stored in the Movement folder. Choose this file and then click OK to open the file.

2. Double-click on the text "Frame 1" in the Workspace toolbar to open the Frame Editor.

3. Click on the Active object that is located within the frame (it will look like a green diamond shape). The properties for the object will appear in the Properties toolbar. Click on the Movement tab within the Properties toolbar. Click on Type and a drop-down list will appear; select Path. An Edit box will then appear, which allows you to configure the movement of this object. The Properties sheet for the object is shown in Figure 10.3.

4. Click on the Edit box to begin editing the path movement using the dialog box, which is shown in Figure 10.4.

There are a number of options you can apply to your path movement:
New Line: Creates a line, which can be moved to any point on the screen. The first line that created when using the Path dialog will be attached to the inserted object. On each end of the line will be a small black square (these are called

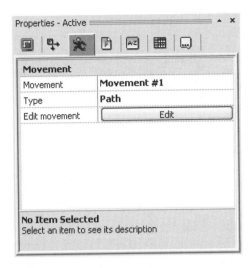

FIGURE 10.3 Object properties for path movement.

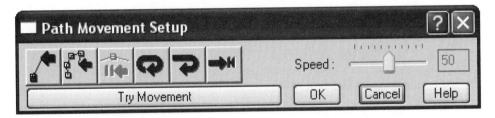

FIGURE 10.4 Path movement.

nodes), where you can configure pauses or the speed of the movement between points. Using this option, you will place a single line; you can then create a second line that originates from the last square from the last new line.

Tape Mouse: This option allows you to create multiple points quickly using a single mouse click, rather than placing them individually. Hold down the left mouse key and then move the mouse cursor to create the path.

Set a Pause: If you want to pause the object at a specific point on the screen (making the object wait), you can set a pause.

Loop the Movement: This will allow you to make a movement repeat continuously. Once the object has reached the end of the movement path (the last square), it will disappear and reappear at the start, and then begin moving again. If you are using this for an object, you may need to make the start and end points out of view of the player so you do not allow the player to see the object disappear on screen.

Reverse at End: If you want an object to go to a certain end point, and then retrace its steps along the same path it was just on, you can select this option.

Reposition Object at End: This will place the object back to its original starting location when it has reached the last node.

Try Movement: If you want to test the movement you just created, click on Try Movement, which in turn will run the movement for the specified object. You can quit out of it at any time using the ESC (escape) key, or alternatively wait until the movement is complete.

Speed: You can change the speed of the object between each node by clicking on the node where you want it to have a different speed. The line where the speed change will be applied will flash to give you a visualization of where this will take place.

NOTE

If you hold your mouse cursor over the items on the Path Movement Setup dialog, a small help text will appear, advising you what each option is.

Mouse Controlled

If you want an object to be controlled by the mouse cursor, select the Mouse Controlled movement type. This type of movement is used in our bat and ball game "The Lab" to move the bat object up and down the screen.

ON THE CD

1. To follow along with the next example, you can use a basic starting file, which places an object on screen ready to be configured for mouse movement. The file can be found in the Movement folder on the companion CD-ROM and is called "mouse basic."

2. Start TGF2, and then click on the File | Open option from the menu. When the Open dialog box appears, browse to your CD-ROM drive, and locate the file "mouse basic," which is stored in the Movement folder. Choose this file and then click OK to open the file.

3. Double-click on the text "Frame 1" in the Workspace toolbar to open the Frame Editor.

4. Click on the Active object that is located within the frame (it will look like a green diamond shape). The properties for the object will appear in the Properties toolbar.

5. Click on the Movement tab within the Properties toolbar. You will now see three options: Movement, Type, and Initial Direction. Click on Type and a drop-down list will appear; select Mouse Controlled.
6. A set of new properties for this object will now be displayed, as shown in Figure 10.5.

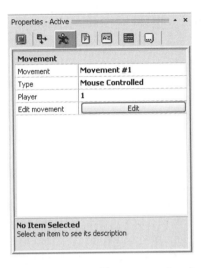

FIGURE 10.5 Object Properties sheet for Mouse Controlled movement

7. You will notice a player item with the number "1" assigned next to it, and an Edit button to configure the movement options.
8. To create the area where you want the object to be moved by the mouse, click on the Edit button. Once you have clicked on this button, you will see Figure 10.6.

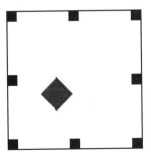

FIGURE 10.6 Editing the mouse-controlled configuration.

9. Using the mouse, expand or decrease the size of the box area where you want the object to be moved by the mouse. Once you are happy with the area you have specified, you can then click on Try Movement to test the movement and see if you might need to make some changes to the box area. You will now be able to move the object using the mouse, but only within the area you selected.

10. Press the Escape key to exit the example.

Eight Directions

Eight Directions is a good starting point for movement of an object, and is frequently used in (but not exclusively), for example, player movement in a platform or side-shooting game.

ON THE CD

To follow along with the next example, you can use a basic starting file, which places an object on screen ready to be configured for Eight Directions movement. The file can be found in the Movement folder and is called "eight basic."

1. Start TGF2, and then click on the File | Open option from the menu. When the Open dialog box appears, browse to your CD-ROM drive, and locate the file "eight basic," which is stored in the Movement folder. Choose this file and then click OK to open the file.

2. Double-click on the text "Frame 1" in the Workspace toolbar to open the Frame Editor.

3. Click on the Active object that is located within the frame (it will look like a green diamond shape). The properties for the object will appear in the Properties toolbar.

4. Click on the Movement tab within the Properties toolbar. You will now see three options: Movement, Type, and Initial Direction. Click on Type and a drop-down list will appear; select Eight Directions.

5. You will now see a number of new object properties as shown in Figure 10.7.

6. You can select the player you want this object to be controlled by; the default is player 1.

7. You can specify the directions the object can travel in (which are represented by direction numbers), and its initial starting angle, which is useful for objects that move without player intervention. By clicking on either of the directions, a dialog appears, which can be seen in Figure 10.8.

8. You can also specify the speed, acceleration, deceleration, and if the object is starting when the frame is first loaded. Click on the Try Movement button to load a test frame and test the object's movement. Use the arrow keys to move the object around the screen.

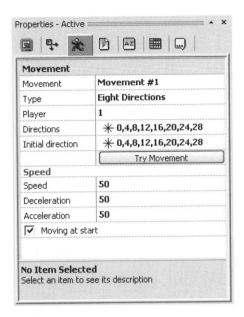

FIGURE 10.7   Object Properties sheet for Eight Directions movement.

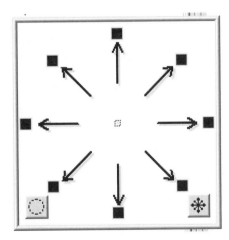

FIGURE 10.8   Direction dialog with Eight Directions selected.

Race Car Movement

Another option that can be chosen as a type of movement is Race Car. By selecting this option, you can mimic the movement of a race car without any additional programming. This allows you to make the object respond in a specific way via the arrow keys, including acceleration, reversing, and cornering (rotating speed).

ON THE CD

The file used to follow this example is located on the companion CD-ROM, under the Movement folder; the file is called "racing car basic."

1. Start TGF2, and then click on the File | Open option from the menu. When the Open dialog box appears, browse to your CD-ROM drive and locate the file "racing car basic," which is stored in the Movement folder. Choose this file and then click OK to open the file.
2. Double-click on the text "Frame 1" in the Workspace toolbar to open the Frame Editor.
3. Click on the Active object that is located within the frame (it will look like a yellow and green racing car). The properties for the object will appear in the Properties toolbar.
4. Click on the Movement tab within the Properties toolbar. You will now see three options: Movement, Type, and Initial Direction. Click on Type and a drop-down list will appear; select Race Car.
5. You will now see a number of new object properties as shown in Figure 10.9.

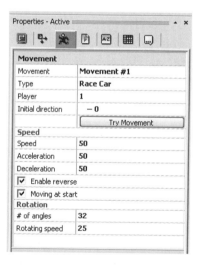

FIGURE 10.9 Object properties showing the Race Car movement

6. To get the race car moving, you do not need to amend any of the options. Click on the Try Movement button to test the race car with the arrow keys on your keyboard.

Platform Movement

The final type of movement available within TGF2 is Platform Movement. If you want to create a platform game, you would apply this type of movement to your main character, and the platforms and ladders.

The file used to follow this example is on the companion CD-ROM, in the Movement folder; the file is called "platform basic."

The "platform basic" file provides you with a single frame with all of the graphic items in their correct positions ready to be configured.

To enable the game to play in Platform Movement, we first need to apply Platform Movement to our character Player_Robin.

1. Start TGF2, and then click on the File | Open option from the menu. When the Open dialog box appears, browse to your CD-ROM drive and locate the file "platform basic," which is stored in the Movement folder. Choose this file and then click OK to open the file.
2. Double-click on the text "Frame 1" in the Workspace toolbar to display the precreated level in the Frame Editor.
3. Single-click on the Player_Robin object to display its properties in the Properties toolbar, and then click on the Movement tab. Click on the Type box to reveal a number of options; click on the Platform option.

You have now configured Robin to make him move with a platform configuration; the only problem with this is that there are no platforms. If you run the frame at this point, you will see Robin fall through the floor; as far as TGF2 is concerned, there are no platforms available for him to land on. Therefore, we need to configure the floor and raised areas that Robin will walk on as "platforms."

4. Click on one of the Platform objects, and then in the Object Properties window, click on the Runtime Options tab. Click on the blank space next to Obstacle type, and from the drop-down menu, choose Platform.

If you have many platforms to configure, it might take awhile to do each separately, so you can select multiple objects using the cursor (by left-clicking and holding down the mouse over the objects) or by holding down the Shift key and single-clicking on each object. Lastly, we have a ladder on the frame, which we need to configure as a "ladder" obstacle type.

5. Click on one of the Ladder objects; the object Properties will then appear. Click on the Runtime Options tab and then click the white space next to the Obstacle Type option. From the drop-down menu, choose Ladder.

If you now run the frame, you will see that your character can walk, jump, and climb up the ladder.

SUMMARY

In this chapter, you learned how to create movement of your objects. You are now ready to tackle the two final concepts that are important when making your games: importing graphics and creating animations. As with the movements, all the graphics of our games are predefined, so it is useful to know how to make your own for your games.

11 Graphics and Animation

In This Chapter

- Graphic Creation
- Animations

This chapter shows you how to import your own graphics using images created in a third-party graphics product, create your own using TGF2's built-in Picture Editor, and how to animate your images into moving graphics.

GRAPHIC CREATION

You may want to create your own graphic images for your games, or import ones created in another graphics package, which is possible using TGF2's Picture Editor. To access the Picture Editor, you need to have inserted onto the play area a graphic-based object; for example, an Active, Picture, or Backdrop object. Once you have placed it, double-click on it to enter the Picture Editor, and begin the process of making your own images or importing one.

Importing Graphics

In the following example, we will import a single BMP (bitmap) formatted file that was created in another graphics program into TGF2.

ON THE CD

The image called "Import1.bmp" has been created for you and can be found in the Graphics folder on the companion CD-ROM.

1. Start TGF2, and then click on the File | New option from the menu to create a new program file.
2. Double-click on the text "Frame 1" in the Workspace toolbar to open the Frame Editor.
3. From the File menu, select Insert | New Object. When the Create New Object dialog box appears, double-click on the Active object. Place the object somewhere on the playfield by left-clicking on the frame.
4. A green diamond-shaped object will now appear within the frame; to enter the Picture Editor, double-click on the object.
5. Click on the Import button (the second in from the top left) to open the Import dialog box.
6. A dialog box will now appear, and you will need to navigate to the location of the file you want to import. In this example, it is "CD-ROM\Graphics\import1.bmp." Select the file and then click on the Open button. An Import dialog box will appear, as shown in Figure 11.1. Click on the OK button to import the image.

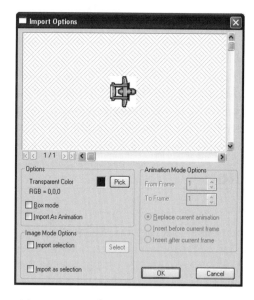

FIGURE 11.1   The Import dialog box.

7. The image of the yellow plane will now replace the green diamond shape; click on the OK button to save this to the object.

Drawing Graphics in TGF2

Perhaps you don't have access to another drawing package, or you would prefer to make your images from within TGF2's own powerful Picture Editor. In the following example, we are going to create a simple graphic image to give you a flavor of the Picture Editor, because it uses many common drawing tools (lines, fill, erase); we won't be going into detail on those aspects.

An example of the final output from this walkthrough is contained on the companion CD-ROM in the Graphics folder; the TGF2 file is called "draw final."

As we are experimenting with the drawing tool, the exact image you create will not be exactly like the picture in the TGF2 "draw final" file.

1. Start TGF2, and then click on the File | New option from the menu to create a new program file.
2. Double-click on the text "Frame 1" in the Workspace toolbar to open the Frame Editor.
3. From the File menu, select Insert | New Object. When the Create New Object dialog box appears, double-click on the Active object. Place the object somewhere on the playfield by left-clicking on the frame.
4. A green diamond-shaped object will now appear in the frame; to enter the Picture Editor, double-click on the object.
5. First, we need to delete the current image that is occupying the Active object. You can do this using either the Clear command or the Erase tool. The Clear tool deletes the entire area, and the Erase tool allows you to select a certain area of the image to delete. We want to remove the entire image, so click on the Clear button, which is the first icon at the top left of the Picture Editor (it looks like a blank piece of paper). The image will now be removed from the Active object.
6. The image is too small for the drawing we want to do, so to resize we need to use the Size button, which is the bottom-left button on the toolbar (it resembles a line with an arrowhead on each end). On clicking the Size button, a dialog box will appear allowing you to configure certain sizing aspects of your image, as shown in Figure 11.2.

FIGURE 11.2   Resizing
Tool dialog box.

7. Now we need to amend the image size, so type in "200" for the width and "160" for the height, and then click on the Apply button to make the change to the image.

8. Now, select the Line tool (looks like an image of a straight line and a pencil), and make a number of criss-crossing images on the image canvas. You will now have an image that should look similar to Figure 11.3.

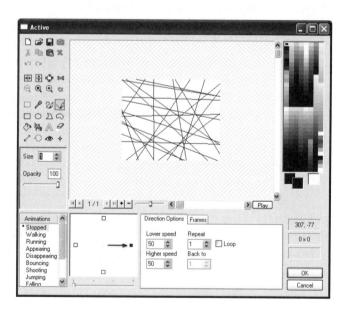

FIGURE 11.3   Picture Editor with a drawing in progress.

9. We now need to fill in some of the areas of the image with different colors, so choose the Fill tool in the toolbar (it looks like a paint pot being tipped over), and then click on any color from the selection of colors on the right of the Picture Editor. Click within some of the blank areas on the image to fill them with the selected color. Do this a few times and then choose another color, and then continue to fill more of the white gaps. Do this a number of times until you are happy with the image.

If you have trouble seeing some of the gaps, you can use the Zoom function within the Picture Editor to increase the size of the image temporarily.

10. Click on the OK button to save the work to the Active object.

Do not click on the red "X" in the corner of the Active Picture dialog box or on Cancel if you want to save your image, as this will revert the object to its original image.

ANIMATIONS

Animations are important in games, making the images look like they are moving (this could be the movement of the main character, an item in the background, or an enemy player). In addition, animations make the game look more interesting and more realistic. All animations used within TGF2 are created within the Picture Editor, and use the same process as importing a single image.

We are going to create a small animation of a plane being destroyed; the completed file called "import anim final" can be found on the companion CD-ROM in the Graphics folder.

1. Start TGF2, and then click on the File | New option from the menu to create a new program file.
2. Double-click on the text "Frame 1" in the Workspace toolbar to open the Frame Editor.
3. From the File menu, select Insert | New Object; when the Create New Object dialog box appears, double-click on the Active object. Place the object somewhere on the playfield by left-clicking on the frame.
4. A green diamond-shaped object will appear in the frame; to enter the Picture Editor, double-click on the object.

5. Click on the Import icon to open the Import dialog box. Browse for the graphics folder on the companion CD-ROM, select the image called

"anim1," and then click on Open. You will see the Import Options dialog that appeared when importing a single image in Figure 11.4.

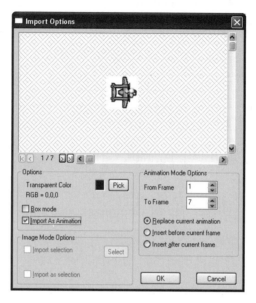

FIGURE 11.4 Import Options dialog box for multiple animations.

6. Ensure the Import as an Animation check box is ticked, and then click on the OK button.

You will now have an Active object that has seven frames of the plane being destroyed. Notice that by default, the Active object will play the animation as soon as the frame is started; in the example "import anim final," it has been told not to run the animation until the user presses the Spacebar.

SUMMARY

In this chapter, you learned two of the most important aspects of making your games with TGF2: how to import or draw your own images, and how to animate them. You are now ready to tackle the first game in this book, "The Lab," where we will use some of the features and functionality of TGF2 with which you are now familiar.

12 Creating a Bat-and-Ball Game

In this chapter, we will create our very first game, which will be an exciting and fun Bat-and-Ball style game. We will learn the basic concepts of TGF2, and the best way to structure your games using the product. We will take the game idea from a set of graphics, to a fully playable one level with its own high-score table.

ABOUT THE LAB

The first game we are going to make is called "The Lab." Although it is a traditional Bat-and-Ball type of game (details of this type of game can be found in Chapter 1, "Games, Games, and More Games"), by putting in some nice graphics and an interesting story, you can make it an excellent game for people to play. It is very important to remember that although this type of game has been done many times, you can make it different using an interesting concept. "The Lab" is an interesting take on the Bat and Ball type of game; the story goes something like this:

```
You are a lab technician working on a new experiment. There is an acci-
dent in the lab and your chemicals have been mixed up, creating a force
field so you are unable to escape.
    You must destroy all of the items on the shelf, which will reveal new
ingredients to help you free yourself.
```

For this game, you will need to separate it into three easily manageable sections:

The Main screen: Also known as the title screen or loading screen. This is where you introduce the game to the game players, provide options to play the game, see the high scores, and quit the game.

The Game screen: This is where the user starts to play the game and tries to beat the current high score.

The High-Score screen: This is where players can see all of the current high scores so they can think about what they have to do to get onto the leaderboard.

To make things easier, all of the graphics have been premade, and the objects used within this game are preconfigured, again to make things easier. We covered these configurations in Chapters 6, "Object, the Cornerstone of Creation," and 7, "Configuring Properties."

Before we begin, we need to break the game down into more detail of what will happen in each stage.

This first game is documented in detail at each stage; the other two main games have less detailed instructions, as you should then be familiar with how to do cer-tain aspects of the programming.

1. When the game starts, the main menu graphic appears, which displays the title of the game and three options: Start Game, High Scores, and Quit. Clicking on any of the options makes the program go to another frame. Start Game takes the program to frame two for the player to play the game, High Scores takes the game to frame three to see the current highest scores, and Quit exits the program.

2. When the player clicks on the Start Game button, he will be taken to the game screen. The blocks will be placed on screen, and the user will need to press the Spacebar to begin playing the game. Each block will take two hits to be destroyed, and then will be removed from the play area. There will be four special blocks that release a bottle or a chemical shape, so if the bat hits

them, the player will get a special bonus. The bat will be moved using the Up and Down arrow keys. Once all three lives have been lost (the ball will need to disappear behind the bat on the right-hand side of the screen), a box will appear asking the player to enter his or her name.

3. After entering your name, you will be taken to the High Scores screen (Frame three), where the current scores will be listed. Clicking on the Leave button will take you back to the main screen (frame one).

Before you begin to create the game, check out the final creation on the companion CD-ROM. The executable file is located in \Game1, and the file to run it is called "TheLab.exe." This will show you all the sections of the game, and how it plays.

Graphics Library—The Lab

All of the graphics and objects used in this game have been placed in a library to make the game development easier. A library is a folder in which you can access all the component parts to your game. These components could be graphics, sound, or TGF2 files. By saving your TGF2 file to a folder and then using the Library toolbar to point to it, you can use them as libraries as well. The major benefit of this is that if you have a number of similar game concepts, you can place them all in the same folder, and then drag and drop items from them onto your new game.

To use our ready-made graphics and objects, we need to point the library to the files on the companion CD-ROM. The Library files for the Lab game can be found in the folder CDROM\Game1\Lib.

1. Right-click on the left-hand pane of the Library toolbar to reveal a pop-up menu.
2. Click on the New option. A dialog box will appear, allowing you to browse your computer and any attached devices. Browse the list until you see your CD-ROM drive (located under My Computer on Windows XP).
3. After finding your CD-ROM drive, find the folder \Game1\Lib on the companion CD-ROM, And then click on the OK button. You will then need to enter a library folder name; for this game we will call it "The Lab," so type that in the box that appears in the toolbar.
4. Click on "The Lab" folder name in the Library toolbar; a small graphic will appear in the right window pane. Double-click on this item to browse down into the library. You will then see more items in the right window pane, which separates the graphics and objects into relevant groups. You can double-click on any of the three available groups to see some of the game items. You can use the Up arrow to move back up, but this is only

useful if you have multiple folders within one folder. Depending on your screen resolution, you may need to use the scroll bar to view all of the available items you can use in your game. Remember, you can increase the size of the Library toolbar if you have the room to do so by moving the mouse over the edges of the Toolbar box and the dragging the window. You will then see all the items needed in the game as shown in Figure 12.1.

FIGURE 12.1   Some of the objects available in the Lab library.

5. To add an item to your game, simply drag the item onto the Frame Editor.

THE LAB—INITIAL SETUP

First, we need to set up all the frames we will work with for this game. We will need three frames: one for the Main Menu, one for the Game, and one for the Hi-Score table.

Creating the Frames

The first thing we need to do is create the TGF file and then create our initial three frames.

1. Start TGF2, and then click on the File/New option on the menu. This will create the initial game program and its first frame.
2. Highlight the text "Application 1," which is the top item in the Workspace toolbar. You can then either right-click and select New Frame, or select Insert/New Frame from the menu. This will create a second frame called "Frame 2"; type in the name "Game." Press Enter to accept the frame name.
3. Insert another frame using the same method as before and call it "Hi-Score."

4. We now need to change the name of the first of the frames, "Frame 1." Highlight it by clicking once on it with the left mouse button, and then right-click on it and select Rename. Call this frame "Main Menu," and then press the Enter key to accept the changes.

Changing Application Settings

The application settings are configuration options that affect the entire game. These could include the size of window, can it be maximized, minimized, what graphic mode does it run in, and so forth. You can see what the current setup of the Workspace toolbar should look like in Figure 12.2.

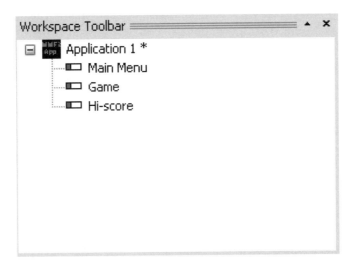

FIGURE 12.2   The current configuration of the Workspace.

1. First, we need to change the name of the game to something a little more interesting and descriptive than "Application 1." Click the left mouse button once on the word "Application 1" to highlight the text. Change the text to "The Lab."

You could have changed the name of the game by left-clicking once on the word "Application 1" to highlight it. Then, right-click on the text to bring up the pop-up menu. Select Rename and then type in the game name.

2. You may see a small * next to the game name, which means that you haven't saved the game yet, and you have made a change since the last save.

Try to get into the habit of saving your game regularly, so if you have any problems or your computer crashes, you hopefully will not lose any work.

3. There is only one bit of configuration we need to do at the Application frame before we start making our game, as the rest of the default settings are perfect for what we need. If you run the game now, by clicking on the Run Application button on the menu bar, the game will appear. Everything looks fine, but notice that you can click on the Maximize button and the game will fill the entire screen. We don't want this to happen, as the game graphics are configured to play within a certain screen size (640x480), and you will have a border around the game if a user presses the Maximize button, which doesn't look very professional. We need to go into the Application Properties; you can do this by clicking on the game name "The Lab" in the Workspace toolbar. This will now load the Application Properties into the Properties toolbar. Click on the icon that looks like a monitor, which is the Window Properties tab. Find No Maximize Box and tick it. This will disable that option from being clicked when you next run the game. Figure 12.3 shows an example of how the properties will look when you have made that change.

4. Save the game by clicking on File/Save on the menu, or the Save button on the toolbar.

FIGURE 12.3 Removing the maximize option.

THE LAB—MAIN MENU

If you run the game, it will display the window on screen, and will not allow it to be maximized. Nothing else will happen, so now you need to create the main menu screen. The main menu is used as an introduction screen to the players, and allows them to play the game, view the high scores, or quit. The main menu should be kept as simple as possible; if it is too confusing, the player might exit rather than continue and play the game. Moreover, if they don't like the game because it has a confusing interface, they might not download any other games on your site.

1. Click on the words "The Lab" in the Library toolbar (the library link was created earlier; if you do not have it, see the "Graphics Library—The Lab" section for more details).
2. You will now see an icon and the words "the Lab" in the right-hand window; this is the library file containing all the objects and graphics we need. Double click-on the "The Lab" icon to drill down to the next level.
3. Within the Library toolbar, you will now see the icons Intro, Game Frame, and Highscores. To make this game easier, we have placed all the required objects in these three areas; for the main menu of our game, all of the items you need are stored under Intro. Double-click on Intro to see the items we will use in the first frame of our game.

If you want to navigate back up at any time, click on the upward pointing green arrow.

4. Before we can place any items on the playfield, we must be able to see the right frame on the screen. To do this, double-click on Main Menu in the Workspace toolbar to go to the correct frame. Your screen should now look something like Figure 12.4.
5. The first item you will need is a background graphic to make the screen look more interesting. You will see an image in the Library toolbar called "Background." Left-click on this graphic and continue to hold down the left mouse button while dragging the image across onto the playfield. Once it's in position, let go of the left mouse button and the background image will appear in the Frame Editor window. If the image doesn't cover the playfield precisely, you can move it with the mouse by dragging it into position, or right-click on the image, and then select Align in Frame/Horz/Center and Align in Frame/Vert/Center. The second method is preferred, as the graphic will be placed automatically in the center.
6. Next, you need to place the three Bitmap buttons on the playfield. In the middle of the background image is a box in which they need to be placed.

Put the buttons in the order of "Button—Start Game," "Button—High-score," and "Button—Quit."

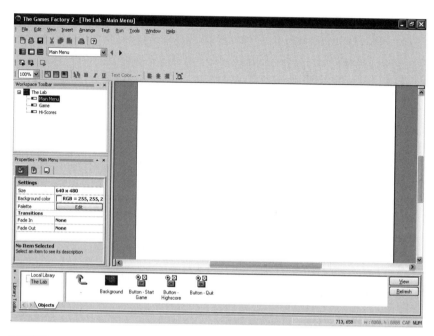

FIGURE 12.4   How your current screen should look.

The three Bitmap buttons can be created in your own games by using the Button object. You have a number of options with the Button object, including Bitmap, which allows you to assign different images for when the user clicks on and off with the mouse. In "The Lab," the three buttons have three images each for each state: Normal (not pressed), Pressed (when clicked on), and Disabled (if it is switched off but still visible within the game). All of the three images are essentially the same, but with slightly different coloring. When the player clicks on the button, it will change color. This is an easy-to-create, yet very effective graphic effect that can be used within games to make them look more professional.

7. You now have all of the elements needed for the main menu on the screen. An example of this is shown in Figure 12.5.

If the game is run at this stage, the game window will appear with a nicely drawn background and three buttons down the middle. On clicking each of the three graphic text objects, they will turn yellow but not make anything happen. You will not need to do any programming using the Event Editor at this time, as all of the graphical elements will be put in place first. This will give you a flavor of what each frame is supposed to do, and what parts you will need to code to get it working correctly later.

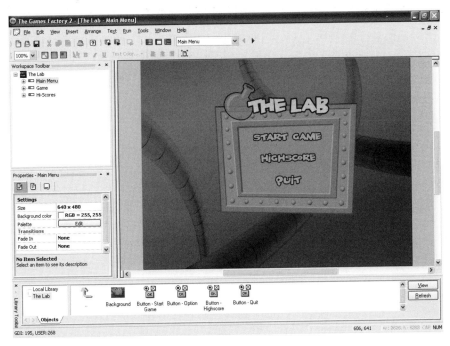

FIGURE 12.5   How the first frame should look once the items have been placed.
©Jason Darby 2005. Reprinted with permission.

THE LAB—THE GAME SCREEN

Now that the Main Menu screen is complete, it is sensible to put all of the graphical elements of the game screen together. This will be more work than the Main Menu screen because of the number of objects involved to represent all the blocks. There are a number of shortcuts we can use to make placing them much quicker:

1. Double left-click on the frame entitled "Game"; this will change the Frame Editor from the first frame to the second. The playfield will be blank, because we have not put any objects on this frame.
2. In the Library toolbar, we are currently viewing the objects for the first frame; double-click on the up pointing green arrow to move up a level. Double-click on the library group called "Game Frame." You will now see all the objects you need to use in this frame.

3. Drag the Background image from the Library toolbar onto the playfield. Now, drag the image called "Frame" onto the playfield. This will place it on top of the Background image. You may need to center both images in the middle of the frame (using the right mouse button, click Align in Frame, discussed in "The Lab—Main Menu" section).

4. You now need to place the first brick onto the play area. Drag the graphic object called "Brick" and put it anywhere on the screen. Left-click on the brick to bring up its properties in the Properties Workspace. We need to access the Size/Position tab to change its position on the screen. Click on the Size/Position tab to see the settings. Type "94" in both the X and Y positions. This will place the first brick to the correct position on the playfield, and will be used as the placeholder for all the other bricks we need to add.

5. The bricks will be placed 7 down and 11 across. This could take a long time if you had to drag and drop each brick onto the screen, but luckily, there is a way to do this in TGF2 called "duplicating." Duplicating an object makes another copy of the object, and although it contains most of the aspects of the original object, you are allowed to specify some different object properties. Left-click on the brick so it is highlighted, and then right-click on it and select the Duplicate option. A Duplication dialog box will appear as shown in Figure 12.6.

NOTE

There are two ways to create replica objects on the playfield: Duplicate and Clone object. Although they will create what appears to be exactly the same thing, there is a difference between the two options. Duplicate creates all objects with the same appearance and name, and will appear in the Event Editor as a single object. Any changes you make to a single object will change all the others. The benefit of duplicating objects is that you can work with them as a group, or you can access single objects using a internal value assigned to each (you can also use Random to access them). Cloning looks similar to duplication, but creates a separate object with different properties, and each has a unique name.

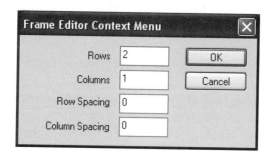

FIGURE 12.6 Duplication dialog box.

6. When duplicating an object, you have a number of options you can choose to make copies and place them on the playfield. "Rows" is how many copies of the object you will make going in a downward direction (the number includes the one that already exists). "Columns" is how many objects will appear to the right of the current object (again includes the one you are duplicating). Then there are two options for spacing the objects on the screen; the higher the number, the bigger the gap between each object. "Row spacing" indicates the space between the objects going from top to bottom, and "Column spacing" will determine the space of each object left to right. You need to enter the following numbers to create the right number of bricks: 7 rows, 11 columns, 0 row spacing, and 12 column spacing. Once you click OK, you will see how the screen is starting to look more like a game. Delete four bricks from anywhere within the group of bricks and then replace them with the four special bricks from the Library toolbar (Brick Large Mode, Brick Sticky Mode, Brick Shoot Mode, and Brick Double Ball Mode).

TGF2 has a number of new features that allow you to develop your game quickly, which can mean a quicker release date, and less time spent doing repetitive tasks.

7. Place the Ball object onto the playfield. Click on the object to view its properties, and then click on the Size/Position tab. Set the X and Y settings as 405 and 212, respectively.

8. Drag the Bat object onto the playfield. Then, click on it to highlight it and to display the Object Properties in the Properties Workspace area. Click on the Size/Position tab and set the X, Y settings to 587 and 193, respectively.

9. Drag the Lives object onto the playfield and place it in the Lives box on the playfield. You don't need an exact position as long as you place it in the middle of the Lives box using the mouse (if you want to place it in exact same place as the game, the X, Y settings are 120 and 442, respectively).

10. Find the Scores object, drag it onto the playfield, and place it in the Score box (on the right-hand side). You can place it manually, or put it at the co-ordinates 555, 462.

11. Finally, you need to drag all the other objects onto the Frame Editor, but outside the playfield. These objects will be used in the game, but are not to be shown when the frame runs. An example of how your game should look is shown in Figure 12.7. By placing them outside the play area, you can call on the graphics when you need them using code. You will need to drag the following objects onto the Frame Editor: Formula_Large, Formula_Sticky, Formula_Shoot, Double Ball, and Bullet.

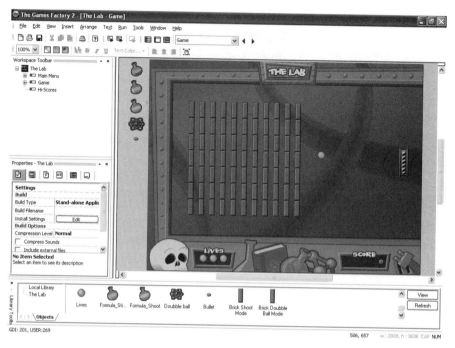

FIGURE 12.7 The setup of the game and how it should look. ©Jason Darby 2005. Reprinted with permission.

THE LAB–HI-SCORES

The Hi-Scores frame is the last frame within the game and is used to show the players if they achieved a good score.

1. Double left-click on the frame entitled "Hi-Scores"; this will change the Frame Editor from the second frame to the third. The playfield will be blank, because we haven't put any objects onto this frame.
2. In the Library toolbar, we are currently viewing the objects for the second frame; double click on the up pointing green arrow to move up a level. Double-click on the library group called "Hi-scores." You will now see all of the objects you need to use in this frame.
3. Drag the Backdrop object onto the playfield. Once placed, you will need to drag it correctly into position or use the Align in Frame option from the pop-up menu (using the right mouse button).
4. Drag the Button—Leave object onto the playfield and place it toward the button end of the background box. You can also place it more precisely using the Object Properties and placing it at coordinates 279, 354 (using

the Size/Position tab, which can be accessed by left-clicking on Leave Button).

5. Finally, drag the Hi-Score object onto the playfield, and place it above the Leave button. You can place it precisely using the coordinates 220, 115. An example of what it should look like is shown in Figure 12.8.

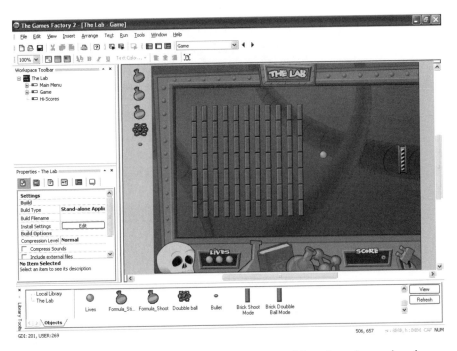

FIGURE 12.8   The look of frame once all the game objects have been placed.
©Jason Darby 2005. Reprinted with permission.

THE LAB—PROGRAMMING

All of the components are now in place, ready for you to program them into your game. We will start with the Main Menu, move on to the game, and finish with the final frame, the Hi-Scores frame. The first and third frames contain very little code and will be straightforward to code; the game frame involves much more complexity. If you have trouble with any of the programming parts, you can examine the full source code on the companion CD-ROM.

ON THE CD

The source code for the games in this book are stored in the folders Game1, Game2, and Game3, under a directory called "\fullsource." "The Lab" is stored in Game1.

Programming the Main Menu

As you may remember, the first frame (called the Main Menu) consists of three buttons, which when pressed should take the player to various areas of the game. The first frame is straightforward to program and involves similar code for all three buttons.

1. Make sure you are on the Main Menu frame and that it appears in the Frame Editor. If it currently is displaying a different frame or you are not sure, double-click on the words "Main Menu" in the Workspace toolbar. Click on the Event Editor toolbar button so you can begin to enter your code.

2. The first bit of code we need to generate is that if the player clicks the Start button, the program goes straight to the Game Frame (in this case, frame 2). Click on the text "New Condition" in the Event Editor. The New Condition dialog box will appear, as shown in Figure 12.9.

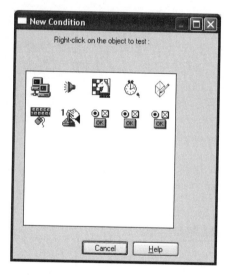

FIGURE 12.9 The New Condition dialog box.

3. Find the Button object; currently, there are three buttons listed (and icons for other objects). Hold the mouse over each Button object, and a tooltip (a yellow message) will appear stating the object name. Once you have found the one that says "Button—Start Game," either double left-click or single right-click on it to bring up the pop-up menu. Select the option Button Clicked. This can be shown in Figure 12.10.

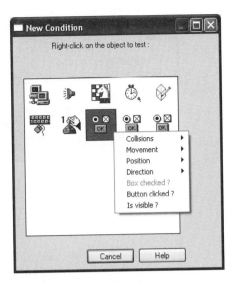

FIGURE 12.10   Left-click on the Button
Clicked option to add the condition.

4. There will now be one line of code that says "Button Clicked" as a condition. This means that TGF2 will try to do something (an action) when the button has been clicked. You haven't programmed the action, so when the button is clicked, nothing will happen. Going across from the Condition line, move your mouse until you are under the image of a Knight on a Chessboard icon. This is the Storyboard Controls option, and using this can control moving from a specific frame to closing the game window. Right mouse click and select Jump to Frame from the pop-up menu. A dialog box will appear allowing you to choose what frame to move to (see Figure 12.11). Click on the frame you want the game to move to when the player presses the Start Game button, which in this case is frame 2, and then click the OK button.

If you are unsure of any of the objects or icons in the Event Editor, you can hold your mouse over each and a little text icon will appear telling you what it is.

5. Click on the Run the Application button to start the program, and left mouse click on the Start Game button to make sure it goes to the frame where the game level is displayed.

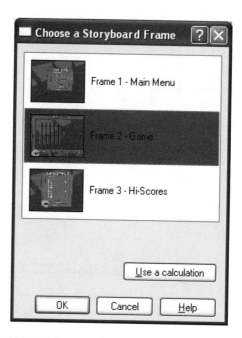

FIGURE 12.11   Choosing a frame to move to.

Remember, nothing else will happen in the game, as we have not programmed it yet. Quit the program by pressing the Exit Application button (the red X) in the top-right corner of the game window.

6. Now that the first frame jump is programmed, you now need to do the same for the High Score and Quit buttons. Add a new condition, double-click on the Button—Highscore object, and select Button Clicked from the pop-up menu. The condition line will be added. Now, move across to the Storyboard column, right-click, and select Jump to Frame. Select frame 3, which is the Hi-Scores frame, and click OK. This will mean that when the players press the Hi-Score button, it will take them to the last frame and show them the current high scores. Let's complete the final part of the programming for frame 1:

    when the player presses the Quit button, the game exits. Click on New Condition, select the Button Quit object, and select Button Clicked? from the pop-up menu. Move across to the right once more, and right-click under the Storyboard column. This time, rather than select Jumping to a Specific Frame, choose End the Application.

7. Run the entire game and try the Hi-Score and Quit buttons to see the result of your programming. If it doesn't work as expected, compare your

code to the completed source code for "The Lab" in the \fullsource\game1 folder on the companion CD-ROM.

Programming the Game

1. It is now time to complete the programming for the game section, and compared to frames 1 and 3, there is much more work involved, as this is where you will need to program all the movements, and what happens when the graphics hit each other. There are many more lines of code, but much of it is replicated and just points to a different object. Therefore, even though it looks like a lot of work, the speed of development is very quick.

2. Confirm you are on the correct frame by double-clicking on the text "Game" in the Workspace toolbar. The game frame should appear. Then, click on the Event Editor button on the Button toolbar to see all events currently assigned to this frame.

3. The first bit of code we need to do is to mix up all of the bricks. Currently, the bottom four from the first row are all the special bricks, and if the ball hits those, a bonus bottle will appear. This obviously is a little too predictable if they are always in the same place (it is also not much fun for the players if they know where they are). Create a new condition, select the Special icon (it looks like two computers connected together), and then choose Limit Conditions, Repeat. The Expression Calculator then appears; we want to mix up the bricks enough times so their positions are as random as possible, so type in the number "10" and then click on OK. The condition line will now read "Repeat 10 times." We need to have all the bricks (including the special ones) mixed up, so move to the right of the condition, and under the first brick column, right-click to bring up the actions. Select Position, and then select Swap Position with Another Object from the pop-up menu. You now have coded one type of brick to be swapped 10 times. We want the other bricks to be swapped as well, so create the same action on the same condition line, but under another Brick object (there is no need to create a separate condition when it is the same). You can either code this by using the right mouse button, or drag the newly created action (which is shown as a tick) onto another column. Once this is done, there will be five actions on the same line under each of the Brick objects. An example of how this will look can be seen in Figure 12.12.

All the events All the objects											
1	• Repeat 10 times	✓	✓	✓	✓	✓					
2	• New condition										

Swap position with another object

FIGURE 12.12   Set of five actions in the same action box.

4. Now that the bricks are all mixed up, we'll get the ball moving on the play area. Insert a comment line with the text "Start ball again on space." To insert a comment, right-click on the event line number, choose Insert | A Comment, enter the comment text in the dialog box, and then click on OK.

5. Insert a new event and condition of "Upon Pressing the Spacebar." To do this, click on the "New Condition" text, select the Mouse Pointer and Keyboard icon, then select Keyboard and then select "Upon pressing a key." TGF2 will now ask you to press a key; in this case, we want to program the Spacebar. Press the Spacebar for it to record it into the condition. This means that the program will do something when the Spacebar is pressed by the player. We are not finished with this event; we need to add some extra code into it by adding another condition in the same line of code (same event). Right-click on the "Upon Pressing the Spacebar" condition text to bring up a pop-up menu. Select Insert so a new condition can be added (the New Condition dialog box will appear). Select the Ball object, right-click, choose Movement, and then choose Is Ball Stopped. This will add an extra line into the event, but we still need to add one more. Create another condition on the same line (as detailed previously), but this time, select the Ball object, then Alterable Values, Flags, and then "Is a flag off" from the pop-up menu. The Expression Calculator will appear; click OK, as we will be using the default flag number of 0. Now create another event with the same conditions as the first, except that the internal flag is on. Your events and conditions should look similar to Figure 12.13.

You may find that the order of your conditions doesn't match that in Figure 12.13. If so, drag each item to the correct place. In TGF2, you must have them in the right order, or strange results may happen, or your code might fail to work.

6. The two events shown in Figure 12.13 take into account when the user presses the Spacebar and that the ball isn't moving. There are two reasons why the ball may not be moving: the player just lost a life and the ball has been placed in its start position, or the special bonus of the ball sticking to the bat has been activated. The internal flag is used to distinguish between these two states; "on" means that sticky mode is currently enabled. Now we

need to apply the actions for each of the events. The other main difference between the two actions is that when the game is about to start or the ball has been replaced due to a lost life, when the player presses the Spacebar the ball can go in a 45-degree angle to the left. If the ball is stuck to the bat and the player presses the Spacebar, it will only move left of its current position.

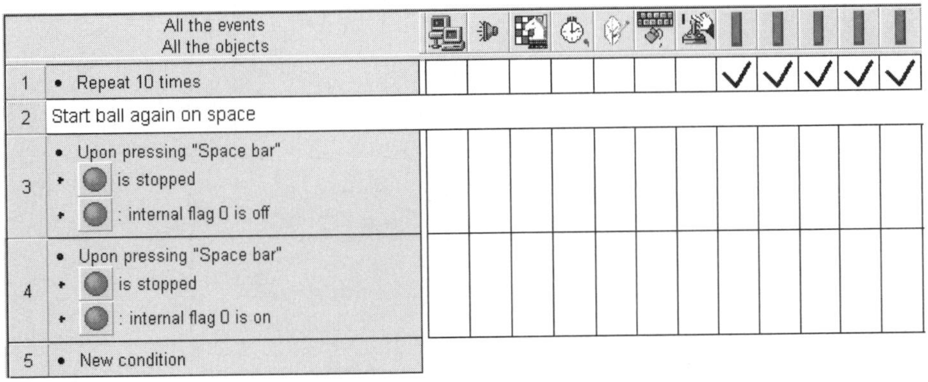

FIGURE 12.13 Current configuration of events.

7. Move to the right of the first "Upon pressing Spacebar" event until you are directly under the Ball object column. Right-click and select Direction, Select Direction from the pop-up menu. A Direction dialog box will appear that shows one current direction (the default) in which the object can move. By clicking on the boxes, you can switch the direction arrows on and off. Untick the arrow pointing to the right, and click on nine boxes on the left. All boxes are numbered (if you hold your mouse over a box, it will tell you the direction number). The boxes that need to be switched on are 12, 13, 14, 15, 16, 17, 18, 19, and 20. Your Directional dialog should now look like Figure 12.14. Click the OK button to go back to the Event Editor.

8. Right click on the Ball column where you now have a tick (this should be against the first "Upon pressing Spacebar" event), and then from the pop-up menu, choose Movement, Start.

9. You will now need to program the second "Upon pressing Spacebar" event. Move to the right, and make sure you are below the Ball object (this will be one row below the last actions you just entered, which will be shown as a tick). Right-click on the empty box and select Direction, Select Direction; the Direction dialog box will appear. Remove the right-pointing arrow by clicking on it once, create an arrow pointing left (clicking on box number 16), and then click OK to go back to the Event Editor. Create another ac-

tion in the same box by right-clicking, and then selecting Movement, Start. We need to create one more action for this event, so right-click again on the same box and select Flags, Set Off.

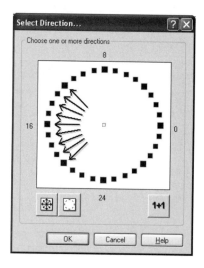

FIGURE 12.14 Selecting the right direction.

Bat and Ball Off Screen

If you run the game, you will notice that the ball goes off the screen, and the bat can be moved up and down (using the up and down arrow keys) out of the play area. The bat needs to stay within the playfield and not go any higher or lower than the game border. The ball should only be able to leave the playfield on the right side of the screen (at which point, the player would lose a life).

The bat, ball, and objects all have their movement predefined. This is because we programmed it into the Object library to lessen the work you need to do. To learn more about movement, refer to Chapter 10, "Movement."

1. Create a new comment line and type in the words "Bounce" (to create a comment, click on the number next to the words "New Condition," and then select Insert, A Comment). Below this comment, we will put all of the code to make the ball bounce back into the play area and the bat to stay on the screen.

2. Create a new event (by clicking on New Condition) and then selecting the Bat icon from the New Condition dialog box. Then, choose Collisions,

Backdrop from the pop-up menu. This event will do something when the bat hits the Backdrop object (which in this case is the border around the screen). Move across to the action column for the Bat on the same event line, right-click, and choose Movement, Stop. This will stop the bat from moving if it hits the border graphic. Run the frame and test to see if the Bat is stopped from moving outside the game area.

3. Create a new event, and select the Ball object in the New Condition dialog box. From the pop-up menu, select Collisions, Backdrop. Move across to the Action box, and under the ball this time we don't want the object to stop, we want it to bounce (which means it will stay inside the border area). To do this, right-click and select Movement, Bounce. Try running the frame again, and this time the ball will stay bouncing inside the playfield unless it goes behind the bat or through it (we haven't programmed it to bounce off the bat yet), at which time it will disappear.

4. So, let's now program the ball hitting the bat. Create a new event, select the Ball object from the Create New Condition dialog box, and then choose Collisions, Another Object from the pop-up menu. A dialog box will appear asking you to choose an object; double click on the Bat object. The event line will now read "Collision between Ball and Bat." This means that the program will do an action when the ball hits the bat. We are not quite finished with the conditions in this event, as we need to distinguish between the ball hitting the bat from a normal bounce, or if it was stuck to the bat because the Sticky Ball bonus has been activated. The reason for this is that at both times, the bat and ball will be touching, and if we didn't change this code, it would run every time either one was true. Right-click on the Collision between Ball and Bat condition and select Insert, at which point the New Condition dialog will appear. Select the Bat and then right-click to bring up the pop-up menu. From the pop-up menu, choose Alterable Values and then Is a Flag Off. When asked for the flag number, leave it at 0 and click OK. The flag being off means that the ball isn't stuck to the bat, so this condition will only happen when the ball is bouncing around the screen. To the right of this event under the Ball column, right click and choose Movement, Bounce from the pop-up menu. Run the frame and you will see that the ball bounces off the top, bottom, left, and the bat.

Remember that you may need to drag the conditions into the right order (as detailed in each part) for the game to work correctly.

Destruction of Bricks

1. Next, we need to destroy the bricks once the ball has hit them. Each brick will be hit twice before it is destroyed. When the brick is hit the first time, the color of the brick changes to show that it only needs one more hit to be destroyed.

2. Create two comment lines; the first should say "Brick Events," and the second comment line directly below it should say "Second Hit (destroys brick)." (Remember, you can create a comment line by right-clicking on the number for the New Condition line and then selecting Insert, A Comment).

3. Click on the "New Condition" text to create a new condition. You will need to create a condition of "Collision between ball and brick." Add a second condition in the same event to check if the brick is facing a specific direction. We use animation directions as indicators if they have been hit. To do this, click Insert, select Brick, and then from the pop-up menu, choose Direction, Compare Direction of Brick. A Direction dialog box will appear; change the arrow to pointing down. This will be at direction (24), and then click on OK.

4. Create a comment line under the event you just created and call it "First Hit." Create a new event under this that is the same as the condition above it, but change the condition "Brick is facing direction down" to "Brick is facing direction right." A shortcut when creating event lines that are similar is to copy an event and then paste it. Then, all you have to do is change the specific condition. The two events and comment lines will look like Figure 12.15.

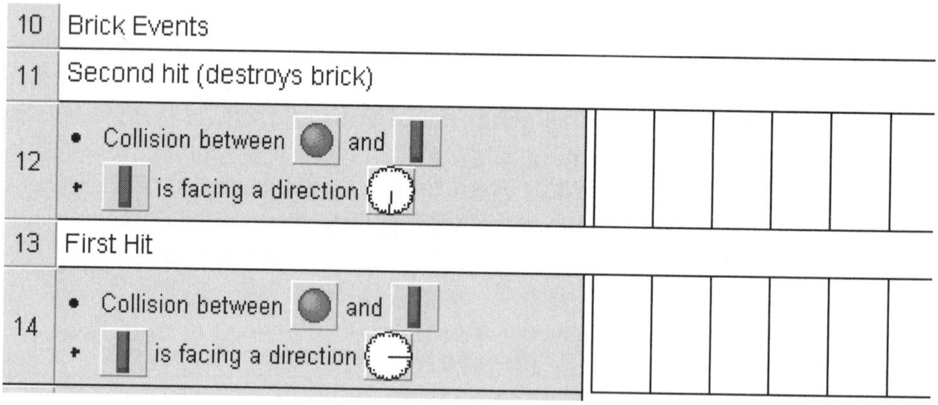

FIGURE 12.15 You can copy similar events and make changes to the conditions, saving time.

5. For the first of the two events, move to the right, and under the Player 1 column (which is a Joystick icon) right-click, select Score, Add to Score, and then in the Expression Calculator, type "100." This will add 100 to the player's score every time a brick is destroyed. Drag the Tick from this box to the event directly below it, as you want to add 100 to the score when the ball makes contact with a brick. On the first Event, move to the column Brick, right-click and select Destroy. Move across to the Ball column, right-click, and choose Movement, Bounce. Drag the Bounce action directly below the second of the two events.

6. For the second event, under the Brick column, set the direction to down (24). You can do this by right-clicking on the box and choosing Direction, Select Direction from the pop-up menu. In the Direction dialog box, make sure the arrow is pointing right. Test the game by clicking on Run Frame; you should now have bricks being destroyed.

7. A game without sound is very much like watching TV with the mute button on. Having sound can make all the difference in the quality of a game, and players will find it much more interesting if they can hear things happening. For the last two events we created, we are going to add a sound for every time the ball hits a brick.

8. On the first event (the one directly under the comment "Second hit (destroys brick)," move along the columns until you find an icon that looks like a speaker; this is the Sound icon. Right-click and select Samples, Play Sample, and a Play Sample dialog box will appear (as shown in Figure 12.16).

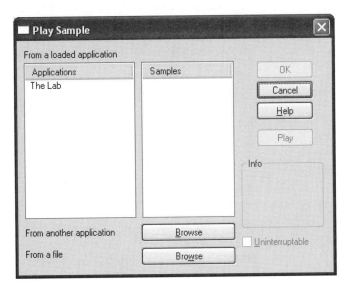

FIGURE 12.16 Adding sounds to your game.

9. Click on the Browse button (From a File) and navigate to the folder \Game1\Sounds\ directory on the CD-ROM that comes with this book. Double-click on the sample "Bounce Hi" to add the action to the event. We are going to use the same sound for the second event we created, so drag it down to the event that is below the comment text "First Hit." Run the game again to hear the sounds play when the ball hits the bricks.

Destruction of Special Bricks

1. If you run the game, you will notice that the majority of the bricks on the playfield will be destroyed, but four of them will not be. These four bricks are the special bricks that are used to spawn the bonus items for the player to take advantage of. Now we need to code the destruction of the four bricks when they are hit once by the ball.

2. Create one comment line called "Special Brick Events," and then create four more comment lines called "Shoot Mode—Brick," "Sticky Mode—Brick," "Large Mode—Brick," and "Double Ball Mode—Brick." Then, under each of the four comments, create an event (four in total) with the condition "Collision between Ball and **Special** brick." Replace the **Special** brick part with the type of brick mentioned above the event in the comment. For example, under the comment "Shoot Mode—Brick," create an event under it that says, "Collision between ball and 'Brick Shoot Mode.'" An example of what this will look like appears in Figure 12.17.

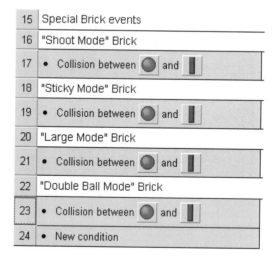

FIGURE 12.17   Setting up collision between the special bricks and the ball.

3. Once you have done this for all four comment lines, create an action that plays the sound "Bounce Hi" (this will be under the Speaker icon). This will be the same for all four event lines, so drag it to all of the others in the same column. You could also drag it from an earlier event where it plays the same sound.

4. When each brick is hit, we want to add to the score, so under the Player 1 column (the icon looks like a joystick), create an action to "Add 100 to score." Again, drag and drop this so all four conditions contain the same action.

5. Under the Ball column for each event, create an action so the Ball bounces back (use the Movement, Bounce option). Drag this so all four conditions have the same action.

6. Across from each of the four events under the corresponding brick columns, create a Destroy action. For example, across from the "Shoot Mode—Brick" under the Brick Shoot Mode column, right-click on the Action box and select Destroy. This means that when the ball hits the brick, the brick will be destroyed. Do the same for the other three events. Drag the Destroy action to under each of the other brick columns (which corresponds to the correct event).

7. Next, we have to program that when the ball hits a special brick, a bonus will appear from it. On the first condition in this group (Shoot Mode Brick), move across until you are under the Create New Objects column (the icon looks like a box with a pen). Right mouse click and select Create Object from the pop-up menu. A Create Object dialog box will appear; find the Bonus object (this will be a bottle or a red star-shaped object) that relates to the event line you are coding. In the first example, it will be the object that relates to Collision between Ball and Brick Shoot Mode. The object you need to find is the Formula_Shoot bottle; select it and then click on OK. The Create Object dialog box will then appear. There are two ways to place a newly created object (which is based on a current object): use "At actual X, Y coordinates," or "Relative to." With "At actual," you will see a box with a crosshair in it; drag it around the field to a place where you would like the new object to appear. With "Relative to," you can choose an object on the playfield that will act as an anchor for the object to appear from. We want our Bonus objects to appear from each of the special bricks so choose "Relative to." A Choose an Object box will appear, and you will now need to pick the object that the new object will appear closest to. Find the correct brick (in this case, it's Brick Shoot Mode) and then click on OK. Once you have clicked on OK, you will see a flashing box around the object, a line, and a box with a crosshair in it. The crosshair shows the position where the Bonus object will appear; drag this box until it is in the

center of the flashing box, and then click on OK. Do the same for the other three events, and then run the game to see the results. When the special bricks have been destroyed, the relevant Bonus icon should appear in its place.

8. The last thing you need to program for this group of events is that once the ball has destroyed the special brick and the bonus has appeared on-screen, it should scroll to the right so the player can try to catch it to earn the special abilities. To do this, move across to the right of each event and find the relevant Bonus Object column that relates to the right events. Right-click, and select Movement, Start. For example, find the event Collision between Ball and Brick Shoot Mode, move to the right until you are directly under the Formula_Shoot column, and then apply the action using the right mouse button. Complete this for the other three events, and then run the game to see the bonus items appear and then scroll off to the right.

Automatically, the bonus items move to the right, because they have had their object properties predefined, so when you drop them on the playfield, they have a left-to-right movement ready to be used (which just needed enabling). Chapter 10 has details on how to apply movement to objects.

Destroy Bonus Items If Missed

When you hit a bonus brick and the special item flies out of it, two possible things could happen. You could catch the item with the bat, which means you get a bonus, or you miss the item and it disappears from the play area.

1. Create a comment event line that says, "Destroy collectables if not caught."
2. For each of the Bonus objects, create an event that says "Object_Name Leaves the play area on the right." To do this, create a new condition, select the first special object (in this example, it's the Formula_Large object), and then choose Position, Test Position of Formula_Large from the pop-up menu. A Test Position dialog box will appear. Click on the arrow pointing to the right-hand side pointing outward, and then click on OK. An example of the Test Position dialog box is shown in Figure 12.18.

The Test Position dialog allows you to check where on the play area an object is currently positioned. It is great for quick testing of an object if it has just left the screen, just appeared, is on the outside of the playfield area, or on the playfield. In "The Lab," it is used to see if an object has gone off the playfield, as at this point it is no longer needed in the game.

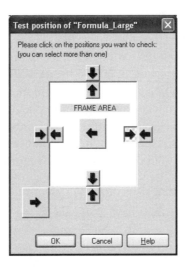

FIGURE 12.18   Testing the position of an object.

3. Create three more events that follow the same convention but with a different starting object. You should now have four events that look like Figure 12.19.

Destroy collectables if not caught

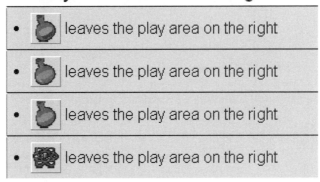

FIGURE 12.19   The code should match what is shown here.

4. When three of the items are not caught by the bat and leave the playfield, we want it to play a glass-breaking sound. Move to the right for each of the three Bottle objects, and when you reach the Sound column, right-click and select Sample, Play Sample from the pop-up menu. In the Browse

ON THE CD

Sample dialog box, click on the button that allows you to browse for a file, and locate the sample called GLASS05, which is contained in the \Game1\Sounds\ folder on the companion CD-ROM. Once you have done this for one event, drag it to the other two events to save time.

5. When an object leaves the playfield, it isn't destroyed automatically. Having many objects running in the playfield will use more memory, so it is sensible to destroy them if they are not needed for a period of time. Destroying an object doesn't mean that you cannot recall the object at a later stage, so don't be concerned about removing them from the play area.

6. For each of the four events, move to the right until you are directly under the corresponding object column. For example, of the first of the four events, you may have Formula_Large Leaves the Play area on the right. When you are under the Formula_Large column, right-click and then select Destroy. Do the same for the other three events.

NOTE

Run the Game frame and destroy a few bricks, and watch the bonus items disappear off the play area. Notice that the number of objects will begin to reduce.

Collecting Bonus Items

When the bat does hit a flying bonus item, a special event will happen. This does require a little more code than the events we discussed previously, and as it is more complex, we will describe each event separately in more detail.

1. The first thing you need to do is create two coding groups. You won't need to code the events inside these two groups just yet, only create the groups so you can reference them.

NOTE

Coding groups were discussed in detail in Chapter 8, "TGF Coding Basics."

2. Create a comment line called "Group events for special conditions," and then create the two groups called "Mode Shoot" and "Mode Sticky" below this. You can create the groups by right-clicking on the last number in the Event Editor (the line that says "New Condition"), and then selecting Insert, Group of Events. Make sure both groups are not "Active When Frame Starts," as we only want the groups to run code when a specific event has happened (which will be when the Sticky or Shoot bonus object hits the bat). We will come back to these groups shortly, but for now, we need to create a set of standard events.

3. Create a comment line called "Collecting." Then, create four comment lines below it called "Shoot Mode formula," "Sticky Mode formula,"

"Large Mode formula," and "Double Ball clone." In between the four comment lines, create four events (one for each comment), which take the form of "Collision between 'Object' and bat." To do this, click twice on the comment line "Shoot Mode formula" so the line number has a flashing box around it (so it does not have a black background). Right-click and select Insert, A New Event. From the New Condition dialog box, choose the Formula_Shoot bottle and right-click to bring up the pop-up menu. Select Collision and then Another Object from the dialog box, select the Bat object, and click on OK. Do the same for the other three events (but replace the Bonus object with the other bonus items); and you should now have something similar to Figure 12.20. The code is saying that "when a bottle or the red round-shaped object hits the Bat, then do an action." We have not coded the action yet, so if you were to run the program, nothing will happen.

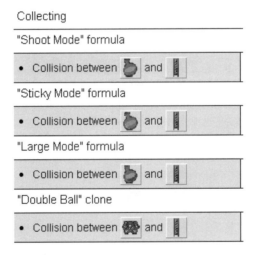

FIGURE 12.20   What to do if the Bonus objects hit the bat.

4. Two common actions are the same for all four events, so it is easier to create those first. On the first of the four event lines (Collision between Formula_Shoot and Bat), move to the right until you are under the Sound column. Right-click and select Samples, Play Sample to bring up the Play Sample dialog box. Click on the Browse button, which corresponds to From a File. Find the Sounds directory (which is located on the companion CD-ROM in the folder \Game\|sounds, and select the sound file called "Pop Bubble." Drag this action to the other three event lines.

ON THE CD

5. The events we created take into consideration that when the Bonus objects hit the bat, we need them to disappear off the play area. If we don't remove them, they will continue to move to the right, which is not correct. Move to the right of the first event, stop when you are under the Bonus object in the column (e.g., for the first event, it would be the Formula_Shoot column), and right-click and select Destroy. You will then need to drag the Destroy action to the other events under their corresponding columns (remember when the Bonus object hits the bat, the Bat object will need to be destroyed).

6. Move to the right of the Collision between Formula_Shoot and Bat until you are below the Special Conditions column. Right-click and select Group of Events, Activate. An Activate dialog box will appear as shown in Figure 12.21. Make sure that (1) – Mode Shoot is highlighted, and then select OK.

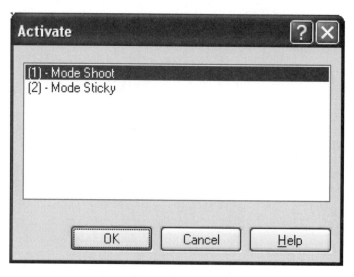

FIGURE 12.21 Activating groups.

Groups were discussed in Chapter 8. The two groups used in this game are to separate the code for the two Bonus objects, sticky and shoot items. The code in these two groups will only be executed when the Bonus objects hit the bat.

7. You will need to follow a similar procedure for the event Collision between Formula_Sticky and Bat. However, this time, activate the (2) – Mode Sticky group.

8. Move to the right of the Collision between Formula_Shoot and Bat event and find the Bat column. Right-click and select Animation, Change, Animation from the pop-up menu. An Animation dialog box will appear (as shown in Figure 12.22); select the Shoot text, and click on OK. This means that when the "Shoot" formula bottle hits the bat, the bat will change its appearance and will then have a gun attached to it. One last action we have to make to the same column is to right-click again, choose Flags, Set Off, and click OK at the Expression Calculator.

The Set Off flag has to be set because if the bat were currently in Sticky mode, it would continue to shoot and stick at the same time, which isn't how the game works.

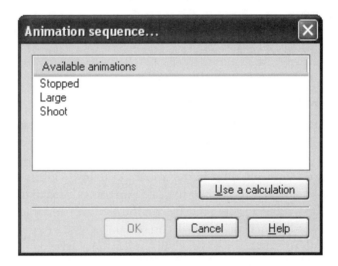

FIGURE 12.22   Selecting the animation to play.

9. Moving on to the Collision between Formula_Sticky and Bat event, and move to the right until you are directly under the Bat column. Create two actions; the first being Set Internal Flag 0 to On, and the second Change Animation sequence to Stopped. If you are unsure how to do this, look at the previous event instructions.
10. The next event to add some additional actions to is "Collision between Formula_Large and Bat." Again, move to the right until you reach the Bat column; create an action "Change animation sequence to large," and an action "Set Internal flag 0 to off."

11. The final event in this section should be "Collision between Double ball and Bat." Move across until you reach the Create New Objects column, and right-click and choose Create Object. From the dialog box, select the Ball object. Then, you will be asked where will the new ball be placed; in the X and Y boxes, type 382 and 228 (then click on OK). Move across to the Bat column and add an action that equals "Set Internal Flag 0 to off." Create another action under the Ball column that sets the direction of the Ball to 13, 14, 18, and 19 (you can do this by selecting Direction, Select Direction from the pop-up menu). Create another action under the Ball column that starts the ball movement (right-click and then select Movement, Start).

NOTE

The Internal flag is to distinguish when the Bat is in sticky mode. The only issue with that at this point is that if you run the game and the bat catches the Bonus object that can make it sticky, the ball will go straight through the bat. Currently, there is a slight conflict in the programming, and until we program the two special groups, it will not do what we intended.

Ball Leaves Play Area

The game is now starting to come together nicely, but when the ball leaves the screen, nothing else happens and the game cannot continue. As you can imagine, it is very important to put the ball back on the screen so the play can continue; a knock-on effect is that the player also needs to lose a life as a negative consequence of allowing the ball to get past the bat. Two things need to be programmed into the game: first, if there is only one ball on the play area and it leaves the screen, a life is lost. Second, if there are two balls on screen because a bonus modifier is in effect, a life is only lost once the second ball has left the playfield.

1. Create three comment lines called "Ball Leaves Play Area," "If Player loses ball and only has one = Lose Life," and "If Player loses ball and has double ball = destroy the extra ball."

2. Under the second comment line, create an event with the following conditions. Number of Balls = 1 + Ball leaves the play area on the right. This will allow the program to know when there is only ball in play, and that the player has just missed hitting it with the bat. To create this condition, click on the New Condition box, select the Ball object, then from the pop-up menu, select Pick or Count, and then Compare to the number of Ball Objects. A Compare calculation box will appear; ensure that the box says "equal to 1." An example of this box is shown in Figure 12.23.

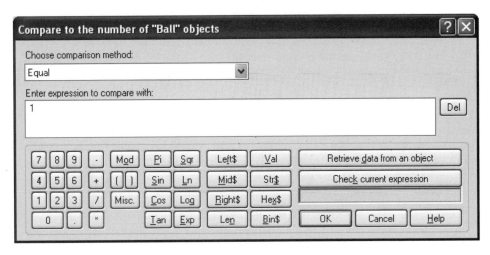

FIGURE 12.23 Comparing the number of balls in the game.

3. Right-click on the condition that you just created and select Insert. Then, click on the Ball object and select Position, Test Position of Ball from the pop-up dialog. A dialog box will appear asking you where it should test; click on the arrow pointing outward to the right (leaves in the right).

4. Under the third comment, create the condition "Number of Balls = 2 + Ball leaves the play area on the right." This is the same as the previous event except that the number of balls should equal two rather than one. This is for when the Bonus object has been enabled.

5. Both events have some actions that are the same, so the action for one event can be dragged to the other to save programming time. The first action to create is under the Special Conditions column. Right-click on this column for the first event, select Group of Events, Deactivate, and then select Mode Shoot from the dialog box. Create another action in the same column (Special Conditions) in the same event, but choose Mode Sticky. You should now have two actions assigned to the first event in the Specials column. To save programming time, drag this into the same column into the second event. Once the ball has left the play area, you do not want the bonus code to still be working, so this disables it.

6. On the first event, move across to the Sound column, and add a new sample (if you have forgotten how to do this, check earlier in this chapter on how to do it). The sample you need is Slide Down; after you apply it, drag it to the second event.

7. On the first of the two events, move to the right until you are directly under the Player One column (the one that looks like a joystick). Right-click and choose Number of Lives, Subtract from Number of Lives, and on the

Expression Calculator, type in the number "1." Every time the ball leaves the playfield, the game will minus 1 from the lives. We do not need to set this into the second event, as when there are two balls on the screen and one leaves, we do not want to reduce the number of lives.

8. Again, on the first event, go along the columns until you are directly under the Bat. You will need to apply the following actions: Set Internal Flag 0 to Off, and Change Animation Sequence to Stopped.

9. Under the Ball column for the first event, create two actions: Set Position at (382, 228), and Stop. The first action can be created by selecting Position, Select Position (and then enter 382 and 228); the second by selecting Movement, Stop.

10. The code for the second event is required to destroy the second ball, so move across to the ball column and then select Destroy. Once the ball has disappeared off the play area, it will remove it from the game. We also need to set the Internal flag to Off.

Player Dies

If you now run the game, nearly everything is working correctly. One area of the functionality of the game that current isn't working is that when the ball has gotten past the bat and the lives are down to zero, the game continues. This is not correct, as we want the game to end once the player runs out of lives. This part of the code is very quick to do, and the outcome is that once all lives are gone, the game goes to frame 3 so the player can enter a high score (if appropriate).

1. Create a comment line called "Player Dies." Then, add a new event, and in the New Condition dialog box, double-click on the Player 1 object to bring up the pop-up menu. From there, select the When Number of Lives Reaches 0 option. Move to the right until you reach the Storyboard Controls column, and then create an action to jump to frame 3. To do this, right-click, select Jump to Frame, and then select frame 3 from the dialog box.

All Bricks Destroyed

What do we want to happen in the game when all the bricks have been destroyed? In this game, once they have been removed from the play area, the game will then move to frame 3 so the player can enter his or her name for recording into the high-score table.

1. Create a comment line called "All Bricks Destroyed."

2. Create an event that will contain five conditions. When the New Condition dialog box appears, pick the first Brick in the window, then select Pick or Count, and then select Have All 'Brick' Been Destroyed. This will create the first condition, but we need four more to represent the other bricks (each of the bonus bricks). So, continue to add further conditions until you have something that resembles Figure 12.24, each time selecting a different brick type from the New Condition dialog box.

FIGURE 12.24   Code to create actions when all bricks have been destroyed.

3. You will only need to create one action for this event, so move across to the Storyboard Controls column, right-click, and select Restart the Current Frame.

Sticky and Shoot Mode

If you play the game, you may notice that two things are not currently functioning, and in fact are the only two things left to do on the Game frame. We need to introduce the bonus functionality of the ball sticking to the bat, and the bat having the capability to fire bullets (which is great fun for the player). The first thing you need to do is create some events that take into consideration what to do with the bullets once they have been fired. At the moment, the Bonus object that gives you the gun cannot fire anything, and that will have to be programmed. When programming, you need to think about what events you need. For example, what type of events would you need when you can fire the bullets? The bullets will destroy things in their path, so you will need to program the collision between a bullet and a brick, also hitting the bonus bricks, and finally, what happens if it doesn't hit any bricks and hits the back of the play area (on the left-hand side).

1. Create a comment line called "Bullet Events."
2. The first event you need to make is Bullet Is Overlapping Brick. To create this condition, click on New Condition (or use the right mouse button and click on Insert, New Event). Select the Bullet object and then choose Collisions, Overlapping Another Object from the pop-up menu. From the dialog box, select the Brick object. This event works if the bullet hits any of the standard bricks (it doesn't work for the bonus bricks; they needed to be coded separately).
3. Create a comment line under the event just created and call it "Collision with Special Bricks."
4. Now, create four events the same as the first event, choosing a different Brick object for each event. For the first of the four new events, select the Bullet object and then choose Collisions, Overlapping Another Object from the pop-up menu. From the dialog box, select a Bonus Brick object. This will take into account whenever the bullet hits one of the bonus bricks.
5. Create an event that sees when the bullet hits the background (so there are no bricks in its way and it goes all the way to the left side of the screen). To do this, create an event and select the Bullet object.
6. Create one more event, selecting the Bullet object, but this time, choose Collisions, Backdrop from the pop-up menu. This will force an action when the bullet hits the background. Your events should now look like Figure 12.25.

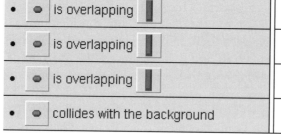

FIGURE 12.25 Creating a group of conditions to test for bullet collisions.

7. The actions for these events are straightforward. For the first event, move to the right until you are under the Brick object. Right-click and select Destroy. When the bullet hits the brick, you want it removed from the play area. Next, drag this event (or program it in) for the next four overlapping events, but under their own brick column. For example, for the event Bullet Is Overlapping Brick Shoot Mode, the action Destroy will need to be placed under the Brick Shoot Mode column.

8. For all of the events made in this section, move to the Bullet column, right-click, and apply the Destroy action. The bullet needs to be destroyed if it hits anything (otherwise, it would keep moving).

Special Code

1. The game screen is now nearly complete; there is only one section of code left to make it work correctly. If you play the game, you will notice you still cannot fire the gun, and the ball does not stick onto the bat. Therefore, the following example shows you how to switch on the code to make them work. For the Shoot bonus, we will set a number of bullets that can be fired (this number could be changed to make the bonus better or worse), and then set the appearance and direction of the bullets. For the Sticky bonus, the code is a little more complex, as we need to position the ball onto the bat and leave it there until the player presses the Spacebar to fire it back into the game.

Mode Shoot

1. Find the Mode Shoot group you created earlier. You may need to double-click on it to expand it. By expanding it, you will see New Condition below it. Create two comment lines in the group, the first called "Shoot Mode Events," and then second "Setting number of shots."

2. Create an event "Only one action when event loops." To do this, click on New Condition, select the Special object (which looks like two computers), and choose Limit Conditions, "Only one action when event loops" from the pop-up menu.

3. Move to the Bat column, right-click, and then select Alterable Values, Set. The Expression Calculator dialog appears; enter the number "15" in the expression box, and then click on OK. The action should read "Set Alterable Value A to 15."

4. Create a new comment line called "Actually Shooting."

5. Now create a new event with three conditions: Upon Pressing Space Bar + Bat Animation Shoot Is Playing + Alterable Value of A of Bat > 0. It may seem a little confusing, but it is straightforward. Shooting is created by

pressing the Spacebar, but you only want it to work if the Bat has the shooting animation showing (the animation that looks like a gun) and there are more than zero bullets left. To create the first of the three conditions, you will need to use The Mouse pointer and Keyboard object, then The Keyboard, Upon Pressing a Key"; when the dialog appears asking you to press a key, press the Spacebar. The second condition can be made by selecting the Bat object and then Animation, Which Animation of Bat Is Playing," and then choosing Shoot from the dialog box. For the final condition for this event, pick the Bat object and then the Alterable Values, Compare to One of the Alterable Values; this will bring up the Expression Calculator. In the Choose a Comparison Method drop-down box, select Greater and then click OK. Now you will need to create the action that fires a bullet toward the bricks (going from right to left). Move across until you are under the Bat column, right-click, and then select Shoot an Object. A Shoot Object Dialog box will appear; scroll down until you find the bullet, select it, and click on OK. Another Shoot an Object dialog box appears (as shown in Figure 12.26). Set the speed of the object to 60 and then choose the radio button Shoot in Selected Directions. A Movement dialog will appear; untick the arrow pointing upward, and tick one going to the left (the direction number 16). Click on OK, and then on OK again to return to the Event Editor. Create one more action in the same column by selecting Alterable Values, Subtract From, and entering the number "1" into the Enter Expression box. Click on OK.

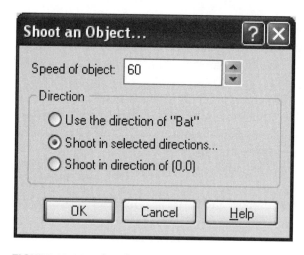

FIGURE 12.26   The Shoot Object dialog screen.

6. Create a comment line and call it "Ending Shoot Mode if you run out of bullets."

7. Create a condition under this comment to say "Alterable Value A of Bat = 0." To do this, select the Bat from the New Condition dialog box, then from the pop-up, select Alterable Values, Compare to One of the Alterable Values. When the Expression Calculator dialog appears, click on OK, as it is correct. Move to the right of the condition until you are under the Bat column, then right-click and choose Animation, Change, Animation Sequence. When the dialog box appears, select Stopped and then click on OK. If you now run the game, you will see that the gun can now be enabled and shot 15 times.

Mode Sticky

1. Under the Mode Sticky group, create a new comment that says, "Sticky mode is on."

2. Create a condition Bat Internal Flag 0 Is On + Collision between Bat and Ball. To do this, add a condition, select the Bat object, and then from the pop-up menu, select Alterable Values, Flags, Is a Flag On. Leave the number at 0 (as this is our flag number), and click on OK. For the second condition in the same event, click on the Ball object, then Collisions, With Another Object, and choose the Bat.

3. There are five actions for this event, shown in Figure 12.27.

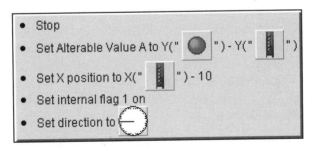

FIGURE 12.27 The five actions in the first event in the Mode Sticky group.

4. For the first action, right-click under the Ball column, and then select Movement, Stop. All of the other actions are also under the Ball column.

5. Add the second action, and select Alterable Values, Set. The Expression Calculator dialog box will appear. In the Enter Expression box, delete the current value of 0. There are two ways to enter the data: manually, or by clicking on Retrieve Data from an Object. For speed purposes, we are going

to enter it manually, so type in the expression box – Y(Ball) – Y(Bat), and then click on Check Current Expression to see if you have typed it in correctly. If you have, it will say "Valid Expression."

6. For the third action, select the Position, Set X Coordinate option from the pop-up menu, and at the Expression Calculator type in X(Bat) – 10. Then, click on the Check Current Expression to make sure you have done it correctly.

7. For the fourth action, select Flags, Set On, leave the number as 0, and click on the OK box in the Expression Calculator.

8. For the fifth action, select Direction, Select Direction, and then from the Direction dialog, click off the right pointing arrow, and click on the left direction to make the pointer appear (this will be direction number 16).

9. The code is now in place, but we have to activate the stickiness of the ball to the bat. To do this, create another event, and put in the condition Ball Internal Flag 0 is On. To do so, right-click on New Condition, select the Ball object, and in the pop-up menu choose Alterable Values, Flags, Is a Flag On? When the Expression Calculator appears, leave the expression number at 0 and click OK.

10. Move to the right until you are under the Ball column, right-click, and select Position, Set Y Coordinate. The Expression Calculator will appear; this time, click on Retrieve Data from an Object button to show a list of objects. Right-click on the Bat object, and select Position, Y Coordinate from the pop-up menu. It should now read "Y (Bat)" in the Expression Calculator, but we are not finished yet; after the expression, type "a +" and then click on the Retrieve button. Right-click on the Ball object, and select Values, Values A to M, Retrieve Alterable Value A. The text in the Expression Calculator should now read "Y (Bat) + Alterable Value A(Ball)."

11. Click on the OK button.

Programming the Hi-Scores

There is only one bit of programming that we have to do for the Hi-Scores frame, and that is to go back to the main menu when the player clicks on the Quit button.

1. Make sure you are on the right frame by double-clicking on the word "Hi-Scores" in the Workspace toolbar. The Hi-Score frame will then appear. Click on the Event Editor button on the toolbar to bring up the list of events that are currently programmed into the frame (currently none).

2. Click on New Condition, right-click on Button—Leave Object, and select Button Clicked on the pop-up menu. Move across to the right until you are directly under the Storyboard Controls column (it looks like a chessboard

and knight piece). Right-click and select Restart the Application. The game is now complete; congratulations, you have finished writing your first game.

BAT-AND-BALL RETRO

The Bat-and-Ball game has been around for over 20 years and was one of the first to be released. It was slightly different then, and consisted of two bats (one for each player) and a ball. It was more like a game of tennis, where the player had to send the ball back and would lose a point if he or she missed it. As computers became more advanced and had more memory available, the traditional idea of bat and ball arrived on the scene. This consisted of one bat and a number of bricks to be destroyed. There have been many variations on this theme, from the bat being at the bottom of the screen and the bricks being above it, swapping left and right, and even 3D versions. There are many games to choose from that you could make with regard to retro-based games. Do a search for "bat and ball" on the retro Web sites to see the games that have been made on this theme. Some of the most popular bat and ball games were converted to the home computer format after appearing on arcade machines. An example of one game that took the leap from arcade to home computer is *Arkanoid®*. If you do a search for this on the Internet, you will find a lot of information on how it was designed, and what extra options you can build into your bat-and-ball games.

SUMMARY

In this chapter, we went through the process of creating our first in-depth game, and although there was a lot of code, hopefully it wasn't too difficult to understand. The important thing to remember when making games is that you can take what you have learned and apply it to other games you are making. Making games is a learning experience, and the more things you try, the better, so your next game will be much more interesting. Always try to retain old games so you can go back and look at the code, as you may find that you have useful information in them that you can swap over to the latest program. The first real game we made may seem quite large, but it was only about 50 lines of code. As you make more games, you will get very much quicker at it and will need less instruction on how to put the events together. This game introduced the concepts of movement, destroying objects, alterable values, and animation. In the next few chapters, we look at the exciting concepts involved in side-scrolling shoot-'em-ups.

13 Scrolling Game Concepts

In This Chapter

■ Scrolling Techniques

B efore we begin our second game, "Amazing Fighter Pilot," we will look at scrolling. Scrolling the screen is a common technique used to create platform or side-scrolling shoot-'em-up games (not exclusively, but these are two areas that it is commonly used for), and may be something you will use in your future games. In this chapter, we introduce you to two different scrolling techniques: the standard scrolling you can implement within TGF2, and "fake" scrolling, whereby the illusion of scrolling is created to make the player believe the plane is moving along the scenery.

SCROLLING TECHNIQUES

For the game "Amazing Fighter Pilot" in Chapter 14, "Creating a Side-scrolling Shoot-'em-up Game," we use the "fake" scrolling technique. This type of scrolling works well for Amazing Fighter Pilot", but is not necessarily the main type of scrolling you will come across when making your own games. You might consider using the scrolling used in "Amazing Fighter Pilot" in other scrolling shoot-'em-ups that move from left to right or right to left, but you couldn't use it in games that scroll in multiple directions following the main character.

Standard Scrolling

This is the typical type of scrolling found in games made with TGF2, whereby the player can move in multiple directions and the screen follows. Although we used the "fake" scrolling for the plane game in the next chapter, we could have used standard scrolling for it. The way scrolling works is that you have a window size, which is the size of the window the users can see on their computer monitor. An example of this would be 640x480, but within TGF2, you can also create a frame size, and to start creating a scrolling game, you need to make the frame bigger than the application size. Once this is done, a bit of coding is required to ensure the player is always at the center of the screen, and the frame scrolls in the direction of the player's movement. In the following example, we are going to make a simple scrolling game using a racing car.

ON THE CD

To follow the next example, you will need to load a starting file. This file loads a basic 640x480 screen with a yellow racing car on the frame, which has racing car movement already applied to it. If you run it, you will be able to drive the racing car around the screen, but it will move out of view when it reaches the edge of the window. The file, called "racing car," can be found on the companion CD-ROM in the Scrolling folder.

Setting up the Screen

First, we need to load the basic file and then configure the Frame window to be bigger than the Application window. This then allows us to program in the scrolling aspect, which will move around this unseen area. After completing this task, run the file. Notice that the program will not react any differently, as we're simply preparing the area for it to be able to scroll.

1. Start TGF2, and then click on the File | Open option from the menu. When the Open dialog box appears, browse for your CD-ROM drive and locate the file "racing car" in the Scrolling folder. Select this file, and then click on OK to open the file.

2. Double-click on the text "Frame 1" in the Workspace toolbar to open the Frame Editor. You will now see a screen with a yellow racing car placed on the frame.

3. In the Properties toolbar, you will now see the frame settings, which will already be on the Settings tab. Click on the "640x480" text in the Size Properties item. You will now be able to specify the frame size, or you can click on the right-pointing arrow and select one from the drop-down box. Type or select "1600x1200." This will now increase the size of the frame to 1600x1200, while keeping the Application window size to 640x480.

Now that the screen has been configured to have a scroll area larger than the frame size, it's time for us to create the scrolling events.

Programming the Scrolling

The last bit of work required to implement the scrolling on the screen is to tell the frame to follow the yellow race car.

1. Click on the Event Editor button on the Button toolbar.

2. You will now be in the Event Editor where there are currently no events; there will be one line that says "New Condition." Click on this text to create a new event; when the dialog box appears, right-click on the Special object (which looks like two computers networked together). From the pop-up menu, choose Always/Never and then Always. This will create an event that is always read by TGF2, and so is continuously running.

3. Move to the right of this event until you are directly under the Storyboard Controls object (this looks like a knight with a chessboard behind it). Right-click on the empty square to add an action; when the pop-up menu appears, choose Scrollings, Center Window Position in Frame. A Center Window Position... dialog box appears, which allows you to position items either at an actual coordinate or relative to another object's position. In this case, we want the window's position to be relative to the car, so click on the Relative To radio button. A Choose an Object dialog box appears; click on the yellow car object called "Top_Four" and then click on the OK button.

4. The Center Window Position In... dialog box will reappear; type "0,0" in the X and Y coordinate boxes. This tells TGF2 how far away from the object the position should be; 0,0 means the object is the focal point. Click on the OK button to save the information to the action.

5. Click on New Condition to create the final event. In the dialog box, right-click on the yellow car object Top_Four, and from the pop-up menu, choose Position, Test Position of 'Top_Four.' A Test Position Of.. dialog box will appear. Click on the four pointing-out arrows called "Leaves in the

top?," "Leaves in the right?," "Leaves in the left?," and "Leaves in the bottom?" and then click on the OK button.

6. Move to the right of this new condition until you are directly under the yellow car Top_Four, right-click, and select Movement, Stop.

As you can see, there isn't much work required to get a basic scrolling example working; add a few graphics, and within a very short period of time, you have your very own scrolling game. A version of the scrolling example (including additional graphics) can be found on the companion CD-ROM, located in the Scrolling folder and called Stnd Scrolling1.

ON THE CD

Fake Scrolling

There are a number of ways to implement some of the features of TGF2, and scrolling is no different. The solution just discussed is the standard way to implement scrolling within your games. However, if you want to have the same background repeated multiple times, thereby allowing your level to take some time to finish, this type of scrolling is a very memory efficient and easy way to do so (because you do not need to create a very large frame size to accommodate the scrolling area, you use less memory in TGF2). With standard scrolling, the window area moves with the Player object around the frame, and the Background objects are statically placed around the play area. With fake scrolling, the frame does not move; the player object only moves in the window area, and the background moves from right to left to simulate a scrolling screen. The two examples of the scrolling mentioned in this book are shown in Figures 13.1 and 13.2.

FIGURE 13.1 Standard scrolling where the window moves around the frame area.

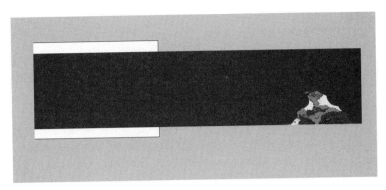

FIGURE 13.2   Fake scrolling example, where the background moves, and the window is static.

Fake scrolling works by having a number of large graphic tiles that have path movement applied to each, so when the game starts, they move in a right-to-left direction. When they get to a specific point on the screen (the end of the path movement), they then have the command to return to their starting point, and because they also have Loop configured, they continue along the same path again. Using four tiles in "Amazing Fighter Pilot" in the next chapter, we are able to generate an endless scrolling effect, in which the game is controlled by the destruction of planes (controlled by the programmer) and not the size of the game area.

When applying path movement to the object using the New Line tool (when applying and editing the path movement), you can work out how long the line needs to be by making the length of the line the same size as the length of the tile.

Two examples on the companion CD-ROM show how fake scrolling works. These files are in the Scrolling folder, and the filenames are "fake" and "fake2."

The "fake" file shows you an example of the scrolling used in the second game in the book; notice that it has been color coded to show you how the scrolling works visually within the game. The second game in this book has three tiles that are the same (these are sea tiles), and the fourth tile is a sea tile with a small amount of land in the middle of it. When running this example, you will see the land tile scrolls nicely from the right of the screen to the left, and then disappears. If you run the second example, "fake2," each of the tiles has been given a separate color to show you how the scrolling is working behind the scenes. When a tile is sent back to its original starting point, it overlaps another sea tile; as they are all the same graphically, the end user does not notice this overlapping effect. The fourth tile is always placed on top, and isn't affected by the overlapping.

SUMMARY

In this chapter, we examined two different scrolling techniques, and in the next chapter, you will be using one of them for our second game, "Amazing Fighter Pilot." The great thing about the second game is that it is based on a number of retro game styles from the 1980s, and using this fake scrolling technique can be applied to other retro scrolling games with ease. The next chapter takes our scrolling technique and applies it to a side-scrolling shoot-'em-up game, in which the player has to destroy a number of enemy waves and then defeat the end-of-level big boss.

14 Creating a Side-scrolling Shoot-'em-up Game

In This Chapter

- About Amazing Fighter Pilot
- Fighter Pilot—Initial Setup
- Fighter Pilot—Main Menu
- Fighter Pilot—The Game Screen
- Fighter Pilot—Hi-Scores
- Fighter Pilot—Programming

You've created your first game, "The Lab," which you hopefully found exciting and a good exercise to learn about the power of TGF2. In this chapter, we move to the next stage of game creation and create a side-scrolling shoot-'em-up game called "Amazing Fighter Pilot" (also known as "Fighter Pilot" for ease of writing). Some of the concepts are the same, which should make your game development a little faster.

ABOUT AMAZING FIGHTER PILOT

"Amazing Fighter Pilot" is an exciting side-scrolling shoot-'em-up with left-to-right scrolling, enemy airplanes, moving backgrounds, and a big enemy boss as the end-of-level enemy that the player will need to defeat. Details of these types of games can be found in Chapter 1, "Games, Games, and More Games." The story of "Fighter Pilo" is as follows:

```
It is 1944, and you have been given an important mission to deliver a set
of top-secret plans to your HQ. Unfortunately, you have to fly through a num-
ber of enemy zones before you can delivery the plane's cargo.
```

The second game takes form similar to the first game, and has been separated into three easy-to-distinguish frames:

The Main Screen: From this screen, we will launch the title frame of our game, "Amazing Fighter Pilot."

The Game Screen: This is where the player begins to play the game. "Fighter Pilot" introduces you to a number of new game-making techniques, including fake scrolling, multiple enemies, and health.

The Hi-Score Screen: When the players run out of lives, the customary Hi-Scores frame will appear, allowing the players to enter their score.

Again, all of the games graphics and objects have been premade and placed in a library file to speed up the creation of the game, and to allow you to start programming rather than drawing images. We now need to describe the game in more detail so you understand what is going to happen in each stage.

1. At the start of the game, the main menu graphic appears; this displays the "Fighter Pilot" background image. You will use the mouse to move up and down the menu system. On left-clicking the mouse, you will then be taken to the relevant screens. You have three options: New Game, Highscores, and Quit. Clicking on New Game will take you to the game screen.
2. The player's airplane will appear, and pressing the Shift key will fire the plane's main weapon. There is also a bomb weapon that is limited to three shots, and activated using the Ctrl key.
3. The background will scroll from right to left, and then return to its original position to begin scrolling again. A number of enemy planes will appear from the right in different programmed waves. The player's plane has a health bar, which is depleted every time a plane or enemy bullet hits it. When the health reaches zero, the player will lose a life. Once the player has defeated enough enemies, he or she will then face an end-of-level boss.

The end-of-level enemy is a big airplane that takes a number of hits to destroy. You might be wondering why it's called an "end-of-level boss." In many old retro

games, at the end of each level the player would have to defeat a bigger and more powerful baddie, the end-of-level boss.

4. Once the players have defeated the end-of-level boss or have lost all their lives, they will be sent to the final frame, which is the Hi-Scores frame. If the players' score is higher than the scores already on the scoreboard, they will be asked to enter a name. From here, the players will also be able to go back to the start of the game.

Before you begin to make the game, check out the final game on the companion CD-ROM. The executable is located in the \Game2 folder and is called "Pilot.exe."

Graphics Library—Fighter Pilot

To access the ready-made graphics for "Fighter Pilot," point the Library toolbar to the correct folder on the companion CD-ROM.

The Library files for the Fighter Pilot game can be found in the folder CD-ROM\Game2\Lib.

1. Right-click on the left-hand pane of the Library toolbar to reveal a pop-up menu.
2. Click on the New option. A dialog box will appear, allowing you to browse your computer for the Library file we need for this game. Browse the list until you see your CD-ROM.
3. Next, locate the folder \Game2\Lib. Then, click on the OK button, enter a library name, "Fighter Pilot," and then press Enter.
4. You are now ready to move down into the library and drag any files onto the play area.

FIGHTER PILOT—INITIAL SETUP

As we did with the first game, we need to set up the frames you will be working with in this game development: one for the Main Menu, one for the Game, and one for the Hi-Score table.

Creating the Frames

First, you need to create the three frames that will be used in "Fighter Pilot."

1. Start TGF2, and then click on the File | New option in the menu. This will create the initial game program and its first frame.
2. Highlight the text "Application 1," which is the top item in the Workspace toolbar. Right-click on it, and select Insert | New Frame from the pop-up menu. This will create a second frame called "Frame 2"; type in Frame 2's real name, "Game." Press Enter to accept the new frame name.
3. Insert another frame and rename it "Hi-Scores."
4. Now, rename Frame 1 and call it "Main Menu."

Changing Application Settings

You now need to make some application settings changes as you did in the first game to prevent the player from maximizing the game screen.

1. Left mouse click on the text "Application 1" to select it, and then left-click on it again to rename the game. Change the text to "Amazing Fighter Pilot."
2. Save the game to a location of your choice.
3. Go into the Application Properties by clicking on the game name "Amazing Fighter Pilot" in the Workspace toolbar. This will now load the Application properties into the Properties toolbar. Click on the icon that looks like a monitor; this is the Window Properties tab. Search the list of properties until you see the option No Maximize Box, and tick it. This will disable that option from being enabled when you next run the game.

FIGHTER PILOT—MAIN MENU

The "Fighter Pilot" game main menu is different from the menu you created in "The Lab." It is important to remember that within TGF2 there are many ways to complete the same task, which means that you have much more artistic license when creating your games. For the main menu of "Fighter Pilot," we will be using two new ideas: a moving icon when you move the mouse over a menu item, and, rather than having the menu items as buttons, this time they will be graphic icons, so to initiate the move to another frame we will be using zones. This will be discussed in more detail in the "Games Programming" section. For now, let's place all of the game's menu objects on the game screen.

1. Double-click on the frame Main Menu to open the Frame Editor for this screen.

2. Now you need to navigate to the right library folder that contains the items for this frame. Click on the text "Fighter Pilot" in the Library toolbar; this will show the planelib file on the right of this item. Double-click on planelib to open the various library levels, and then double-click again on the item Main Menu. You will now see three objects that can be placed onto the play area.

3. Drag the first item (Menu_backdrop) onto the play area. Try to position it exactly on the frame, or right-click on the backdrop graphic and select Align in Frame | Horz Center and Align in Frame | Vert Center from the pop-up menu to position it correctly.

4. Drag the Menu object onto the playfield. Try to position it over the graphic image of itself on the Backdrop object, or click on the object to reveal the Object Properties. Click on the Size Position tab, and set the X,Y coordinates to 377 and 94, respectively.

5. Finally, drag the Selector object onto the play area. Click on the object and set its position to 418, 157. You have now completed the placement of the objects for the Main Menu.

FIGHTER PILOT—THE GAME SCREEN

The Game screen involves a large number of graphics, although the total number is reduced because we will be using code to create new enemy planes. This makes the entire process much simpler, as they are created at runtime rather than dragging hundreds of planes onto the play area. You will need to position some of the objects at a specific location, so make sure you confirm the object's location with the Object Properties and the information in this book; misplacing an object could cause strange results.

The game screen is always the longest part of any game creation, so if you become tired, make sure you save your work, and then take a break.

1. Double-click on the Game frame in the Workspace toolbar to open the Frame Editor.

2. Double-click on the up-pointing green arrow on the Library toolbar to go back up a level so we can place the correct objects on the screen. Double-click on the Library object Game to reveal a large selection of objects; these are the items we will be adding to this frame.

3. First, let's create the background to this game. Find the Backdrop object and drop it onto the play area. Place it correctly in the center of the frame, or use Align in Frame | Horz Center and Align in Frame | Vert Center from

the pop-up menu to position it correctly. This is the Background object, and none of the Game objects will be able to move into this area once we have finished coding.

4. We now need to create the background against which the plane will scroll. Drag the Water object onto the play area and place it on the left-hand side of the frame at position 0, 30. Drag the Water 2 object onto the play area so it is sitting next to Water. Its position should be set at 420, 30. Scroll the frame to the right so you can see the edge of Water 2, and then place Water 3 next to it. Its location should be at 840, 30. Finally, scroll to the right until you see the edge of Water 3, and then drag Water Land next to it, at position 1260, 30. On zooming out, your screen should look like Figure 14.1.

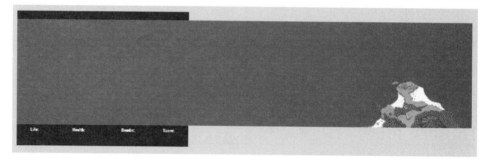

FIGURE 14.1 Background positioned and ready. ©Jason Darby 2005. Reprinted with permission.

5. If you now run the frame, you will notice that the sea and land scroll automatically. This is because each of the four graphic objects has a pre-programmed movement already created. If you want to learn more about scrolling techniques, see Chapter 13, "Scrolling Game Concepts."

6. Let's now place any other items that need to be positioned on the playfield first. Drag the Lives object and place it directly under the "Life" text at position 49, 439.

7. Drag the Health_frame and Health objects onto the playfield, and place then directly below the word "Health." The positions should be 204, 439 and 231, 444, respectively.

8. Drag the Counter_Bombs and Bomb_icon objects to 403, 458 and 388, 435, respectively (this is directly below the word "Bombs").

9. Drag the Score object to 591, 456, which is under the word "Score." Your Information bar should now look something like Figure 14.2.

10. Drag the Flyboy object onto the playfield and place it at the location 9, 174. This is the player's plane, and is used to move around the screen, shooting the enemy planes. As there is already a default movement applied to the

plane, if you now run the frame you can move the plane using the arrow keys. This doesn't work perfectly, as we need to program in some specific items to make it respond accordingly.

FIGURE 14.2 The User Information bar. ©Jason Darby 2005. Reprinted with permission.

11. Next, we need to place all of the Bullet objects we intend to use in our game, but these need to be out of sight of the game player (out of frame). Therefore, scroll upward until you can see the edge of the frame, and then drag and drop the following items (positions in the brackets), Shot 1 (24, –30), Shot 2 Left (56, –15), Shot 2 right (75, –47), Shot 3 Left (95, –18), Shot 3 Right (112, –50), Enemy_shot (112, –50), Boss Bomb (146, –28) and Bomb (165, –28). These are all the different types of weapon shots that will be used by the player, an enemy plane, or the end-of-level boss.

12. Now we need to place all of the enemy planes, on the left-hand side, just outside the frame. Drag Enemy Boss (–243, 70), Enemy_red (–74, 129), Enemy_blue (–74, 191) and Enemy_green (–74, 251).

13. On the bottom left, just outside the frame, we need to place other items we intend to use in the game. From the Library toolbar, drag Bonus_Bombs (–149, 433), Bonus_Shootupgrade (–123, 433), Point 100 (–81, 412), Point 200 (–82, 426), Point 500 (–83, 440), Point 1000 (–84, 454), Point 2000 (–85, 471) and Health_Bonus (–23, 457).

14. Finally, we need to place a number of counters on the outside of the frame at the bottom, for taking into account what enemy plane cycle is currently running (this is when we have a wave of enemy planes in a formation), and the health counter of the end-of-level boss. Place Blue Plane Counter (444, 541), Green Plane Counter (476, 541), and Big Boss Health Counter (487, 570). You have now completed the placement of all of the game's objects. Your frame should look like the example in Figure 14.3.

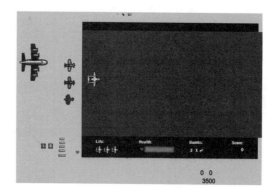

FIGURE 14.3 Current look of the Frame Editor.
©Jason Darby 2005. Reprinted with permission.

FIGHTER PILOT—HI-SCORES

For the Hi-Scores screen, we will be following the process as the first game. The only difference is that we are not using button clicks; we are using mouse clicks in a specific area of the screen to move between the three frames.

1. Double-click on the Hi-Scores frame in the Workspace toolbar to open the Frame Editor.
2. Double-click on the up-pointing green arrow on the Library toolbar to go back up a level so we can place the correct objects on the screen. Double-click on the Library object that says "Hi-scores" to reveal two objects; these are the items we will be adding onto this frame.
3. Drag the Hi_Backdrop object onto the play area. Try to position it exactly on the frame, or right-click on the Backdrop graphic and select Align in Frame | Horz Center and Align in Frame | Vert Center from the pop-up menu to position it correctly.
4. Drag the Hi-Score object onto the play area and try to place it in the center of the score box; the exact position of the object should be 413, 118. Remember, you can access this by clicking on the Hi-Score object, and then within the Properties toolbar, click on the Size & Position tab and enter these numbers in the X and Y coordinates.

FIGHTER PILOT—PROGRAMMING

You now have all the objects in place to begin making your second game. There will be three enemy plane waves, which will send a set number of planes in a specific position across the screen. Once all three waves of red, green, and blue planes have been defeated, the end-of-level boss will appear. If you are able to defeat the big boss, the game will end, and you will be taken to the Hi-Scores frame; if you are defeated, you are also taken to the end frame. The game is slightly more complicated than the first, but is broken into various stages so you can see how the game progresses.

Programming the Main Menu

As previously mentioned, the second game's main menu is more animated than the one in "The Lab." Hopefully, this will show you that you can do many different things to represent your menus and make them interesting to the player. If you run the Main Menu frame, you will notice that there is a simple animation of a rotorblade, which will move up or down depending on the location of the mouse to the menu items. Then, when the user clicks on one of three areas he or she will be taken to the game, the Hi-Scores, or quit the program. For the first part, you will need to get the Graphic icon moving when the mouse rolls over an item. When creating a movement based on the mouse position, it is a good idea to place the object approximately where you want it to get a general X, Y coordinate, and then be more specific in the code to get it to the exact position.

At the bottom right of the screen is an X, Y mouse coordinate that updates every time you move your mouse to a new location. This is also very useful for getting a general idea of where a specific location is with regard to its coordinates.

1. Ensure you are currently viewing the Main Menu frame, by double-clicking on the text "Main Menu" on the Workspace toolbar. Then, click on the Event Editor button to go to a blank coding page.
2. Create a comment line called "Create Moving Cursor"; to do this, you will need to right-click on the event number 1, and then select Insert, A Comment from the pop-up dialog box. Then, enter the text and press the OK button to save.
3. Now we will need to create the three events that check to see where the mouse pointer is currently positioned. If it finds itself in a specific area (called zone"), it will then do the action of moving the mouse. Click on the word "New Condition" on event line 1. Then, double-click on The Mouse Pointer and Keyboard object in the dialog box (the Graphic icon is of a mouse and keyboard). From the pop-up menu, select The Mouse, Check for Mouse Pointer in a Zone. This will take you to the Main Menu frame, and you will see a Zone Setup dialog box and a flashing box. You can either position it manually or use the coordinate boxes. Type in 392 and 590 on the Horizontal line, and on the Vertical, type 141 to 179. This should now

place a flashing box around the words "New Game" on the frame; click OK to go back to the Event Editor. Create two more events that do the same for the other two options. The coordinates for the word "Highscores" would be 396 to 594, and 186 to 215. The coordinates for the word "Quit" would be 395 to 593, and 222 to 249.

4. You will now have three events with a single condition in each. When the mouse pointer goes within that area of the screen, the condition will be true. Therefore, now you will need to create an action, the moving of the graphic rotor-blade to a set position to the left of the text. On the first condition, move to the right until you are directly under the Selector object, and then right-click and select Position, Set Y Coordinate from the pop-up menu. When the Expression Evaluator appears, type in the number "157," Which is the current Y position of the Selector object. You may be wondering, as it is already in this location, why set it? The reason for this is that once the player has moved the mouse over one of the other two items, the cursor will move, and it will need to be moved back when the player moves the mouse back into the New Game zone. To save time, you can drag the Action (the tick) to the two events directly below it, and then edit the Y coordinate (which can be done by right-clicking on the action, and then from the pop-up menu, select Edit). You may want to create these two additional actions manually; either way, you will need to set the Y coordinate for the second of the three events to 195, and the third to 233. If you now run the frame, you will see that you can move the mouse over the three text graphics, and the rotor-blade will move with it.

5. The next stage of the Main Menu is to get the user to click on one of the three items and then take the user to the relevant screen. Create a new comment line under Event four, called "On Click of Mouse." Next, we want to create three events that take action when the user clicks on the left mouse button within a certain area of the screen. Click on the text "New Condition" below the new comment line you just added, double-click on the The Mouse Pointer and Keyboard object, and select The Mouse, User Clicks within a Zone; a dialog box will appear. We only want to do something on a single left mouse click; this is the default setting, so click the OK button. You will now see the Zone dialog box; again, we will use the same coordinates that we used to test if the mouse was within a certain area, so type in "392 to 520" and "141 to 179." You will now need to create the next two events using the same conditions, but using the coordinates of 396 to 594 and 186 to 215 for the first, and then 395 to 593 and 222 to 249 for the second. There will now be three events with a single condition in each under the "On click of mouse" comment line.

6. On the first of the three new events, move across until you are directly under the Storyboard Controls System object. When the user clicks with the left mouse button on the words "New Game," we want it to play the game. Right-click on the Action box, and then select Jump to Frame from the pop-up menu. When the Choose a Storyboard Frame dialog box appears, select Frame 2—Game, and click on the OK button. For the second event, do the same, but select Frame 3—Hi-Scores. For the final event, we want to quit the program, so this time, right-click on the Action box and then select End the Application.

7. An example of what the events and conditions should look like is shown in Figure 14.4. You have now completed the programming for the Main Menu. You can test it to see if it works correctly, although you won't be able to move back from the other two frames, as this hasn't been programming in yet.

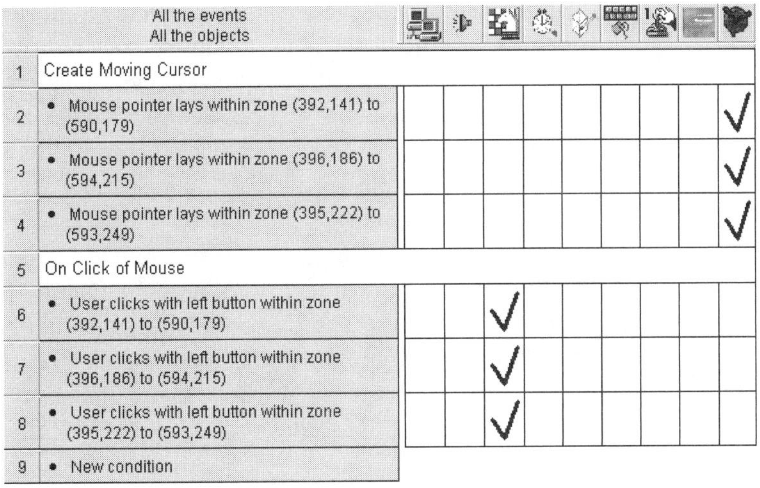

FIGURE 14.4 Main Menu's events and actions.

Programming the Game

You are now ready to begin creating the game frame, which contains most of the program code. The coding has been placed into sections to make it easier to code, but is also a good way to learn how to structure your programs. When making games, you do not need to write everything at once and hope it works. You can take one feature at a time, code it, test it, and then move on to the next. If you become stuck, you can always move on to another feature and come back later. The first thing we need to do in our game is enable program the player movements.

1. Make sure you are on the Game frame by double-clicking on Game in the Workspace toolbar. Once you have the Game frame open, click on the Event Editor to bring up the empty editor.

2. First, we need to create a player group; this will be enabled from the beginning and will contain all of the main player instructions. Right-click on the number "1" on the Event Editor screen, and from the pop-up, select Insert, A Group of Events. In the Group dialog box, type the title "Events for the Player," leave the default option "active at frame start," and then click OK.

3. You will now have a single group created; under this, create a comment line "If player is not moving, set it to forward direction" (to create a comment, right-click on the number and then Insert, A Comment).

4. Directly under this comment, we are going to create our first condition, which will test to see if the player's plane is facing a specific direction (not going forward), but the player isn't moving it (speed is 0), and then change it to face forward. This is a reset option, so when the plane is not moving, it is only showing the front animation. When you start the game, you will notice that the plane is set to its forward-facing direction. If you do not set this condition, it is possible for the plane to be leaning to one side when the player isn't pressing the keys, which obviously isn't right. Therefore, this option is for cosmetic reasons only, but still very important.

5. Click on the New Condition directly under the Events for Player group. Right-click the Flyboy object, and choose Direction, Compare Direction of Flyboy from the pop-up menu. The Direction dialog box will appear; you need to select directions 4, 8, 12, 16, 20, 24, and 28. The dialog box should look like Figure 14.5. If it does, click on the OK button; otherwise, make the necessary changes.

The plane is set to use eight directions in its movements, which is why we want to select the seven directions that are not moving forward.

6. We need to add a second condition to the same event, as we want to confirm that the plane isn't moving. Right-click on the condition, and select Insert from the pop-up menu. Then, choose the Flyboy object, and then from the pop-up menu, choose Movement, Compare Speed of Flyboy to a Value. The Expression Evaluator will appear; leave the amount as 0, and then click on OK. This condition will then be true if the plane is pointing in a different direction but is not moving.

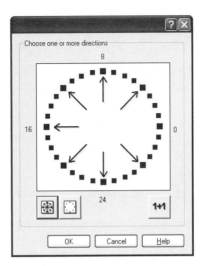

FIGURE 14.5 Direction dialog configuration.

7. Move to the right of this condition until you are directly under the Flyboy object. Right-click and select Direction, Select Direction; the Direction dialog box will appear, and will be pointing to the right. The default direction is what we require, so click on OK to insert the action.

8. Create a comment line under the last condition you just created and call it "Moving Plane Up and Down."

9. Create two events, with one condition in each; the first being Repeat while the Up arrow is pressed, and the second event Repeat while the Down arrow is pressed. To do this, click on New Condition, right-click on The Mouse pointer and Keyboard object, and then from the pop-up menu, choose The Keyboard, Repeat While Key is pressed. A dialog box will then appear, waiting for you to press a key. Press the up arrow to complete the condition. Create the other new condition using the same process, but press the down arrow key.

10. On the first condition (Repeat While the Up Arrow Is Pressed), move to the right until you are directly under the Flyboy object. Right-click and choose Direction, Select Direction, from the Direction dialog box, unselect the right pointing arrow, and insert an up pointing arrow (direction number 8). On the second condition, complete a similar process, but this time, set the direction to down (direction number 24). You should now have a set of events as shown in Figure 14.6.

Remember, for speed you can drag an action down onto another condition line, and then right-click and select Edit to make it specific to that condition.

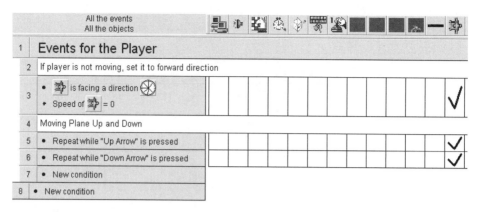

FIGURE 14.6 Events and conditions created so far.

Keeping the Plane in the Frame

If you now run the game, and try to move the plane up, down, left, or right, you will notice that the plane can leave the screen, but also move out of the sea and onto the user area (shown as a black bar at the top and bottom). This can be separated into two events: one to stop the plane from exiting the frame on the left or right, and the second event to stop it from entering the black bar areas on the top and bottom (called "Game backdrop").

1. Create a comment line under the last event that was created (the line should be number 7) and call it "Keeping Plane in Area."
2. Under this comment line, create an event. This event should have a single condition that checks to see if the plane has left the frame on the left or right. To assign this, click on the words "New Condition," select the Flyboy object, and then choose Position, Test Position of Flyboy. The Test Position dialog box will appear; left mouse click on the left and right out-pointing arrows (this means an object moving out of the frame on the left and right). The Test dialog should look like Figure 14.7; click OK to close it and record your selection.
3. The actions for both events are the same, so let's configure the second event first. Click on New Condition, choose the Flyboy from the dialog box, and on the pop-up menu, choose Collisions, Backdrop.
4. With both events ready, we now need to put the same action in each; when the players plane tries to exit the frame from the left or right, or collides with the backdrop (the black bars), the plane stops. Move across to the right until you are under the Flyboy object, right-click, and select Movement, Stop. You can then drag this action directly below it to the second of the two events. Your events for this part should look like Figure 14.8.

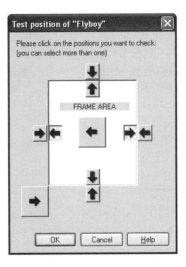

FIGURE 14.7   Test Position dialog box.

7	Keeping Plane in Area
8	• 🛩 leaves the play area on the left or right
9	• 🛩 collides with the background

FIGURE 14.8   Plane movement restriction events.

Bomb Modes

The player has a number of weapons at his disposal: a single shot, a double shot, a triple shot, and a powerful bomb. In the game, we will introduce a bonus that will upgrade to double and triple shot, but by default, the player will get a single-shot machine gun and three bombs. To ensure the right weapon is in place, we use Alterable values, which you can assign to an object and change throughout the game. The great thing is that you can also create conditions for when they change, and make the program do a specific action. We will be using Alterable value A for storing the weapon's status. The value will be 0 for single shot, 1 for double shot, and 2 for a triple shot.

1. Under the last event that you created (which should be event number 9), you will see the New Condition line. We are still creating events under the

Player group we created earlier. Right-click on the event number 10 and insert a new comment called "Shoot Type."

2. Insert a new event by clicking on New Condition, and then select the Flyboy object from the dialog. On the pop-up menu, choose Alterable Values, Compare to One of the Alterable Values. Once you have selected this, the Expression Evaluator will appear; Alterable Value "A" will need to equal "0," in this case, which is the default, so click on OK. We need to add another condition to the same event for when the player is pressing the Shift key (as this is the Fire button). Right-click on the condition you just added, select Insert, and from the dialog box, choose The Mouse Pointer and Keyboard object. From the pop-up menu, select Keyboard, Upon Pressing a Key. A dialog box will appear for you to specify the key; press the Shift key.

3. You now need to create two more events with the same set of conditions, except that the Alterable value in the second of the three events will be 1, and 2 in the third. You should now have three events that are the same as Figure 14.9.

Remember, to save time, you can copy the events by double-clicking on the Alterable value and amending it.

10	Shoot Type
11	• Alterable Value A of ⬡ = 0 ✦ Upon pressing "Shift"
12	• Alterable Value A of ⬡ = 1 ✦ Upon pressing "Shift"
13	• Alterable Value A of ⬡ = 2 ✦ Upon pressing "Shift"
14	• New condition

FIGURE 14.9 Alterable values for each weapon type.

You now need to create the actions for each of these three events, to fire the actual bullets. The single shot is a simple one bullet moving forward, the double shot is two bullets moving forward, and the triple shot is one bullet moving forward, and a left- and right-angled bullet. We will also set a specific speed for each bullet, which can be changed later if needed to make the game easier or harder. As the Alterable value is set to 0 by default, once you have created these events, you will only be able to fire a single machine gun.

4. For the first of the three events, move to the right until you are directly under the Flyboy, right-click, and from the pop-up, select Shoot an Object. A dialog box will appear, asking you what you want to shoot from the plane. Find and select Shot 1. On clicking OK, you will now be shown another dialog box with various speed and direction options. Leave the speed at 100, and then click on the Shoot in Selected Directions… radio button. A Direction dialog box will appear; unselect the up arrow (direction number 8), and click on Direction Zero (to the right). Click on OK, and then OK again to save the action. If you now run the game, you can use the Shift key to fire single bullets.

5. Now, you need to program in the double shot, using the same process, but this time, find and select Shot 2 Left, direction to the right at speed 100. Once you have completed that action, create another on the same condition line, but select Shot 2 Right, same speed and direction.

6. For the triple shot, you will need to select Shot 3 Left at speed of 85 at a direction of 4, Shot 1 at a speed of 100 at a direction of 0, and Shot 3 Right at a speed of 85, direction of 28.

If you want to test the other firing methods, you will need to insert a temporary event at the beginning of the game, setting a different Alterable number to "A."

The last of the shooting modes is the ability to shoot a single bomb that has the added benefit of destroying everything in its path (unlike the other modes, which are destroyed when they hit an enemy plane). The player only has three bombs to begin with; more can be obtained in the game by moving the plane over a bonus ammunition box. Once the player runs out of bombs, he will not be able to fire anymore. We use a counter to store the number of bombs, and use a condition to see if there are more than 0; if so it will fire a bomb, if not the condition will not be true and so will not shoot anything.

7. Create a comment line called "Shoot Bombs Mode."
8. Under this, create a single event, with two conditions. The first condition is Upon Pressing Control; this is taking into account when the player is pressing the Ctrl key to fire the Bomb (select The Mouse Pointer and Keyboard, then Keyboard, and finally Upon Pressing a Key; you will need to press the Ctrl key to save the condition). Once you have this condition, right-click on it, and select Insert from the pop-up menu. Find the Counter_bombs object, right-click on it, and from the pop-up, choose

Compare the Counter to a Value. The Expression Evaluator will appear; change the Equal to Greater and leave the zero, which will be correct for our calculation. Click on the OK button to save this condition.

9. Move to the right of the event you just created until you are directly under the Flyboy; we are now going to set an action to fire a big bomb in the direction of the planes (left to right). Right-click, choose Shoot an Object from the pop-up menu, find the Bomb object, and double-click on it. Change the speed to 45 (as we want it to go much slower than the other weapons), and then click on the radio button Shoot in Selected Directions... Change the direction from 8 (pointing up) to direction 0 (pointing to the right), click on OK, and then OK to save. If you now run the game, you can press the Ctrl key and fire the large bomb, but you will notice you can keep firing it. Move to the right of the event, and when you get directly under the Counter_bombs object, right-click on the empty action box. Select Subtract from Counter; when the Expression Evaluator appears, replace the zero with a number "1." Click on the OK button to save. Every time you fire the bomb weapon, it will now subtract 1 from the counter. Therefore, if you run the game again, you will notice that you can only fire three bombs and then it will stop.

In this game example, the counter was already predefined with a starting value of 3 (you didn't need to do anything, it was already configured). When making your own games, you will need to set an initial value on your counters to make these types of actions work correctly.

You have now completed all of the code needed in the Events for the Player group, so to tidy things up a little, you can double-click on the group header and compact all the code, so it disappears. It is still there, but just hidden; to bring it back, all you need to do is double-click again on the group header. The event lines will renumber themselves every time you reduce or expand a group.

Creating Plane Waves

The game is starting to work quite well, but the player doesn't have anything to do except fly around. To make it more exciting, we need planes for the player to shoot down. All planes will appear from the right side of the screen, and will be in three waves. Each wave will be configured to appear slightly different to give the player more of a challenge. The enemy waves are all created in groups, which allows us to enable and disable each group as we want through the code. If you decide to make the game harder, you can create additional waves (groups) or change the order in which each group is run.

1. Right-click on the last event line number, which has the words "New Condition" associated with it. Then, choose A Group of Events; when the dialog box appears, type the name of the group, which will be Red Planes, be sure you unclick Active when Frame Starts, and then click on OK.
2. Create two more groups, Blue Planes and Green Planes, again ensuring that Active when Frame Starts is disabled. If your Events for the Player group is compressed, you should now have a set of groups that looks like Figure 14.10.

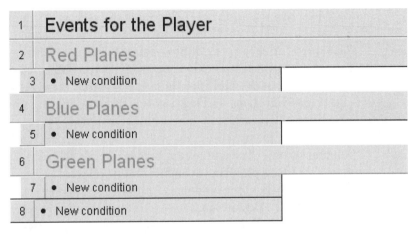

FIGURE 14.10   Groups currently created.

3. Under Red Planes, click on the "New Condition" text to add the first event to this group. Select the Timer object from the dialog box, and then choose Every from the pop-up menu. A Timer dialog box will appear; we need something to happen every half a second. Therefore, remove the number 1 from the Seconds box and add 50 to the 1/100 box. Move to the right of this condition until you are directly under the Create New Objects object (the Create object looks like a dotted square with a marker pen). Right-click and select Create Object; a further dialog box will appear. Locate the Enemy_red plane and double-click on it. A Position dialog box will appear; type in the coordinates 735 and 120. This will position it just outside the play area. This action will create a new red enemy plane at the specified located every half a second. The problem with this is that all of the planes would be created in the same spot and would be overlapping each other, so we now need to create another action on the same event line to position them. Move to the right until you are directly under the Enemy_Red object, right-click, and then select Position, Set Y coordinate. The Expression

Evaluator will appear; replace the zero item with Random (330) +27, and then click on the OK button. This expression creates a plane on the Y axis (top to bottom) within a range of 330 +27. The +27 is to ensure that it always misses the very first 27 pixels, which in our case are covered by a black border. If you didn't have the +27, you would find planes appearing on the black bars, which of course is not correct.

4. If you now run the game, you will notice you have the Flyboy object flying on a scrolling background, but nothing else happens. You haven't done anything wrong, it is just that the code you just wrote is in a group that is disabled. This means that TFG2 ignores any code within a disabled group. You will need to enable this group for that section of code to work.

5. This can be done via code or by enabling the group; we are going to do the second option. Right-click on the group, select Edit, tick the box Active When Frame Starts, and click on OK. The group is now enabled, and you can retest your game and see a group of planes fly onto the screen (the planes already have a built-in movement assigned).

6. If you now run the game, you will notice on the Debugger bar that the number of objects keeps getting higher as each red plane leaves the play area. This isn't a problem with a first, but if you were to leave the game running for a while, you would begin to notice some very strange results. On every frame is a default Number of Objects setting, configured at 500. This setting configures TGF2 to understand how many objects it will be running. You can change this to a higher number, but the higher the number, the more memory the program will use. Of course, it's okay to increase this number, but in a game like "Fighter Pilot," the red planes that leave the screen are no longer needed, so it is more efficient to destroy them than to increase the Number of Objects setting.

7. When a plane reaches minus 200 on the X coordinate (to the left-hand side of the play area), we need to destroy the red planes. Create a new condition, select the Enemy_Red object, and from the pop-up, choose Position, Compare X Position to a Value. When the Expression Evaluator appears, change the Equals sign to Lower or Equal, type in −200, and then click on OK to save. Move to the right of the condition until you are directly under the Enemy_Red object, right-click, and then select Destroy from the pop-up.

This now means that if the red enemy plane reaches a position of −200 on the X-axis, it will remove it. If you now run the game, you will notice that the number of objects goes up when a red plane enters the screen, and then reduces when it goes off. This makes your games much more efficient and stops them from needing to use large amounts of memory to store all of the objects the game has created. The final part to the red enemy wave is to tell TGF2 when to stop creating these planes, and then move on to the next color. Remember that because we are using groups, we can enable and disable each group when we like; all we need to do is create a condition of when it would happen. For the moment, we want the red planes to stop being created after 20 seconds, which we can do by enabling the next group and disabling the one we are finished with.

8. Click on New Condition in the Red Planes group. Select the Timer object, and choose Is the Timer Equal to a Certain Value? When the Timer dialog box appears, move the Seconds arrow to 20, and then click OK to save.

9. Move to the right until you are directly under the Special Conditions object (which looks like two computers connected to each other). Right-click and select Group of Events, Activate; a Group dialog box will appear showing all the groups you currently have in your game. Double-click on Blue Planes, as we want to switch that group On to send its planes (although we haven't created them yet). Do the same action again, but this time, select Deactivate, and then choose Red Planes; this is so no more red planes are created. An example of the Activate and Deactivate Group dialog can be seen in Figure 14.11.

FIGURE 14.11 Activating or Deactivating a Group dialog

We now need to create the blue plane wave, and to make the game more interesting, it will need to be different from the first group. Rather than randomly creating planes and making them fly toward the player, we will be creating an entire row. Additionally, we will be using a counter to check how many sets of planes have been created (four in this game example). Later, you could change this number to increase or decrease the number of blue plane waves.

10. Under the Blue Planes group, create a new condition, select the Timer object, and choose Every. Change the time in the dialog box to 3 seconds, and then click on OK.

11. Move to the right until you are under the Create New Objects dialog box. Select Create Object from the pop-up menu. Select the Enemy_blue object, and then in the Location dialog, type in the X, Y coordinates as 729, 48. This is just outside the play area at the top of the sea. We now need to create another six blue planes in the same way, with different locations: (729, 97), (729, 146), (729, 195), (729, 244), (729, 293), and (729,342). This will create a single row of blue planes.

12. On the same event line, move to the right until you are directly under the Blue plane Counter, right-click, select Add to Counter, and in the Expression Evaluator, type in the number "1." This will now add 1 to the counter every time it creates a row of planes.

13. The same problem with the number of objects on screen now occurs with the blue planes. Therefore, we must now create a new condition, this time to destroy any blue planes that have gone left of the screen. You can type this in manually, or copy the event from the red planes group. Then, double-click on the red plane in the condition and change it to blue. You will also need to move to the right and remove the Destroy action from the red plane and add it to the blue plane. To do this manually, create a new condition, and select the Enemy_blue object, then Position, Compare X Position to a Value from the pop-up menu. In the Expression Evaluator, choose Lower or Equal, enter the calculation of —200, and then press on OK. Move to the right, and when you are directly below the Enemy_blue object, right-click and select Destroy.

14. We now want to limit the number of blue plane waves; as we have already set up a counter that is increasing with each wave, we can now set a limit on it. Create a new condition, and select Blue Plane Counter, Compare the Counter to a Value. When the Expression Evaluator dialog appears, change the calculation to the number "4" (which means there will be four waves of blue planes), and then click on the OK button to save the condition to the event.

15. Move to the right until you are directly under the Special Conditions object. Right-click, select Group of Events, Activate, and in the dialog box that appears, choose Green Planes, and then click OK. Now, using the same process, Deactivate, Blue Planes.

16. For the final wave of planes, we are going to place a set of green enemy planes in a "V" formation. Using another counter, you will set a number to generate the number of waves that need to be sent.

17. Create a new condition under the Green Planes group, select the Timer object, and then choose Every from the pop-up menu. Move the arrow until

it reads "five seconds," and then click on the OK button. As you can see by this condition, the plane waves are activated every five seconds.

18. Move to the right until you are under Create New Objects, right click, and select Create Object. You will need to select the enemy_green and then specify its location. The locations for the seven planes are (708, 202), (732, 244), (732, 163), (777, 274), (777, 130), (821, 308), and (821, 96). If you hold your mouse cursor over the Action box, you should see a set of planes as shown in Figure 14.12.

A good way to design your waves of enemy planes is to open a blank TGF game, place them on the screen where you would like them to appear, make a note of the X, Y locations, and then transfer it to your game.

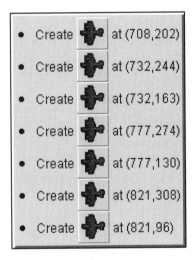

FIGURE 14.12   Green plane locations.

19. You now need to add one more action to this condition; we need to add "1" to the green plane counter so we can control the number of plane waves that appear. Move to the right of the condition until you are directly under the Green Plane Counter, right-click, select Add to Counter, and in the Expression Evaluator, enter the number "1" and click OK.

20. As we did with the other two plane groups, we have to destroy any green created planes that leave the play area on the left. Create a new condition, select the Enemy_green, select Position, Compare X Position to a Value from the pop-up menu, and then Lower or Equal and –200 in the Expres-

sion Evaluator. On the right under the Enemy_green object, right-click and set the Action to Destroy.

21. The final event for this group is to read the counter, and when it reaches a certain number, disable the group. Click on New Condition, select the Green Plane Counter object, choose Compare the Counter to a Value, type in the number "4" in the Expression Evaluator, and then click OK. Move to the right of the condition until you are under the Special Conditions object, right-click, select Group of Events, Deactivate, and then choose Green Planes from the dialog box. An example of the three separate conditions can be seen in Figure 14.13.

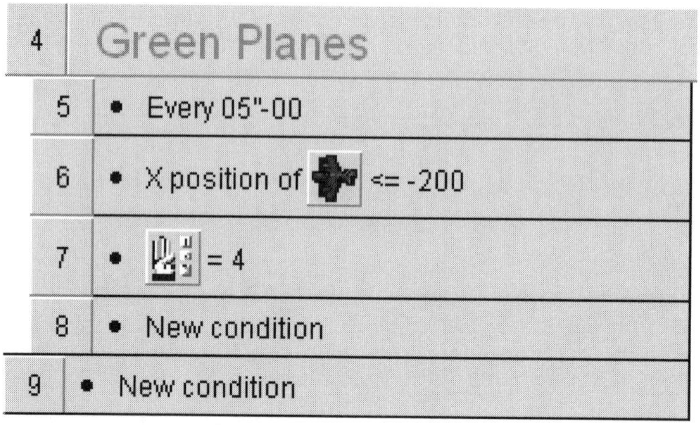

4	Green Planes
5	• Every 05"-00
6	• X position of ✈ <= -200
7	• 🖼 = 4
8	• New condition
9	• New condition

FIGURE 14.13 The conditions you should have when you have finished the Green group.

End-of-Level Boss

We now have three enemy plane waves in place, but we still need something to complete the level. We could just finish it there, but it would be much more interesting if we added an end-of-level boss to defeat, so that is what we are going to do. If you decided to make a similar game, you would add many levels and a number of different bosses to defeat. Keeping a varied enemy makes for a much more interesting game, and allows you to increase the difficulty and separate the levels. The first thing that needs to be done is the creation of a group to hold the end-of-level boss code.

1. Right-click on the number of the last event (the one that says "New Condition"), select Insert, A Group of Events, enter the name of the group as "Big Boss," and then untick Active when Frame starts. Click on the OK button.

You need to create a single Big Boss enemy rather than the multiple objects created previously. There are a number of ways to do this, but we will use the Run this Event Once condition. This means it will only run the event once, and then ignore it for the rest of the game. Of course, if you wanted to display this enemy on more than one level, this would not be the correct command to use, and an alternative condition would need to be used. If you were to make multiple levels and multiple bosses in a game, another method would to be create multiple Boss groups, and change the way the boss reacts in each group. The second method is recommended, as it is easier to find any specific level boss and make changes to it if there is a problem.

2. Click on New Condition, select the Special object, and then from the pop-up menu, choose Limit Conditions, Run this Event Once. Move to the right until you are directly under the Create Object object, right-click, and choose Create object. Find the Enemy_Boss, and double-click on it to select. You will now be asked for its starting location; type in the X, Y coordinates of 651, 140.

Now that we have created the enemy big boss, we need it to appear in the play area and then keep it moving within a certain area of the screen to allow the player to shoot it down. It wouldn't be as much fun for the player if the plane appeared and then moved off the screen. The way we accomplish this is that the plane appears and two conditions are created to find its location on the play area. Once the plane reaches a specific area on the left, an action takes place to move it forward, and once it reaches a point forward (to the right), it moves it back to the left. This keeps the plane in a continual loop, and won't disappear until it is destroyed or you have lost all lives and the game is over.

3. Click on New Condition, select the Enemy_Boss, then Position, Compare X Position to a Value. Finally, change the Equal in the Expression Evaluator to Less or Equal and enter a number of 450.

4. Move to the right until you are directly under the Enemy_Boss object, and then right click. From the pop-up menu, choose Direction, Select Direction, and when the direction dialog appears, untick the default direction of zero and select direction seven.

5. Click on New Condition, choose the Enemy_Boss, and from the pop-up menu, select Position, Compare X Position to a Value. Then, on the Expression Evaluator, change the Equal to Equal or Greater, enter the number 470, and click on OK. You now need to add one more condition to this event line; otherwise, the plane will continue off to the left. Right-click on the condition, select Insert, choose the Enemy_Boss by double-clicking on

it, and then select Direction, Compare Direction of Enemy_boss. In the Direction dialog, unselect direction 0 and create direction 7.

6. Move to the right until you are directly under the Enemy_boss object, right-click, select Direction, Select Direction, from the Direction dialog, and untick direction 0 and tick 23.

Now when you run the frame, the enemy plane will enter the game screen, moving in a downward direction; once it hits the X coordinate of 450, it will change its direction to an upward movement, and then will continue until it reaches 470. At this point, it changes its direction again, and puts it in a loop until you destroy it or you are destroyed.

The next event we need to create is to find out when the enemy boss' health meter reaches zero. Shortly, we will be programming bullet events that will minus the health of the boss when a bullet hits it, but for ease of programming, we can set an event here that will check when it runs out.

7. Click on New Condition, select Big Boss Health Counters, and then from the pop-up, choose Compare the Counter to a Value. The Expression Evaluator appears, and the default setting is set to Equal and 0, which is what we require (we want to know when the enemy plane has no health). Click on the OK button to accept.

8. Move to the right of the condition until you are directly under the Enemy_Boss, right-click, and pick Animation, Change, Animation Sequence. You will now be presented with a dialog box; choose User Animation.

When the counter reaches zero, it will play the User Animation of the plane becoming more transparent (invisible), making it look like it is disappearing. The last thing we need to do for this group is to find out when this animation has finished playing, and then destroy the Enemy_boss from the play area.

9. Click on New Condition, select Enemy_Boss, and on the pop-up, choose Animation, Has an Animation Finished. Then, select User Animation and click on the OK button. Move to the right of the condition until you are directly under the Enemy_boss object, right-click, and select Destroy.

As you needed to play an animation when the health ran out, another condition is waiting for the animation to finish playing before it removes the graphic from the screen. This now concludes the code for the Enemy Boss.

Destruction of Enemy Planes

On playing the game, you can move the plane around, the enemy waves appear, you can fire the weapons, but nothing happens when the bullets hit them. What needs to be programmed at this stage is when the bullets hit the enemy planes, the planes are destroyed (with the bullet), and a set number of points are added to the players score. There are eight events for this stage, four for the standard set of bullets, and four for the Bomb object. Eight events are required to make a condition that is checking for when a bullet or bomb hits an enemy plane, so it can then do the relevant action associated with it. To reduce the amount of programming, a Qualifier group has been created on all the normal player bullets. The Qualifier group is called Group.Bullets in the Event Editor, and as mentioned in Chapter 8, "TGF Coding Basics," will allow you to create conditions and actions associated with this group.

To check on an object's group status, click on the object in question to reveal its Object Properties, and then click on the Events tab (in the Properties Workspace toolbar) to see if any Qualifiers have been assigned. In this game, a Qualifier group called Bullets has been attached to Shot 1, Shot 2 Left, Shot 2 Right, Shot 3 Left, and Shot 3 Right.

1. First, we need to create a new group that will contain all the bullet collision conditions. Right-click on the number of the last event in the editor (it will say "New Condition" in it), and then pick Insert, A Group of Events. In the Create Group dialog box, type in the group name "Destroy Enemy Planes," leave the group as Active, and then click on the OK button.

2. Click on "New Condition" that is directly under (in) this group. When the Object dialog box appears, locate the Group.Bullets object; this is the group that has been precreated. Right-click on it and select Collisions, Another Object from the pop-up menu. You will be shown a Test Condition dialog box; from here, you will need to pick the first enemy plane, which is Enemy_red. Now that the condition is added, move to the right until you are directly under the Player 1 object (picture of a joystick). Right-click, pick Score, Add to Score, and then in the Expression Evaluator, type in the number "100." Move to the right of this condition again until you are directly under Group.Bullets, right-click, and select Destroy. We need one more action to this condition, so move to the right until you are directly under the Enemy_red object, right-click, and select Destroy.

This event detects when a bullet hits the Enemy_red object; it will then add 100 points to the player's score, destroy the bullet, and then destroy the enemy plane. If you run the game now, you will notice you can destroy the red planes and get a small number of points as well. Now you will need to add events for the Enemy_blue, Enemy_green, and Enemy_boss objects.

3. Follow the same procedure that was just completed, and add an event that contains the condition Collision between Group.Bullets and Enemy_blue; for the actions, add 200 to the score, and then destroy both the plane and the bullet group.

4. On another event line, you will need to do the same for the Enemy_green object, adding 200 to the score, and destroying both the plane and bullet.

5. On the next event line, you now need to create a condition for the Enemy_boss; this time, adding 500 points to the score. Only add a Destroy action to the bullet group and not the Enemy_boss. You will need an extra action to this event line to reduce the health of the Enemy_boss. Move to the right until you are directly under the Big Boss Health Counter object. Right-click, select Subtract from Counter, type in "100," and then click on the OK button.

If you run the game at this point, you could actually destroy all of the planes including the Enemy Boss, but you will notice that when firing your bomb weapon, it goes right through the planes and does no damage. Therefore, in a similar fashion to the previous events, we need to add conditions to take into account the collision between the bomb and the enemy.

6. Click on New Condition, select the Bomb object, then Collisions, Another Object from the pop-up, and finally, the Enemy_red from the dialog box. Move to the right until you are under the Player 1 object, right-click, and select Score, Add to Score. From the Expression Evaluator, type in "100" and click the OK button. Scroll further to the right, find the Enemy_red object, right-click, and select Destroy.

7. Do the same for the objects Enemy_blue and Enemy_green, except add "200" to the score (making sure you destroy the correct colored object).

8. Create a collision between the Bomb and Enemy_boss, move to the right until you are under Player 1, select Score, Add to Score, and type in "500." Move to the right until you are directly under the Bomb object, and right-click, and choose Destroy. Move across until you find Big Boss Health Counter, right-click, pick Subtract from Counter, and type in "200" in the Expression Evaluator. You can see an example of all these conditions in Figure 14.14.

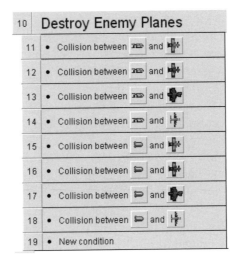

FIGURE 14.14   Destroy Enemy Planes group.

Enemy Fire

The game currently doesn't give the player much of a challenge, so we need the enemy planes to shoot back at the player. This ensures the player has to keep moving or will be hit, which in turn makes hitting the enemy planes harder.

1. On the last event line outside of the groups, right-click on the number and select Insert, A Comment. Enter the comment name "Enemy Fire," and click on the OK button.

2. Under this comment line, we need to add a number of events; click on the New Condition text, select Timer, and choose Every. When the Timer dialog appears, you will notice that it is set at a default 1 second; this is what we need in the condition, so click on the OK button. We need to add another condition to the same event, so right-click on the condition we just added and select Insert, find the Enemy_red object, and right-click. From the pop-up menu, select Pick or Count, Pick Enemy_red at Random. One final condition needs to be added to the event, so right-click on the condition just added, and pick Insert. Find the Enemy_red object, and from the pop-up menu, pick Position, Compare X Position to a Value. The Expression Evaluator will appear; change the Equal to Greater Than. Within the Expression Editor, you will need to compare the position of the red plane with the player's plane; to do this, you click on the Retrieve Data from an Object button, find the Flyboy object, and from the pop-up, choose Position, X Coordinate. Now you need to add the action associated with the

Event, so move to the right until you are directly under Enemy_red. Right-click, choose Shoot an Object; from the dialog box that appears find Enemy_shot, select it, and then click on OK. You will now see a Shoot dialog box; change the speed to 60 and then pick Shoot in the Direction of.... The Coordinate dialog box will then appear; as we want the bullets to fly toward the player, we need to select Relative to. You will be asked to choose an object, so find the Flyboy object, and click OK. A flashing cursor will be placed on screen; type in the X, Y coordinates or move the cursor until it is at position 28, 28. Click on the OK button, and then click on the next OK button to save the action to the Event Editor.

In the last set of conditions, we told TGF2 to pick a red enemy plane at random every second. As long as this enemy plane is positioned in front of the player's plane, it shoots a bullet in the direction of the Flyboy object. The reason for comparing the position of the enemy plane with the player is to prevent the enemy firing at the Flyboy after it has flown past it. If you decide to make this game harder, you could remove the condition line from that event, so the enemy planes would continue to fire regardless of their position.

3. You now need to add two further events for the two other enemy planes: the Enemy_blue and the Enemy_red objects. Follow the same procedure, but replace the enemy planes with either of the two colored planes. You should now have a set of conditions that match Figure 14.15.

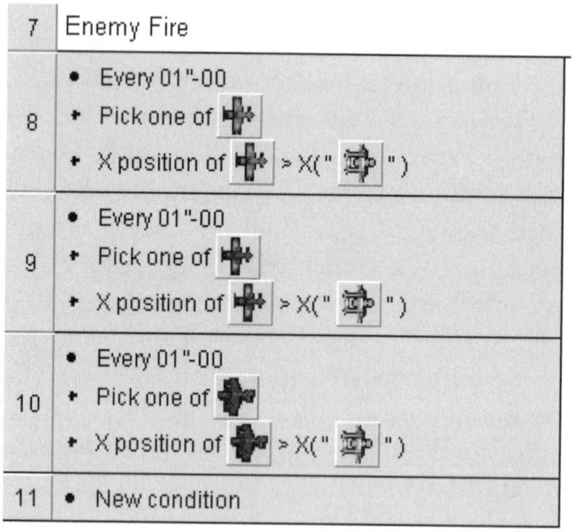

FIGURE 14.15   Enemy plane firing events.

Player Collisions

The player's plane can currently fly through the enemies' shots and through the planes themselves. We now need to set up a group of events that reduce the player's health if he is hit by an enemy shot or hits another Plane object.

1. Right-click on the last number in the Event Editor, select Insert, A Comment, type in "Collisions," and press the OK button.

2. Click on New Condition, select Enemy_shot, and then from the pop-up menu, Collisions, Another Object, and then find and select the Flyboy object. Move to the right until you find the Enemy_shot object, right-click, and select Destroy. Continue on the same event line until you find the Health counter. Right-click, select Subtract from Counter, and enter the number "1" in the Expression Evaluator. Click OK to save the action to the Event Editor.

3. Create another event with the condition Collision between Flyboy and Enemy_red, for the actions we will need to destroy the enemy plane and subtract "1" from the health counter. You can do this by clicking on New Condition, selecting Flyboy, and from the pop-up menu, Collisions, Another Object, and then find the Enemy_red object. Move to the right until you find Enemy_Red, right-click, and choose Destroy. Find the Health Counter object, right-click, pick Subtract from Counter, enter the number "1" in the Expression Evaluator, and then click on the OK button.

4. Do the same for Collision between Flyboy and Enemy_blue, set the destroy action on the blue plane, and subtract 1 from the health counter.

5. You will need to do this one more time for Collision between Flyboy and Enemy_green; you will need to destroy the green enemy plane and subtract 1 from the health counter.

6. You should now have a set of events that look like Figure 14.16. The Health object is a Counter object with a starting value of 5, so every time the player's plane hits an enemy object it reduces this counter by 1. This is a very easy way to keep track of the health of the Flyboy, and is shown as a health bar, which can be placed in the game visually.

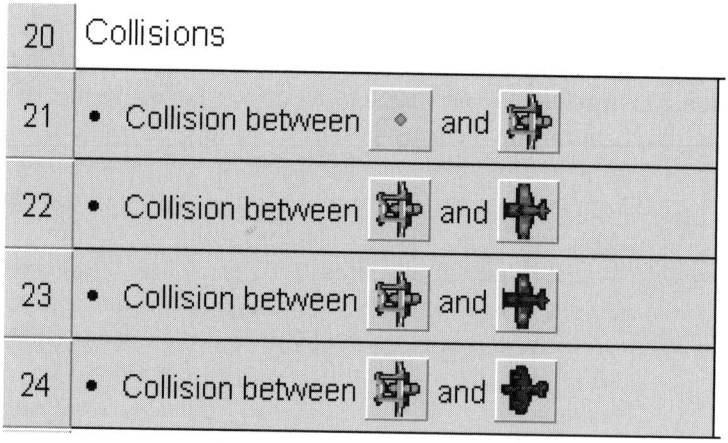

FIGURE 14.16 The Collision events.

Players Health

Now that we have a set of events that reduce the player's health when his plane is hit by an enemy plane, we now need two conditions for the player's lives. The first condition needs to track the player's health counter, and when it reaches zero, to remove a life and then reset the counter to full health. The second condition tracks when the player's health has reached zero and there are no more lives left, at which point it tells the game to go to frame 3, which contains the high-scores table.

1. Right-click on the last event number in the Event Editor, and from the pop-up menu, choose Insert, A comment. For the comment text, type "Health and Lives," and then click on the OK button.
2. Click on New Condition, and from the dialog box, find and double left-click on the Health object. From the pop-up menu, select Compare the Counter to a Value; on the Expression Evaluator, leave the default settings, and click on the OK button.
3. Right-click on the condition you just added, select Insert, select Player 1, and then from the pop-up, choose Compare to Players Number of Lives. When the Expression Evaluator appears, change the Equal to Greater, and then click on the OK button.
4. Move to the right of this condition until you are under the Player 1 object, right-click, and then choose Number of Lives, Subtract from Number of Lives. Enter the number "1" in the Expression Evaluator, and then click OK. Move to the right until you are under the Health counter, right-click, select Set Counter; in the Expression Evaluator, enter the number "5."

5. Enter a new event line, by clicking on New Condition; from the dialog box, find and double left-click on the Health object. From the pop-up menu, select Compare the Counter to a Value; on the Expression Evaluator, leave the default settings, and click the OK button. Right-click on the condition you have just added, select Insert, then select Player 1, and then from the pop-up menu, choose Compare to Players Number of Lives. When the Expression Evaluator appears, leave it at Equal, and then click on the OK button.

6. Move to the right until you are under Storyboard Controls, right-click, pick Jump to Frame, and in the Frame dialog, select Frame 3—Hi-Scores.

Programming the Hi-Scores

The Hi-Scores screen is the least complicated screen to program, and only requires two events: one for entering the high score and the other to allow the players to go back to the Main Menu screen so they can play another game. First, we will need to check to see if the player has a high score. This is determined by the Hi-Score table, which is inserted onto the frame; each item within this list has a score. TGF2 will check the lowest score and see if the player has a higher score. If the condition is true (the player has a higher score), the programmer is then able to create a number of actions based on this.

1. Click on New Condition, double left-click on the Hi-Score object, and from the pop-up menu, choose Has Player a Hiscore?. A Player dialog box will then appear; select Player 1. This will create a condition for when the player has a high score to do something.

2. Let's now create the action, which will be to ask for the players' name when they get a high score. Move to the right of this condition until you are directly under the Hi-Score object. Right-click, select Ask for a Players Name, and in the dialog box that appears, select Player 1.

3. Now that you have created the condition and action to ask for a name, you need to program in the navigational aspect of moving from this frame back to the Main Menu so the player can start a new game. When designing your games, make sure you test the navigational aspects of getting around your program. Bad design in one of the areas will make the end user feel that you haven't made an effort, and can affect the quality of a product from the user's perception. These little design issues can really make a difference in the players' perception of your games.

4. Click on the "New Condition" text to create our next condition. Double-click on The Mouse Pointer and Keyboard object from the dialog box, and then select The Mouse, User Clicks within a Zone from the pop-up menu.

A dialog box will appear, but we will be using all the defaults (single click, left mouse button), so click on the OK button. A Zone dialog box will appear, and you will need to enter the coordinates of 456 to 529 and 273 to 305, and then click on OK.

5. Move to the right until you are directly below Storyboard Controls, right-click, and select Jump to Frame from the pop-up menu. Then, choose Frame1—Main Menu from the dialog box. You now have created an action to move back to the first screen when the user clicks on the area that contains the image that says "Back." An example of the Events can be seen in Figure 14.17.

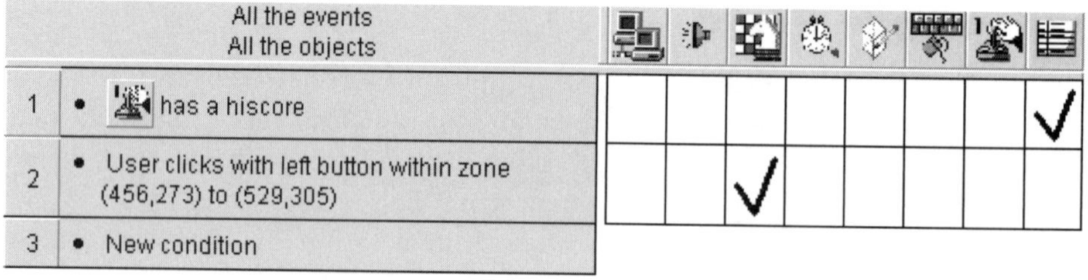

	All the events / All the objects								
1	• 🔔 has a hiscore								✓
2	• User clicks with left button within zone (456,273) to (529,305)		✓						
3	• New condition								

FIGURE 14.17   The Hi-Scores events

SUMMARY

This chapter showed you how to create a side-scrolling shoot-'em-up game. We looked at a number of concepts, including scrolling, bullets, shooting from another object, and health meters. In the next few chapters, we introduce more concepts and a new game type, the platform game. With this new type of game, we will be looking at platforms, jumping, and ladders, and how to implement them in your games.

15 Robin Hood, the Rescue of Lady Marian

In This Chapter

- About Robin Hood, the Rescue of Lady Marian
- Robin Hood—Initial Setup
- Robin Hood—Main Menu
- Robin Hood—The Game Screen
- Robin Hood—Hi-Scores
- Robin Hood—Programming
- Programming the Hi-Scores

In this chapter, we will be creating a platform game called "Robin Hood, the Rescue of Lady Marian" (also called "Robin Hood"). It takes a number of the concepts you have already learnt and builds on them, but adds some new techniques such as jumping, ladders, and platforms. Although the game is only a single level, it shows that with some graphics and a small number of events, you can create a very interesting game in no time at all.

ABOUT ROBIN HOOD, THE RESCUE OF LADY MARIAN

The game involves the story of Robin Hood, who is controlled by the player. You will need to progress up the ladders and across the platforms, navigating past enemy guards and traversing traps that are lying in wait. The game is completed when Robin reaches the top-left platform where the Sheriff and Marian are waiting for him. The story for Robin Hood goes as follows:

    The evil Sheriff of Nottingham has kidnapped the love of your life Lady
    Marian, and it's your task to rescue her. Unfortunately, soldiers and
    traps stand in your way! As you steal from the rich and give to the poor,
    you must collect as much gold as you can!

This game takes a similar form as the first and second game, in that it has been separated into three easy-to-distinguish frames:

The Main Screen: From this screen, we will launch the title frame of our game, Robin Hood.

The Game Screen: This is where the player will begin to play the game.

The Hi-Score Screen: Once the player has run out of lives, the Hi-Scores frame will appear, allowing the players to enter their score.

Again, all of the games graphics and objects have been premade and placed into a library file to speed up the creation of the game, and to allow you to start programming rather than draw images. We now need to describe the game in more detail so you understand what is going to happen in each stage.

1. At the start of the game the main menu graphic appears, which displays the Robin Hood background image. The user will press the Spacebar on the keyboard to begin playing the game.
2. The player (Robin) will appear in a forest; pressing the Shift key will make the character jump, and he can be moved by using the arrow keys. A number of obstacles and enemy soldiers are placed in the play area, and if they touch Robin, he will lose a life.
3. Once the player either has lost all three lives or has reached the platform where Marian and the Sheriff are located, the game will end and take the player to the High-Scores screen. If the players have a high score, they will be asked to enter their name.
4. The players will be able to exit the Hi-Scores screen by pressing the Spacebar, which will take them back to the main menu.

Before you begin to make the game, you can check out the final game on the companion CD-ROM. The executable is located in the \Game3 folder, and the file to run is called "robinhood.exe."

ON THE CD

Graphics Library–Robin Hood

ON THE CD To access the ready-made graphics, point the Library toolbar to the correct folder on the CD-ROM. The library files for "Robin Hood" can be found in the folder CD-ROM\Game3\Lib.

1. Right-click on the left pane of the Library toolbar to reveal a pop-up menu.
2. Click on the New option. A dialog box will appear, allowing you to browse for the library file we need for this game. Browse the list until you see your CD-ROM.
3. Once you have found your CD-ROM drive, find the folder \Game3\Lib. Then, click on the OK button, enter a library name ("Robin Hood"), and then press Enter.
4. You are now ready to move down into the library and drag any files onto the play area.

ROBIN HOOD–INITIAL SETUP

As with the other games, we need to set up the frames you will be working with throughout this game development: one for the main screen, one for the game, and one for the Hi-Score table.

Creating the Frames

First, you need to create the three frames that will be used in the game.

1. Start *TGF2*, and then click on the File | New option in the menu. This will create the initial game program and its first frame.
2. Highlight the text "Application 1," which is the top item in the Workspace toolbar. Right-click on it and select Insert | New Frame from the pop-up menu. This will create a second frame called "Frame 2," type in frame 2's real name, "Game." Press Enter to accept the new frame name.
3. Insert another frame and rename it "Hi-Scores."
4. Now, rename frame 1 and call it "Main Menu."

Changing Application Settings

You now need to make some application settings changes as you did in the first two games, to show the game's name in the menu bar and to prevent the player from maximizing the game screen.

1. Left mouse click on the text "Application 1," right-click and choose Re-name, type in the text "Robin Hood," and then press the Enter key.
2. You will see the Application properties in the Properties window; click on the Window tab, and then tick the No Maximize box.
3. Save your current progress by clicking on the Save button; as this is the first time you have saved this game, you will need to type in a name and a location for the file.

ROBIN HOOD–MAIN MENU

The first thing you need to complete, as with the other two games, is the main menu, which of course is the first screen the player will see when running the game.

1. Double-click on the text "Main Menu" in the Workspace toolbar to bring up the Frame Editor in the right-hand pane.
2. We now need to locate the objects in the Library that we intend to use within our game, so double-click on the text "Robin Hood" in the Library toolbar, and then on the text "RobinHood_Lib" to bring up the specific levels (Main Menu, Game, and Hi-Scores).

We are now ready to begin building our Main Menu, which will consist of four components: the background image, a title image, a text object that tells the user to press a certain key on the keyboard, and another graphic item to complete the look and feel of the menu. We now need to place them on the play area:

3. Double-click on the text "Main" in the Library toolbar to reveal the four items we need to use in this level.
4. Drag and drop the object Backdrop onto the play area. Center it exactly in the frame by holding down the left mouse button, or by right-clicking on the item and choosing Align in Frame | Horz Center and Align in Frame | Vert Center from the pop-up menu.
5. Drag the Title item from the library and place it on the frame. Single-click on the Title to highlight it and to display its properties in the Properties toolbar. In the Properties toolbar for the Title object, click on the Size/Position tab. For the X and Y position, type in 73 and 144, respectively, to place it in the position we require.
6. Drag the Quick object from the library and drop it onto the frame at the bottom of the screen. To place it in the correct position, single left-click on the object, and then click on the Size/Position tab in the Object Properties toolbar. Type in the X and Y coordinates as 0 and 446, respectively.

7. Finally, drag the String object from the library onto the play area. The item needs to be placed at the X, Y coordinates of 245 and 455 (remember, you can do this by accessing the object properties and clicking on the Size/Position tab).

8. If you run the frame, your final placements of items on the main menu frame should look like that of Figure 15.1.

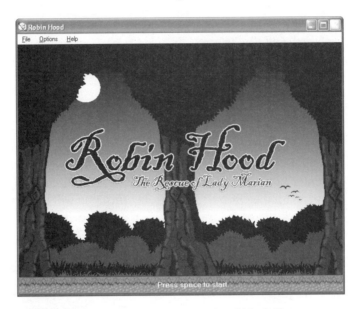

FIGURE 15.1   What the main menu should look like. ©Jason Darby 2005.
Reprinted with permission.

ROBIN HOOD—THE GAME SCREEN

ON THE CD

The game screen contains the majority of the objects used within the game, and will take the longest to create. To save some time, a game file on the companion CD-ROM contains all the objects already in their correct positions in the \Game3 folder. The file is called "Robin-template," you can open it using the File | Open option from within TGF2.

To manually place each object:

1. First, we need to locate the correct library objects; currently, we can see the main menu items. In the Library toolbar, click on the upward-pointing green arrow to move up a level; the three frames will be listed. Double-click on the Game text to display all the objects.

2. Drag the Backdrop object onto the frame, and position it exactly in the frame by dragging it with the mouse, or by right-clicking on it and selecting Align in Frame | Horz Center and Align in Frame | Vert Center.

3. Drag the Platform object onto the play area, and left-click on it to display its properties in the Object Properties toolbar. Click on the Size/Position tab in the Object Properties toolbar, and for the X and Y coordinates, type in 0 and 446, respectively.

We've covered how to access the Objects Properties to precisely place an object on the play area a number of times throughout the book. From this point forward, you will only be asked to place an object at its X and Y coordinate, and not told how access the properties. If you forgot how to access it, look back through the book for examples.

4. On the Platform object you just positioned, right-click on it and select Duplicate from the pop-up menu. When the Duplicate dialog box appears, enter 1 for rows and 16 for columns (everything else should be 0), and then press on the OK button. By doing this, you will have created a floor across the bottom of the frame area. An example of what the entry in the dialog box should look like appears in Figure 15.2.

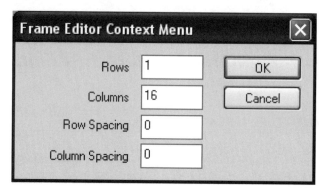

FIGURE 15.2 Duplicating an object a number of times.

5. Drag the Lives object onto the play area and position it at 3, 448.
6. Drag the Score object onto the play area and position it at 628, 477.
7. Drag the Player_Robin object onto the play area and position it at 107, 446.
8. Drag eight Platform-left objects onto the play area, and position them at the following coordinates: (36, 330), (221, 344), (528, 353), (567, 353), (567, 239), (322, 238), (528, 120), (408, 63), and (180, 112).

The best way to place multiple items on the frame is to drag them just outside the frame, so you can see which ones still need to be placed correctly.

9. Drag 23 Platform objects onto the play area (just outside the frame), and then position them at the coordinates (0, 73), (41, 73), (211, 112), (252, 112), (293, 112), (439, 63), (559, 120), (600, 120), (–1, 240), (40, 240), (81, 240), (122, 240), (150, 240), (353, 238), (394, 238), (435, 238), (598, 239), (67, 330), (252, 344), (293, 344), (334, 344), (559, 353), and (600, 353).

10. Drag seven Platform-right objects onto the play area (again just outside the frame), and position each at the coordinates (82, 72), (334, 112), (480, 63), (191, 240), (476, 238), (108, 330), and (375, 344).

11. Drag 11 Collectible_Gold objects onto the play area and then position at the coordinates (168. 437), (192, 437), (216, 437), (240, 437), (138, 230), (165, 230), (190, 230), (448, 228), (426, 54), (453, 54), and (480, 54).

12. We need five Collectible_jewel objects in positions (188, 102), (556, 110), (384, 228), (240, 334), and (615, 436).

13. Place Destroy Painful Stopper 1 at (593, 321), and Destroy Painful Stopper 2 at (8, 208).

14. Place Painful Stopper 1 at (111, 292), and Painful Stopper 2 at (416, 200).

15. Place Badguy 1 at (20, 240), and Badguy 2 at (346, 112).

16. Place 12 Ladder objects at the following coordinates: (58, 222), (58, 244), (58, 288), (352, 327), (352, 360), (352, 404), (545, 338), (545, 360), (545, 404), (596, 109), (596, 153), and (596, 197).

17. Drag Lady Marian onto the play area and place at (13, 22), and then Evil Prince at (43, 14).

18. Place Trap at (270, 305), and another Trap at (408, 407).

If you run the game at this point, you will notice that the two enemy soldiers automatically run left and right. This is because path movement has already been applied to each object.

19. Drag Barrel to (269, –29) and another Barrel to (564, –29).

20. You have now completed the placement of all the objects for the game frame. Make sure you save your work before moving on to the last frame, the Hi-Scores. If you run the frame, your game frame will look like Figure 15.3.

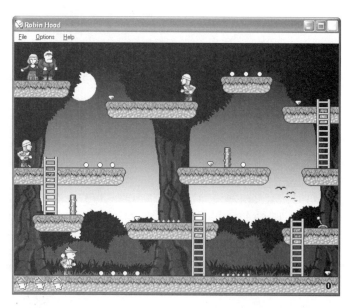

FIGURE 15.3   The game frame when running should look like this.
©Jason Darby 2005. Reprinted with permission.

ROBIN HOOD—HI-SCORES

We now need to place the items for the Hi-Score frame to complete the object placement for all three frames. Once this process has been completed, you will then be able to begin the programming for the game.

1. Double-click on the text "Hi-Scores" in the Workspace toolbar to bring up the blank frame.
2. We now need to locate the correct library files for this frame, so double-click on the up-pointing green arrow in the Library toolbar to see all the frames, and then double-click on the text "Hi-Scores."
3. Drag the Quick Backdrop object onto the play area and center it in the middle of the frame.
4. Place the Bg extra object at the location (543, −39).
5. Place Bg-horizont object at (0, 180).
6. Drag Tree to (−185, 0).
7. Drag the String object to (286, 449).
8. Place Title at (180, 25).
9. Finally, drag the Hi-Scores object onto the play area and place it at the co-ordinates (242, 195).

You have completed the placement of all the required objects for the Hi-Score frame; when running the frame, it should look like Figure 15.4.

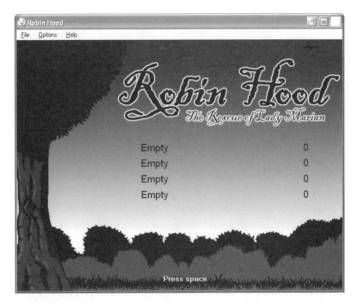

FIGURE 15.4   Layout of the Hi-Scores frame. ©Jason Darby 2005.
Reprinted with permission.

ROBIN HOOD–PROGRAMMING

ON THE CD

We are now ready to begin programming this game; as with the first two games, the Main Menu and Hi-Scores frames are the easiest to program and require very little code. If you have any trouble with the code, or don't understand the explanation, you can compare your work with the completed source code version contained on the companion CD-ROM. The source code (filename "robinhood") for "Robin Hood" can be found in the Game3 folder under the directory "\fullsource."

Programming the Main Menu

The first of the three frames is the main menu, and is the starting point of the game for the player. From this screen, the player can only play the game or exit it. The String object placed earlier onto the play area advises the user to press the Spacebar to continue, and this is the only bit of required code for this frame.

    1. Double-click on the text "Main Menu" in the Workspace toolbar to take you to the first frame.

2. Click on the Event Editor icon in the toolbar to access the area where you will need to enter your code (currently, there is no code assigned, so you will only have one line, "New Condition").

3. Click on the text "New Condition" to begin entering the required code. When the New Condition dialog box appears, right-click on the The Mouse pointer and Keyboard object to bring up the pop-up menu. Select The Keyboard, and then Upon Pressing a Key, at which point a dialog box will appear asking you to press a key. Press the Spacebar to record the condition into the Event Editor, which will now say "Upon Pressing the Space Bar."

4. With this condition, TGF2 will only do something when the condition is true, which is when the user presses the Spacebar. Currently, the condition would be true on pressing the key, but as there are no actions, the program would just continue without any reaction. We now need to tell the program to go to frame 2 when the player presses this key.

5. Move to the right of the condition you just entered, and right-click when you are in the box directly below Storyboard Controls (which looks like a chessboard and a knight). From the pop-up menu, select Jump to Frame, and from the dialog that appears, double-click on Frame 2—Game.

6. You can now run the game (Test Application) to see that pressing the Spacebar moves the program to the game level.

Programming the Game

Now that the main menu points the player to the game frame, we are ready to begin programming this part of the game. As the code for this section of the game is longer than the Main Menu and Hi-Scores, you may want to save your work often so you can come back to it later if you want to take a break. The amount of code required to write for the game is less than you would need to do if you were writing in a traditional programming language. The reason for this is that when using TGF's built-in engines (e.g., the picture/animation editor, path and player movement), the basic skeleton of the game can be created very quickly without any code.

Remember, you can consult the final source code on the companion CD-ROM if you get stuck.

Frame Initialization

At the start of the frame, we need to initialize the players' score and the number of lives we want them to have. In this case, the score will be set to zero, and the number of lives to three.

1. Double-click on the text "Game" in the Workspace toolbar to take you to the second frame.
2. Click on the Event Editor icon in the toolbar to access the area where you will need to enter your code (currently, there is no code assigned, so you will only have one line "New Condition").
3. Click on the text "New Condition" to begin entering the required code. When the New Condition dialog box appears, right-click on the Storyboard Controls object and select Start of Frame from the pop-up menu.
4. Move to the right of this condition until you are directly below the Player 1 object (the image looks like a joystick), and then right-click on the blank box to add an action. From the pop-up menu, select Score, Set Score. When the Expression Evaluator appears, leave the default 0 in the box and click on OK to save the information to the action. Right-click again on the area directly under the Player 1 option, and this time select Number of Lives, Set Number of Lives. In the Expression Evaluator, type in the number "3" and then click OK.

Basic Player Events

If you run the game now, you will find that the character Robin can leave the left and right sides of the frame. As this is a single frame game with no scrolling, we need to stop Robin from leaving the screen.

1. Insert a comment line called "Basic Player Events." To create a comment line, right-click on the number "2" and select Insert | A Comment from the pop-up menu. Type in the text, and then click the OK button.
2. The New Condition line will move to line 3; click on it. Right-click on the Player_Robin object, select Collisions, and then select Backdrop from the pop-up menu. Move to the right of this condition, and when you are directly under the Player_Robin object, right-click and select Movement and then Stop.
3. Create a new condition for a new event by clicking on the "New Condition" text. When the Object dialog appears, select the Player_Robin object again by right-clicking on it. From the pop-up menu, choose Position and then Test position of Player_Robin. The Test Position… dialog appears; click on the left and right out-pointing arrows (called "Leaves in the Left" and "Leaves in the Right"). Click on the OK button to save this to the condition. Move to the right of this condition until you are directly under the Player_Robin object, right-click, and choose Movement and then Stop. Your conditions will now look like Figure 15.5.

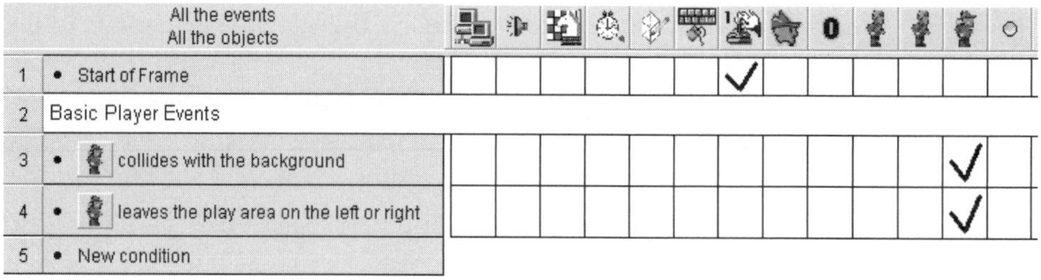

	All the events / All the objects										0				○
1	• Start of Frame								✓						
2	Basic Player Events														
3	• 🧍 collides with the background													✓	
4	• 🧍 leaves the play area on the left or right													✓	
5	• New condition														

FIGURE 15.5 Current conditions.

Activate Levers

The levers in the game are activated when Robin walks over them; the benefit to the players is that doing do removes the spinning spikes from the screen, allowing them to carry on without losing a life.

1. Create a comment line called "Activate Lever 1."
2. Create a new event under this comment line with two conditions in it. To create the first, click on the New Condition text. Then, from the dialog box right-click on the Player_Robin object, select Collisions, and then select Overlapping Another Object. A dialog box will appear, and you will need to choose Destroy Painful Stopper 1. To add another condition in the same event, right-click on the text that now is in event line 6, and select Insert from the pop-up menu. When the dialog box appears, right-click on Destroy Painful Stopper 1, and then choose Direction, Compare Direction of Destroy Painful Stopper 1. The Direction dialog box will appear. Untick the arrow that is pointing to the right (in direction 0), tick the box directly to the left (direction 16), and then click on OK.
3. Create another comment line on event line 7 called "Activate Lever 2."
4. Create another event with two conditions as you did in item number 2, but this time, replace Destroy Painful Stopper 1 with Destroy Painful Stopper 2. The created comment lines and events will now look like Figure 15.6.

The first of the two event lines checks to see if the player has walked into a lever, and that it hasn't already been previously activated (by using its current direction). Once it has found this event to be true, it will play a sound, and then change the animation of the lever from left to right to show that it has been set. Finally, it will destroy the Painful Stopper 1 device. The second event will do the same actions, but for the second stopper and lever.

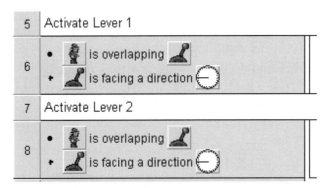

FIGURE 15.6 Events and conditions for activating the levers.

1. For the first of the two events we just created (on event line 6), move to the right until you are directly under the Sound object. Right-click, choose Samples, Play Sample, and then when the Sound dialog box appears, press the Browse button next to From a File. Locate the folder "\game3\sounds" on the companion CD-ROM, click on Lever2, and then click on the Open button.

ON THE CD

2. For event line 7, we need the same action under the Sound object, so drag the action to this line.

3. Going back to event line 6, move to the right until you are directly under Painful Stopper 1, and then right-click and select Destroy. On the same event line, move to the right until you are directly under Destroy Painful Stopper 1, right-click, and choose Direction, Select Direction.... When the Direction dialog box appears, leave the arrow pointing to the right (the default direction), and then click on the OK button.

4. Now, on event line 7, move to the right until you are directly under Painful Stopper 2, and then right-click and select Destroy. On the same event line, move to the right until you are directly under Destroy Painful Stopper 2, right-click, and choose Direction, Select Direction... .When the Direction dialog box appears, leave the arrow pointing to the right (the default direction), and then click on the OK button.

Collectibles

To make the game more of a challenge than just rescuing Marian, and to provide a way to gain points, the player can collect coins and jewels along the way. Collecting coins will earn 10 points, and jewels are worth 30 points.

1. Create a new comment line that says "Grabbing Collectibles."

2. Click on New Condition to create a new condition and event. From the dialog box, right-click on Player_Robin, and then select Collisions, Another Object. A dialog box will appear; click on the Collectible_gold object, and click on the OK button to save the condition.

3. Create a new event and condition on the next available event line (line 11) using the same process, but choose Collectible_Jewel. You should now have a set of events as shown in Figure 15.7.

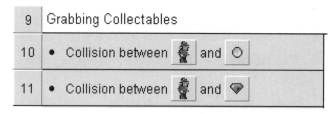

FIGURE 15.7 Two events for collecting jewels.

4. Move to the right of both events and add an action to play a sample called "Blip" (right-click, Samples, Play Sample). Once you have browsed for the file and located it on the companion CD-ROM, you can drag the action to the second of the two events.

5. Move across until you are under the Player 1 object on the first of the two events. Right-click and select Score, Add to Score. When the Expression Evaluator appears, type in the number 10 and then click on the OK button. Moving to the right again until you are under the Collectible_gold object, right-click, and select Destroy.

6. For the second of the two events (line 11), do the same, but set the Add to Score to 30, as the jewels are worth more than coins. Move to the right and set the action Destroy under Collectible_Jewel.

Overlapping Events

Next, we need to check when the player stands over a trap or runs into an angry guard, at which point Robin will lose a life and then flash. The flashing signifies that Robin won't lose a life while he is flashing, giving the player time to move him out of danger. The next set of events you are going to write will need to run some code that is contained within a group. You will not be able to tell your events to enable a group unless that group is already created, so for the following events to be programmed, we need to create a blank group.

1. Right-click on the last event number (number 12) and select Insert, Insert a Group of Events. The Group dialog box will appear; enter the text "Player

Blinking," and then untick Active when Frame Starts to ensure it does not run automatically when the frame begins. The dialog box should look like Figure 15.8. Click on the OK button to continue.

FIGURE 15.8 The Group dialog box.

2. Now that we have created the group, we can create a link to it in events outside it (you cannot enable something that isn't created). Starting from the very last event, right-click on the event number, and then insert three different comment lines: "Lose a life," "Negated Conditions," and "Blinking Player."
3. These text comments are there to remind you what the subsequent events do, in case you come back to the program after a period of time and cannot remember what the code does. The three comments tell us that the next set of events are to do with the player losing a life, and stops the player from losing a life if he is blinking (just lost a life). For this part of the game, we need to create seven events, and a number of actions will be the same for each event, which means we can program it faster by dragging the relevant action to the next event line.
4. Click on the "New Condition" text in the last line to bring up the Condition dialog box. Find and right-click on the Player_Robin object, and then select Collision, Another Object from the pop-up menu. When the dialog box appears, select Painful Stopper 1, and then click on the OK button. We need to add two further conditions to the same event, so right-click on the condition you just added and select Insert. From the dialog box, right-click on Player_Robin and then choose Collisions, Overlapping a Backdrop. You will need to negate this condition, so right-click on it and select Negate

from the pop-up menu. We need to add one more condition to this event, so right-click on the newly negated condition and select Insert from the pop-up menu. Right-click on the Special object, and select Group of Events, Check for Activation. Then from the Group Selection dialog box, highlight the (1) Player Blinking line and then click the OK button. This condition also needs to be negated, so right-click on it, and from the pop-up menu, select Negate. Your event will now look like Figure 15.9.

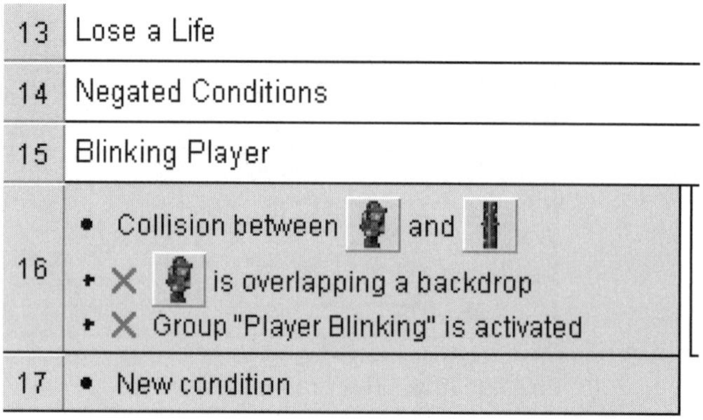

13	Lose a Life
14	Negated Conditions
15	Blinking Player
16	• Collision between 👤 and 🚩 • ✕ 👤 is overlapping a backdrop • ✕ Group "Player Blinking" is activated
17	• New condition

FIGURE 15.9 Three conditions, with two negated.

5. You now need to create a new event with the same three conditions, but the first will be based on Painful Stopper 2. A quick way to do this is to click on the event we just created, which will highlight the line. Then, copy the event by holding down the Ctrl key and then pressing the letter "c." This will copy the event into memory; to copy it, click on the next event line (which will be blank and have the words "New condition" on the same line), hold down the Ctrl key, and then press the "v" key to paste it. You will now have two identical events, but we need to do one more thing. On the second event, double-click on the Painful Stopper 1 object, and when the dialog box appears, find and then double-click on the Painful Stopper 2 object. An example of how the two events should look can be seen in Figure 15.10.

6. For the third event, we can do a similar process to save programming time. Copy and paste the last create event line, double-click on Painful Stopper 2, and when the dialog box appears, pick the Trap Object, and then click on OK. This third event will look like Figure 15.11.

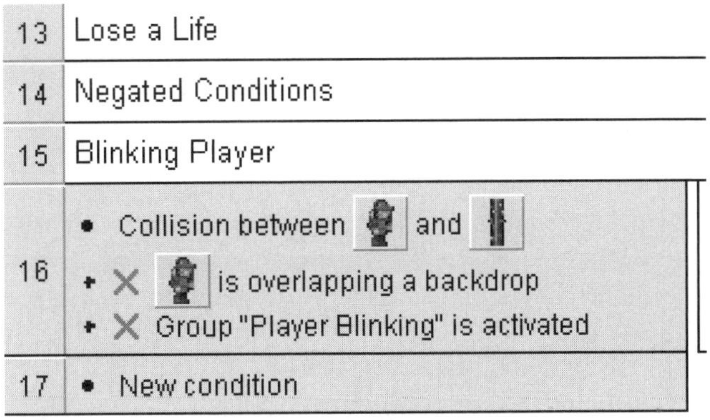

13	Lose a Life
14	Negated Conditions
15	Blinking Player
16	• Collision between 👤 and ▮ • ✕ 👤 is overlapping a backdrop • ✕ Group "Player Blinking" is activated
17	• New condition

FIGURE 15.10   Copying and pasting events for quickness.

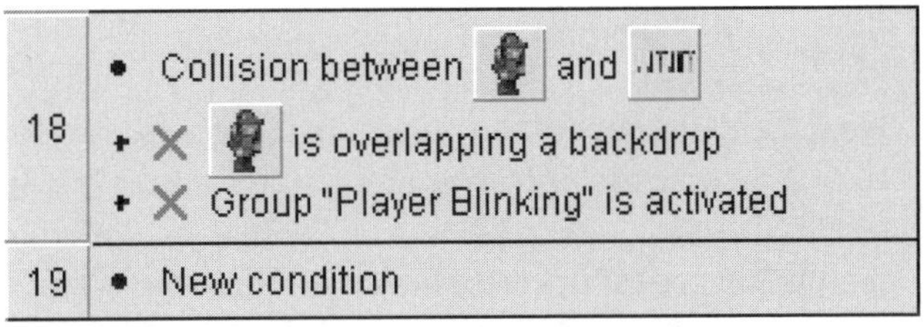

| 18 | • Collision between 👤 and ▥
• ✕ 👤 is overlapping a backdrop
• ✕ Group "Player Blinking" is activated |
| 19 | • New condition |

FIGURE 15.11   Player hits the trap object.

7. Again using the copy and paste method, we can quickly make similar events. Copy the last event we created, and paste it four times to create four new event lines.

8. For the first of the four events, double-click on the Trap object and replace it with Badguy 1, replace the Trap object on the second event line with Badguy 2, the Trap on the third event with Barrel 1, and the Trap object on the fourth event with Barrel 2. On these four events, we don't need the condition "Player_Robin is overlapping a backdrop." Therefore, right-click on this condition in the four events, and then select Delete to remove it. The last four events should look like Figure 15.12.

9. There will now be seven events that deal with the player hitting an object, which will cost the player a life. The negated Group Player Blinking is activated and prevents the player from losing another life while he is flashing. The actions to reduce the lives by one will only run on the condition that Robin isn't flashing. It's now time to create the actions for the seven events.

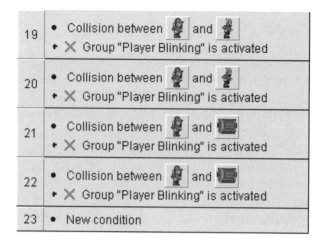

FIGURE 15.12 Collisions between the Player, Barrels, and Badguys.

10. Go back to the first of the seven events you created for the overlapping section. Move across until you are directly under the Special Conditions object, right-click, select Group of Events, Activate, and when the Activate dialog box appears, select (1) Player Blinking. When the player is hit by the painful stopper and isn't already blinking, it will run the code within the Blinking group.

11. We need this action in all seven of the events we created. To do this, drag the tick item to the box below, release, and then do this until all seven boxes contain a tick. You will now have seven ticks as shown in Figure 15.13.

12. When the player hits an object that will cause him to lose a life, we also need to play a sound. On the first of the seven events, move to the right until you are under the Sound object, right-click, select Samples, and then Play Sample. A dialog box will appear; click on the Browse button on the right of the text "From a file." Locate the "Ow" file on the companion CD-ROM under the Game3\sounds folder (you can either double-click on the file, or single-click and then press Open). As with the previous action, drag it to the other six events directly below it.

ON THE CD

13. Go back to the first of the seven events, move to the right until you are directly under the Player 1 object, right-click, and select Number of Lives, Subtract from Number of Lives. The Expression Evaluator appears; type in the number "1" and then click on the OK button. Drag the "Subtract 1 from number of lives" directly down to the six events below it.

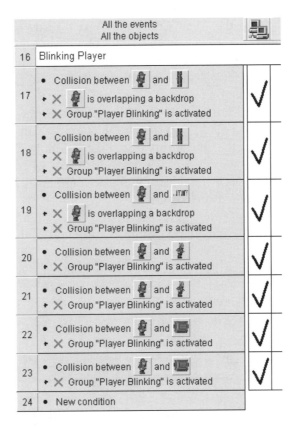

FIGURE 15.13 Dragging of actions across the events.

Player Blinking Group

Now that we have the events all in place to subtract a life every time Robin hits an obstacle or enemy guard, it is time to configure the graphic flashing. This is a very common way in 2D games to signify that the player is invincible for a limited amount of time before he or she can lose health or life again. Previously, we set up the group Player Blinking; we now need to add events to this so when the player loses a life, an action happens.

Find the group Player Blinking as shown in Figure 15.14.

FIGURE 15.14 The Player Blinking group.

1. Click on the "New Condition" text directly under the Player Blinking group. Right-click on the Timer object, and then choose Every from the pop-up menu. When the Timer dialog box appears, remove the 1 from Seconds (by placing a 0 in it), and then enter a 20 in the 1/100 box. Click the OK button to accept the entry. Move to the right of this new event until you are directly under the Player_Robin object. Right-click on the Action box, select Flags, Toggle, enter the number 1 in the Expression Evaluator, and click the OK button to save the action. In the same action box, right-click Choose Alterable Values, Add to, and when the Expression Evaluator appears, leave the value at A, replace the 0 in the Enter Expression box with a 1, and then click on OK.

2. On the next event line, click on the "New Condition" text, and from the dialog box, find Player_Robin. Right-click, and from the pop-up menu, choose Alterable Values, Flags, Is a Flag On. Then in the Expression Evaluator, enter the number "1" and then click on OK. Move to the right of this event until you are directly below Player_Robin, right-click, and choose Visibility, Change Ink Effect. A dialog box will appear, as shown in Figure 15.15. Click on the drop-down arrow, select Inverted, and then click on OK.

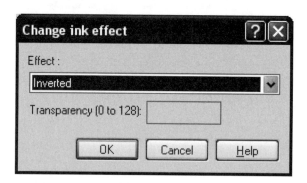

FIGURE 15.15 Ink Effects dialog.

3. On the next event line. click on "New Condition" and right-click on Player_Robin, Alterable Values, Flags, Is a Flag Off. The Expression Evaluator will then appear; type in the number "1" and then click on OK. Move to the right of this new condition until you are directly under Player_Robin, right-click, select Visibility, Change Ink Effect. Then from the dialog box, pick None, and click on OK.

4. Click on New Condition, then right-click on Player_Robin, choose Alterable Values, Compare to One of the Alterable Values. When the Expression Evaluator appears, replace the 0 in the Enter Expression box with an 8, and

then click OK. Move to the right of this condition until you are directly under Player_Robin, and then right-click on the Action box, and select Alterable Values, Set from the pop-up menu. The Expression Evaluator appears; leave the default settings, and click on OK.

5. Move to the left until you are directly under the Special Conditions object, right-click, and choose Group of Events, Deactivate, and then from the dialog box, select (1) Player Blinking. Your conditions will look like Figure 15.16.

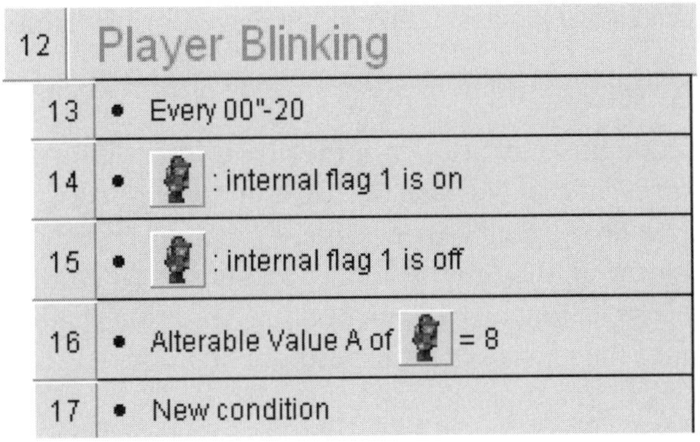

12	Player Blinking	
13	•	Every 00"-20
14	•	🧍 : internal flag 1 is on
15	•	🧍 : internal flag 1 is off
16	•	Alterable Value A of 🧍 = 8
17	•	New condition

FIGURE 15.16 Events for making the player blink.

This group of code is activated when the player hits a certain object, an enemy soldier, or spikes and is not already flashing. The first thing the code does is set a flag on and then off (toggle) every 0.20 of a second, and adds 1 to an Alterable value each time the event is run. The program will then either set the Ink Effect to None or to Invert, depending on what the flag is set to. Finally, once the Alterable value has reached eight (so it will have flashed on and off four times each), it will then set the Alterable value to zero and then disable the group, allowing it to run again correctly the next time the player hits an object.

Game Over—No Lives

Now that the code is in place to reduce the players' lives by one each time they hit a specific group of objects, we now need to tell TGF2 what to do when the lives are at zero. For this game, we need to tell the program to jump to frame 3 so that the players can be asked to enter a high score if they have achieved one, and to see the top four scores.

1. Go to the last event in the Event Editor, and then insert the comment "Game Over."

2. Click on the "New Condition" text, right-click on the Player 1 object, and from the pop-up menu, select When Number of Lives Reaches 0. Move to the right of this condition until you are directly under Storyboard Controls, and right-click on the empty Action box. Select Jump to Frame, and when the dialog box appears, choose Frame 3—Hi-Scores, and then click on OK.

3. The program will now jump to the Hi-Scores frame whenever the player reaches zero lives. It will then automatically check to see if a high score has been achieved and then ask the player for his name.

Game Over–Success

We have configured what to do if the player loses all three lives, but now we need to create an event that will take the player to the Hi-Scores frame on completing the level. This is only a single-level game, so the player only needs to jump onto the same platform as the Sheriff and Lady Marian to complete the game. We will achieve this by setting up a zone-checking condition that will run the code to go to frame 3 once the player enters a specific area on the screen.

1. On the last line of the events, create a comment called "Rescue Complete."
2. Click on the "New Condition" text, select the Player_Robin object, and then from the pop-up menu, choose Pick or Count, Compare to the Number of Player_Robin Objects in a Zone. A Zone dialog box will appear (as shown in Figure 15.17); type in the coordinates as shown (first set of boxes [0 , 75] and second [11, 78]), and then click OK to continue.

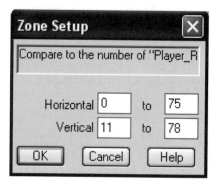

FIGURE 15.17 Configuring the Zone Location Properties.

3. Once you have entered the Zone Properties, an Expression Evaluator appears. Type in the number "1" in the Expression to Compare With box,

and then click on OK.

2. Move to the right of this event until you are directly under the Sound object, right-click, and pick Samples, Play Sample. Then from the dialog box, click on the Browse button next to the text "From a file." Search for the file Ending2, which is located on the companion CD-ROM in the \Game3\sounds folder. Right-click on the Sound object again, and following the same process, add the sound sample Yeeha 2.

3. Move to the right until you are directly under the Storyboard Controls object, right-click, select Jump to Frame, and when the dialog box appears, choose Frame 3—Hi-Scores, and then click on OK.

4. Now when the player enters the area in which the Sheriff and Marian are located, it will play a short tune, and a Yeeha sample, and then ask for the player's score. Once the score has been entered, the player will be taken to frame 3 to see the Scores table.

PROGRAMMING THE HI-SCORES

The final part of the game is to create code to take the players back from the Hi-Scores table to the Main Menu, thus allowing them to play again. This requires only one line of code, and is very similar to the code used in the Main Menu to move from frame 1 to frame 2.

1. Double-click on the text "Hi-Scores" in the Workspace toolbar to take you to the third frame.

2. Click on the Event Editor icon in the toolbar to access the area where you will need to enter your code (currently, there is no code assigned, so you will only have one line, "New Condition").

3. Click on the text "New Condition" to begin entering the required code. When the New Condition dialog box appears, right-click on the The Mouse pointer and Keyboard object to bring up the pop-up menu. Select The Keyboard and then Upon Pressing a Key, at which point, a dialog box will appear asking you to press a key. Press the Spacebar to record the condition into the Event Editor, which will now say "Upon Pressing the Space Bar."

4. Move to the right of the condition you just entered, and right-click when you are in the box directly below Storyboard Controls (which looks like a chessboard and a knight). From the pop-up menu, select Jump to Frame, and from the dialog that appears, double-click on Frame 1—Main Menu.

SUMMARY

You have now completed your third style of game, the platform game. This game contains many ideas that you can use in your own programs. Once the player gets used to a level, it won't take him long to get to Lady Marian. Therefore, it is important to make a wide range of levels in your games with varying degrees of difficulty. This can be achieved very easily by changing the movement properties of the enemy guards or the barrels. In this game, we only have two barrels falling at a set speed and in a particular direction; you could in later levels create more barrels or alter the falling speed. Using barrels in games is a good way to make a level harder and have the player concentrate on more than just getting to a certain location. This was achieved very successfully in the game *Donkey Kong*®, in which the player had to get to the top of the screen to rescue a certain character. Donkey Kong would throw barrels at specific times, and the player would need to jump over them to avoid losing a life. As the game proceeded, more barrels would be thrown and at different speeds and directions, thus making each level less predictable and more challenging. Using the same graphics, but creating a different path movement or speed (which just involves editing the movement properties), you can change the difficulty of a level without any further programming. This makes *TGF2* very good for creating levels quickly and easily without needing additional amounts of programming to get it working.

16 Alien Invaders

In This Chapter

- Retro Game Making
- Alien Invaders Game
- Alien Invaders—Programming

ON THE CD

Retro gaming has become popular again, and no one really knows why game players suddenly have the urge to play games with basic graphics and sound. One reason might be that people want to relive the "glory days" of computer games, when the story behind the games was the most important aspect. Today, there are emulators, devices that plug into TVs, and updated versions of the old classics that run on PCs. This chapter discusses different retro-type games, and how to replicate them in TGF2. Additionally, there is a full code example of an Invaders clone (filename "aliens") in the retro folder on the companion CD-ROM for you to view and learn from.

RETRO GAME MAKING

Creating new versions of old games from the last 10 or 20 years has become a big growth area in the hobby game-making community, and there are numerous Web sites, downloads, and examples of how to create a modern version of a classic from hardware that is no longer available. Even those few companies that still exist today have decided to get in the act and release updates of there own back catalogues; perfect examples of this are Atari and Sega.

There are generally two areas of retro game making available to anyone wanting to make a classic game:

Remake: A remake of the original game, keeping the same levels, sounds, graphic look and feel, and playability. Generally, no areas are improved, except that the program will work on the latest hardware (be it PC, Mac, or something else).

Update: Taking the original game and making new graphics, sounds, and levels, and perhaps changing the controls to make it more playable.

These two options can be mixed; for example, you could make a game that has both variants included so people can choose the original style of game or your updated version.

The three main games in this book all show examples of game types that fit very well into the retro arena. All that has to be done is take each of the games and apply the graphics and playability of the game you want to make. The game "The Lab," for example, is similar to a game called *Arkanoid*, which involved bricks and a bat (also called a paddle); the game "Robin Hood" could easily be amended to represent *Donkey Kong* (platform, barrels falling); and "Amazing Fighter Pilot" could easily be converted into *1944®* (scrolling fighter-plane game). The code is there for you to take and tweak to fit many different types of retro games very easily.

ALIEN INVADERS GAME

To give you an idea of how easy it is to create a simple retro-type game, we will now make a *Space Invaders®* clone. *Space Invaders* involves waves of alien ships, and a single player ship defending Earth (or some planet or base). In the following game example, we again only have a single level, but it shows all the main items you need to think about in your retro game. *Space Invaders* is one of the most popular retro games, and a quick look with an online search engine will show many versions of it all around the world, to download for the PC, Mac, mobile, and to play on the Internet (in various platforms, such as Java, Flash, etc.).

Again, for simplicity, the game has three separate frames:

The Main Screen: The starting screen for the game, from which the player will press the Spacebar to launch the game.

The Game Screen: The player will use the left and right arrow keys to move the spaceship, and the Shift key to fire the weapon.

The Hi-Score Screen: Once the player has run out of lives or destroyed all of the aliens, the Hi-Scores frame will appear, allowing the player to enter his or her name on the leaderboard.

All of the game graphics and screens have been premade, but are really just a shell for you to replace with your own, as the game is only used here to serve as an example of how to make a retro game. Additionally, to make programming easier (and write less code), two qualifier groups have been created, the first for all of the alien invaders, and the second to represent the player's bases (defenses).

Remember, creating qualifying groups allows you to apply code to all items in a group, either as a condition or as an action, thereby reducing the amount of code to write.

The completed version of the game can be found on the companion CD-ROM; the executable is located in the \Retro folder, and the file is called "Invaders.exe."

Graphics Library—Alien Invaders

To access the ready-made graphics and objects for Alien Invaders, point the Library toolbar to the correct folder on the CD-ROM. The library files for the Alien Invaders game can be found in the folder \Retro\Lib.

1. Right-click on the left pane of the Library toolbar to reveal a pop-up menu.
2. Click on the New option; a dialog box will appear allowing you to browse for the library file we need for this game. Browse until you see your CD-ROM drive.
3. Next, find the folder \Retro\Lib, click on the OK button, enter a library name (in this case, "Invaders"), and then press Enter.
4. You are now ready to move down into the library and drag any files onto the play area.

Alien Invaders—Initial Setup

We now need to create the three frames we will be using in the Alien Invaders game, which will be the same as the three games we already created.

1. Start TGF2, and then click on the File | New option in the menu. This will create the initial program and its first frame.
2. Highlight the text "Application 1," which is the topmost item in the Work-space toolbar. Right-click on it and select Insert | New Frame from the pop-up menu. This will create a second frame called "Frame 2." You will notice that it is already selected ready to be amended, so type in Frame 2's real name, "Game," and then press Enter to accept the new frame name.
3. Insert another frame and rename it "Hi-Scores."
4. Now, rename Frame 1 and call it "Main Menu."

Changing Application Settings

As with the other three games, some basic application settings need to be amended.

1. Left mouse click on the text "Application 1," right-click, choose Rename, type in the text "Alien Invaders," and then press the Enter key.
2. You will see the Application Properties in the Properties window; click on the Window tab, and then tick the No Maximize box.

Alien Invaders—Main Menu

We now need to set up the relevant items on the screen for the look and feel of the game. To complete the first frame, the Main Menu:

1. Double-click on the frame Main Menu to ensure you have the correct frame on screen. Then, click on the "Alien Invaders "text in the Library toolbar to open the library file in the right pane. Now, click on the file alienslib in the right pane to reveal all three frames used in this game.
2. Double-click on the frame called "Main Menu" to display all of the objects that are to be used in this game (for this frame, it is five items).
3. Drag the object Backdrop Object 4 onto the play area and then place it in the middle of the frame, either by dragging or by using the right mouse button and selecting Align in Frame | Horz Center, and then Align in Frame | Vert Center.
4. Drag the object Space Console onto the play area, and align it vertically and horizontally.

5. Drag Formatted Text onto the play area and place it at the coordinates 228, 55.
6. Drag Formatted Text 2 onto the play area and place it at the coordinates 279, 412.
7. Finally, drag Formatted Text 3 to the coordinates 197, 131.

Alien Invaders—The Game Screen

It's time to put the game frame together, and for this frame, we need to do something a little different. After placing the 16 different colored aliens, they will need to be duplicated to get a large group of aliens. Remember, duplicated objects do not appear as separate objects in the Event Editor, but as one item.

The first thing we need to do is create the vastness of space and have a black background. There are a number of ways to do so using objects, but the fastest and easiest way is to change the frame color. Each frame can be set to a specific color using the Frame Properties toolbar.

1. Double-click on the text "Game" in the Workspace toolbar to bring up the empty frame. Click on the text "Alien Invaders" in the Workspace toolbar to bring up the Application Properties. On the Settings tab, you will see the option Background color; select the white box next to this, and from the color pop-up, left-click on the color black and your game frame will now go black.

Next, we will place the 16 alien space ships on the screen.

2. Place the following objects in the X, Y coordinates as shown in parentheses: Alien Group 1 (29, 26), Alien Group 2 (58, 26), Alien Group 3 (87, 26), Alien Group 4 (116, 26), Alien Group 5 (145, 26), Alien Group 6 (174, 26), Alien Group 7 (203, 26), Alien Group 8 (232, 26), Alien Group 9 (261, 26), Alien Group 10 (290, 26), Alien Group 11 (319, 26), Alien Group 12 (348, 26), Alien Group 13 (377, 26), Alien Group 14 (406, 26), Alien Group 15 (435, 26), Alien Group 16 (464, 26).

Now, let's place all the other required objects onto the play area.

3. Place the object Small Star Fighter at the coordinates (312, 440), the Current Flag object (34, 515), the Normal object (77, 499), and the Alien Bullet (77, 513).
4. Place the Score object at (625, 472), the Lives object (583, 0), the Active 2 object (20, 0), and the Active 3 object (621, 0).

5. Drag the Backdrop object from the library onto the play area four times (so there are four backdrops on the screen), and place them at the following coordinates (97, 366), (201, 366), (397, 366), and (503, 366), respectively.
6. Drag the Active object onto the playfield four times and place them at the coordinates (97, 366), (201, 366), (397, 366), and (503, 366).

Our final task is the creation of more alien ships. Currently, there is a single row of different colored aliens, but to make the game complete, there needs to be eight in each column. To do this, we need to select the Duplicate command.

7. Right-click on the first alien called "Alien Group 1," and from the pop-up menu, select Duplicate. The Duplicate box will appear. In the boxes, type "Rows equal Eight," "Columns equal One"; the other two items should be zero. An example of what it will look like appears in Figure 16.1. Click on the OK button to create the new aliens onto the play area.

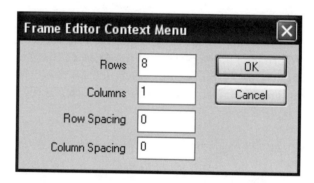

FIGURE 16.1   Duplication box to make more aliens.

8. Now, do the same process for all of the other aliens groups, which create a grid of aliens 16 across and 8 down.

Alien Invaders—The Hi-Scores Frame

Now we have to place the objects on the final frame to create the Hi-Score table, and place text to tell the players that if they want to go back to the start, they will need to press the Spacebar.

1. Double-click on the frame entitled "Hi-Scores" to display the blank frame.
2. Click on the up-pointing green arrow in the Library toolbar to move up a level and to go back to the location that displays the three frames. Double-

click on the item called "Hi-Scores" in the Library toolbar to show the three objects available.

3. Drag the object called "Space style high score" and align it vertically and horizontally within the frame.

4. Place the Hi-Score object onto the frame and position it at the coordinates 160, 136.

5. Finally, place the Formatted Text 2 object at location 277, 451.

6. When using many objects in a game, it is very important to ensure they are placed in the right order, as this decides their overlapping order. In this game, we've put in two lines to see when the aliens are toward the edge of the screen. If these were placed in the incorrect order, you might find that the black lines are in front of the ship and over items. Testing is very important to ensure that this overlapping does not affect the look of your game. To make sure the items are in the correct order, you can use the Bring to Front, Backward, and so forth commands.

7. Right-click on the object Active 2 to bring up the pop-up menu, and select Order | To Back. Right-click on Active 3, and then select Order | To Back.

ALIEN INVADERS—PROGRAMMING

ON THE CD

With all the frames and object now in place, we are ready to begin programming the game. The full source to the completed game is available on the companion CD-ROM in the \fullsource directory.

Programming the Main Menu

For the main menu, we only require a single line of code to make the program check for when the Spacebar is pressed and then move to the game frame.

1. Double-click on the frame Main Menu to load the correct frame.

2. Click on the Event Editor button, and click on the "New Condition" text to start adding the code. From the dialog box, select The Mouse Pointer and Keyboard, and from the pop-up menu, select The Keyboard | Upon Pressing a Key. You will now be asked to press a key, so press the Spacebar.

3. You now have a single event, with a single condition. It requires an action to make it work, so move to the right of this event until you are directly under Storyboard Controls, right-click, and select Jump to Frame. The Frame dialog box will appear; double-click on Frame 2—Game.

Programming the Game

We are now ready to begin programming the game part of "Alien Invaders." The amount of code needed for the game frame is not large (around 43 lines for this section), and the majority of it is self-explanatory. The main area that may cause some confusion is the code attributed to the two Active object lines. These two lines are used to check when an alien (from any column) hits the frame, it then runs its code groups to move the aliens down one block and send them in the opposite direction. There are a number of ways to code this; for example, you could use counters to count down the number of movements the aliens need to make before changing direction. The complexity here is when a column of aliens is destroyed, working out how many additional movements it needs to make. Sometimes, using hidden objects to check for another object is a great way to do these things, making the overall code smaller and easier to understand. Now when a column of aliens is destroyed, the aliens continue moving until the next available alien column hits the hidden line, which can send them back to the opposite direction.

Frame Setup

As with all our prior games, any frame initializations should be placed at the very top of the event list so they run first. We must initialize a number of things: the number of lives a player has needs to be set to three; we need to get the animation effects for the player bases ready; and we must set the counters to the correct numbers so we get the aliens moving from left to right at the start of the frame.

A good example of why initialization should be done can be seen in the lives the player has. If you don't tell TGF2 at the start of the frame that the player has three lives, the second time the game is played (without restarting the application) those original lives will be gone. Consequently, the player would then be playing the game with no lives. The big difference to watch out for is program initialization and frame initialization. When the program starts, it's given a default configuration of three lives, and once these are used up and the game is still running, the game won't reset this number unless coded to do so.

1. Ensure you are on the correct frame by double-clicking on the Game frame. Then, click on the Event Editor button to bring up the empty event list.
2. Create a comment line called "Set-up Frame."
3. Click on "New Condition," select Storyboard Controls, and then select Start of Frame. Move to the right until you are directly under the Player 1 object, right-click, and then select Number of Lives | Set Number of Lives from the pop-up menu. When the Expression Evaluator appears, type in

the number "3" and then click OK. On the same condition line, find the Active object, and then in the Action box, right-click Animation | Paste Image into Background. A dialog box will appear; ensure Not an Obstacle is selected, and then click on the OK button. The Paste into Background dialog box can be seen in Figure 16.2.

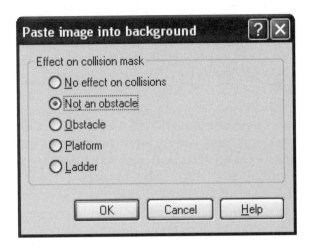

FIGURE 16.2 Pasting an object into the Background dialog box.

4. Move to the right until you are under the counter Current Flag object, right-click, select Set Counter, type the number "2" into the Expression Evaluator, and then click OK.

The counter Current Flag tells the code which direction the aliens should move in; if set to 1, the code will move the aliens to the left, and if set to 2, it will move them to the right. At the very beginning of the frame, the aliens are positioned on the left-hand side of the frame, so we would want them to move to the right, which is why we set the counter initially to 2.

5. Create a comment line on line 3 and call it "Player & Enemy Fire."
6. Click on "New Condition," choose The Mouse Pointer and Keyboard, and then select The Keyboard | Upon Pressing a Key from the pop-up menu. A dialog box will appear asking you to press a key; press the Shift key to save the results to the condition. Move to the right until you are under Small Star Fighter, right-click on the Action box, and select Shoot an Object.... Then, from the dialog box, select Normal (the bullet graphic). When the Shoot an Object dialog box appears, click the Shoot in Selected Directions

radio button. When you click the radio button, you will be asked to enter the direction. By default, it is pointing upward on direction number 8, which is what we need, so click OK, and then click OK again to complete the action.

7. This simple condition and action checks for the player to press the Shift key and then shoots the bullet upward at a speed of 100. If you want to increase the difficulty of the game, you could reduce the speed of firing, which means the player hits fewer enemy ships.

8. Create a new event on line 6, select the Timer object and then select Every. In the dialog box, enter 0 in the Seconds box, 40 in the 1/100 box, and then click on OK. In the same event, we need to create a second condition, so right-click on the condition, choose Insert, select Group.Bad, and from the pop-up menu, select Pick or Count | Pick Group.Bad at Random. Move to the right until you are directly under the Group.Bad object, right-click, and then select Shoot an Object. In the dialog box, select Alien Bullet; when the Shoot an Object dialog box appears, change the speed to 50, and then tick the Shoot in Selected Directions radio button. The Directions dialog box will appear. We need the bullet to go in the direction of the player's ship, so untick direction 8 (pointing upward) and pick 24 (pointing directly downward). Click OK, and then click OK again to complete the action.

9. The last bit of code entered is run every 0.4 seconds, and then picks an alien from the group (at random) and fires an Alien Bullet in the downward direction. If you run the frame at this point, you will be able to move the player's ship using the arrow keys (as it has predefined movement) and be able to shoot with the Shift key. In addition, the aliens will fire a bullet. Notice that the player's ship can leave the left- or right-hand side of the screen, so we now need to correct this.

10. Create a new comment line (on line 6) called "Leave Screen."

11. Create a new condition, select Small Star Fighter, and then from the pop-up, select Position | Test position of Small Star Fighter. The Test position dialog box will appear, click on the left and right outward pointing arrows (called Leaves in the left and Leaves in the right), click on the OK button to save the condition. Move to the right of the condition until you are under the Small Star Fighter object, right-click on the action box and select Movement | Stop from the pop-up menu.

12. The conditions you have created so far should look like Figure 16.3.

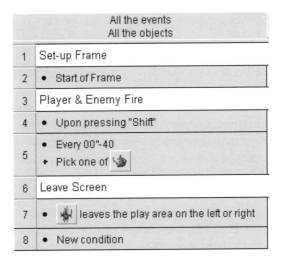

FIGURE 16.3 Conditions configured so far.

13. Create a new comment line called "Movement."
14. Create three groups called "Slow," "Fast," and "Movedown." Ensure that Slow is enabled at start, and Fast and Movedown are disabled (grayed out). Under this, create a comment line called "Destroy Player Bases," and then create a group called "Destroy Bases" and ensure it is disabled. This new set of items should look like Figure 16.4.

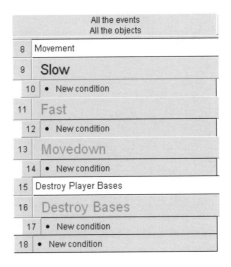

FIGURE 16.4 Newly added comments and groups.

Starting with the Slow group, we will now add conditions and actions to make the aliens to move left and right at a specific speed.

15. Add a comment line directly under the group Slow called "Right."

16. Click on the "New Condition" text under this comment, find the counter Current Flag, right-click, and select Compare the Counter to a Value. When the Expression Evaluator appears, type in the number "2." Insert another condition within the same event (by right-clicking on the one you just added and selecting Insert). Pick the Timer object, on the pop-up, select Every, remove the 1 from the Seconds box, add 70 to the 1/100 box, and click on OK. Move across until you are under the Group.Bad object, and then add an action. When the Object dialog box appears, find the Group.Bad, and then select Position | Set X Coordinate. The Expression Evaluator will appear; click on the Retrieve Data from an Object button, find the Group.Bad, and select Position | X Coordinate from the pop-up menu. In the Expression Evaluator it will now say X(Group.Bad); add +20 to the end of it so it will now read X(Group.Bad)+20, and then click on the OK button.

17. The first thing checked is the Current Flag; if it's set to 2 (which is move to the right), then every 0.7 seconds do the action. The action gets the current X position of the aliens and then adds 20 to it (so it moves to the right). If you were to run this frame, it would continue until it is off the screen, as there is no code to prevent it from doing so. Next, we have to create a condition for when an alien hits the right side of the screen (or in this case, Active 3).

18. Click on "New Condition," choose Active 3, then Collisions | Another Object, and then select Group.Bad. Move to the right until you are under the Current Flag object, set the action to Set Counter, enter the number "1" in the Expression Evaluator, and then click on the OK button. Move back to the left until you are under the Special Conditions object, and then add an action. From the pop-up menu, select Group of Events | Activate, then from the Group Events dialog, choose Movedown, and then click on the OK button.

19. When any of the aliens now reaches the invisible line on the right-hand side, TGF2 will automatically enable the Movedown group of code, which will tell the program to move all the aliens down one, and then disable itself ready to do it again next time. We now need to add the code to do the same for moving the aliens to the left, and a condition to test if it hits the invisible line on the left.

20. Add a comment under the last condition called "Left."

21. Click on the "New Condition" text under this comment, find the counter Current Flag, right-click, and select Compare the Counter to a Value. When the Expression Evaluator appears, type in the number "1." Insert another condition within the same event (by right-clicking on the one you just added and selecting Insert). Pick the Timer object, on the pop-up select Every, remove the 1 from the Seconds box, add 70 into the 1/100 box, and click on OK. Move across until you are under the Group.Bad object, and then add an action. When the Object dialog box appears, find the Group.Bad, and then select Position | Set X Coordinate. the Expression Evaluator will appear; click on the Retrieve data from an Object button, find the Group.Bad, select pick Position | X Coordinate from the pop-up menu. In the Expression Evaluator, it will now say X(Group.Bad); add −20 to the end of it so it will now read X(Group.Bad)−20, and then click OK.

22. Using a negative number on the current X position of the alien will move it to the left.

23. Click on "New Condition," choose Active 2, then Collisions | Another Object, and then select Group.Bad. Move to the right until you are under the Current Flag object, set the action to Set Counter, enter the number "2" in the Expression Evaluator, and then click on the OK button. Move back to the left until you are under the Special Conditions object, and then add an action. From the pop-up menu, select Group of Events | Activate, then from the Group Events dialog, choose Movedown, and then click on the OK button.

24. We have now created the slow-moving aliens, which is the first stage of the alien movement, as once they hit the player bases, they will move at a faster rate (by changing the timer) to provide more of a challenge. Only the timing on the code for the Fast group is different, so to save time, we can copy the events we just created, amend the timer, and we will have completed another section of code.

25. Highlight all of the code under the Slow group between event lines 10 and 12. Then, select Edit | Copy from the menu (or use Ctrl + C), ensure that the group Fast is expanded, place the cursor on event line 18, and then select Edit | Paste (or use Ctrl + V) to paste the events. Double-click on all of the conditions that have Every 00'−70 and change it to 00'−20. Your code for the Slow and Fast groups should now look like Figure 16.5.

26. Ensure the Movedown group is expanded, and then click on "New Condition." From the dialog box, select the Special and then Limit Conditions | Only One Action When Event Loops. Move to the right until you are under Group.Bad, right-click, and select Position | Set Y Coordinate. The Expression Evaluator will appear; click on the Retrieve Data from an Object

button, find the Group.Bad, and select Position | Y Coordinate from the pop-up menu. In the Expression Evaluator, it will now say Y(Group.Bad): add +20 to the end of it so it reads Y(Group.Bad)+20, and then click on the OK button. Move to the Special Conditions object, add an action of Group of Events | Deactivate, and then select the group Movedown.

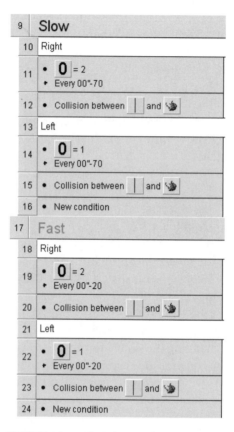

FIGURE 16.5 The Slow and Fast groups.

27. We now need to create a condition in the group Destroy Bases. Click on the "New Condition" text, select Special Conditions, and then from the pop-up menu, select Limit Conditions | Run This Event Once. Move across until you are under the Active object, select Animation | Change Animation Sequence, select User Animation in the dialog, and click on the OK button. On the same action you just entered (just under the Active object) right-click, select Animation | Paste Image into Background, leave the default as Not an Obstacle, and click on OK. Right-click once more on the

same Action box, and select Destroy. Move to the left until you are under the Special Conditions object, right-click, and select Group of Events | Deactivate. When the dialog box appears, choose Destroy Bases, and then click OK.

28. Add a new comment line called "Collisions."
29. Add a new condition, select the object Normal, and then from the pop-up menu, choose Collisions | Another Object. Then, double-click on Group.Bad. Move to the right until you are under the Player 1 object, and right-click Score | Add to Score. When the Expression Evaluator appears, enter the number 10 and then click on OK. Move to the right until you are under Normal, right-click, select DestroyFind the Group.Bad object, right-click, and select Destroy.
30. Add a new condition, select the object Normal, and then from the pop-up menu, choose Collisions | Another Object. Then, double-click on Group.Good. Move across until you are under the Normal object, right-click, and select Destroy.
31. Add a new condition, select the object Alien Bullet, and then from the pop-up menu, choose Collisions | Another Object. Then, double-click on Small Star Fighter. Move across until you are under Player 1, right-click, and select Number of Lives | Subtract from Number of Lives. Then, enter "1" into the Expression Evaluator and click OK. Move across until you are under Alien Bullet, right-click, and select Destroy.
32. Add a new condition, select the object Group.Bad, and then from the pop-up menu, choose Collisions | Another Object. Then, double-click on Group.Good. Move across until you are under Special Conditions, right-click, select Group of Events | Deactivate, and then choose Slow. Then, right-click on the same Special Conditions, select Group of Events | Activate, and then select Fast.
33. Add a new condition, select the object Group.Bad, and then from the pop-up menu, choose Collisions | Another Object, and then double-click on Small Star Fighter. Move to the right until you are under Player 1, right-click, select Number of Lives | Subtract from Number of Lives, enter the number "1" in the Expression Evaluator, and click OK to save this to the action.
34. Add a new condition, select the object Group.Bad, and then from the pop-up menu, choose Collisions | Another Object, and then double-click on Active. Move to the right until you are under Special Conditions, right-click, select Group of Events | Activate, and then select Destroy Bases.
35. Add a new condition, select the object Alien Bullet, and then from the pop-up menu, choose Collisions | Backdrop. Move across until you are under Alien Bullet, select Animation | Change | Animation Sequence, select User

Animation, and then click on OK. Under the same object, right-click, select Animation | Paste Image into Background, leave the default as Not an Obstacle, and click on OK. Finally, right-click on the same action and select Destroy. You should now have a set of conditions like that in Figure 16.6.

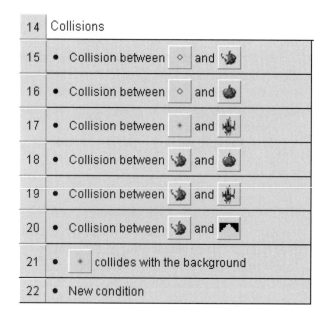

FIGURE 16.6   Conditions for collisions.

36. Create a new comment line called "No More Enemy."
37. Click on New Condition, select Group.Bad, and select Pick or Count | Have All Group.Bad Been Destroyed. Move to the right until you are directly under Storyboard Controls, right-click Jump to Frame, and select Frame 3—Hi-Scores from the dialog box.
38. Create a new comment line called "Lives."
39. Click on "New Condition," select the Player 1 object, and choose When Number of Lives Equals 0. Move to the right of this condition until you are under Storyboard Controls, right-click, select Jump to Frame, then select Frame 3—Hi-Scores, and then click the OK button.

Programming the Hi-Scores

The Hi-Scores frame is the same as the Main Menu code; the player will see the scores and then press the Spacebar to move back to the main menu to play the game again. It is very important to provide the players with an easy way to get back to the main menu so they can get straight into the action.

1. Double-click on the frame Hi-Scores, to load the correct frame.
2. Click on the Event Editor button, and click on the "New Condition" text to start adding the code. From the dialog box, select The Mouse Pointer and Keyboard, and from the pop-up menu, select The Keyboard | Upon Pressing a Key. You will now be asked to press a key, so press the Spacebar.
3. You now have a single event, with a single condition, which now requires an action to make it work. Move to the right of this event until you are directly under Storyboard Controls, right-click, and select Jump to Frame. The Frame dialog box will appear; double-click on Frame 1—Main Menu.

SUMMARY

ON THE CD

You just completed your fourth and final game in this book; however, two more games with full source are included on the companion CD-ROM. The games we developed here touched on all of the important game concepts and coding possibilities of making platform, scrolling, bat and ball, and retro-type games. You now should be able to take what you have learned and start making your own exciting games in TGF2. In the next few chapters, we discuss how to package and distribute any games you create, via download, or playable in a Web browser, or one of the many other options available to you.

17 Additional Concepts

In This Chapter

- Menus
- Web Browser Games
- Icons
- Advanced Games

In this chapter, we look at additional concepts you might consider for your own games. We'll look at menus, which are standard functionality on games that run within an Application window; uploading a game to the Internet so you can create your own online games site; and how to create your own game icons. Included on the companion CD-ROM are two additional games with full code that present some nice ideas on how to create more complex games.

ON THE CD

MENUS

A number of games you can play within an Application window contain a standard Menu system to allow the player to configure certain aspects of the game, anything from changing keyboard controls to viewing a help file. An example of a menu system can be seen in Figure 17.1, which is the default menu contained in the game "The Lab," provided with this book.

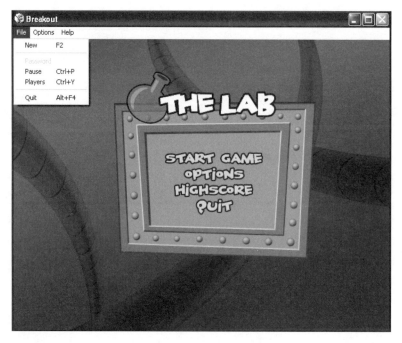

FIGURE 17.1 A menu system in "The Lab." ©Jason Darby 2005. Reprinted with permission.

Basic Menu Configuration

When you create a basic game within TGF2, by default there is a menu already pre-configured, without any settings changes. The basic menu system has a number of options predefined, which are separated under three headings: File, Options, and Help. These menu options will work automatically in the games you create, and although they might not be exactly what you might want, they are a good starting point.

File

New: Starts the program afresh, by reloading the game.

Password: If you have configured a password for a frame, you can enter it here to jump immediately to that frame position. This option will be disabled by default unless you specify a password in the Storyboard Editor.

Pause: Pause the game in progress.

Players: Configure the default player controls (keyboard and joystick).

Quit: Exit the game.

Options

Play Samples: By default this is enabled, so any samples expected to play within the game will be heard on the speakers; by unticking this, all samples will be prevented from playing.

Play Music: The same as Play Samples, except it applies to any music that will play within the game.

Hide the Menu: If you don't want to see the menu while playing the game, you can hide it by selecting this option; it can be brought back by pressing the F8 key.

Help

Contents: Disabled by default, allows you to assign a help file to the menu option or shortcut key (a range of file formats, including hlp, wri, and doc).

About: Selecting this will bring up an information box that details the product name and any copyright message.

Menu Dialog

To change the menu options used within your games you will need to access the Menu Configuration dialog, which is available via the Application Properties.

1. Start TGF2, and click on the option File | New on the menu to create a new game file.
2. Click on "Application 1" in the Workspace toolbar to bring up the Properties sheet. Within the Application Properties sheet, click on the Window tab to bring up options relating to the menu. You should now see a Properties sheet as shown in Figure 17.2.
3. Under the section Menu, you will see two tick boxes and an Edit button. If you want to include a menu bar, leave the Menu Bar option selected, and if you would like the menu to appear when the game is started, leave the second option at its default.
4. Click on the Edit button to open the Menu Editor. You will now see a menu dialog as shown in Figure 17.3.

FIGURE 17.2 Application Properties sheet.

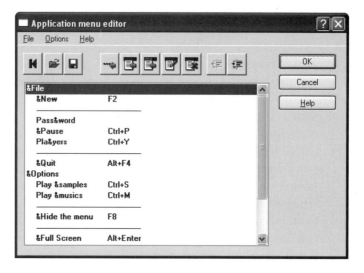

FIGURE 17.3 Menu Editor dialog box.

The top of the dialog box has an example of what your menu will look like when running the game. Below that is a set of buttons that allow you to configure your menu system, and under that are the text commands that make up the actual menu options. The menu buttons consist of:

Reset Menu: This will reset any changes made to the menu back to its original settings.

Load a Menu: Load a menu from a file, allowing you to create an original menu and use it in multiple games without needing to recreate it each time.

Save a Menu: Save a menu so it can be used later in the current or future programs.

Insert a Separator: Creates a line separator between menu options, useful to group similar items together.

Insert an Item: Explanation in sentence case with no end punctuation.

Insert an Item from the Default Menu: If you have created your own menu system, but would like to take advantage of some of the default menu options, you can choose which ones to add.

Edit Current Item: Edit the currently selected line item (you will need to left-click on an item that you want to edit before clicking this button).

Delete an Item: Remove an item from the menu.

Push Left: You can create various levels of menus that when selected will bring up another menu to the right of that option. This allows you to move the menu option higher or lower in the menu order.

Push Right: You can move a menu item to the right of its current position using this button.

Editing a Menu

To edit a current menu's options you can double left-click on the item, or single left-click to highlight it and select the Edit Current Item button. After doing so, you will be presented with the Setup Application Menu option, which can be seen in Figure 17.4.

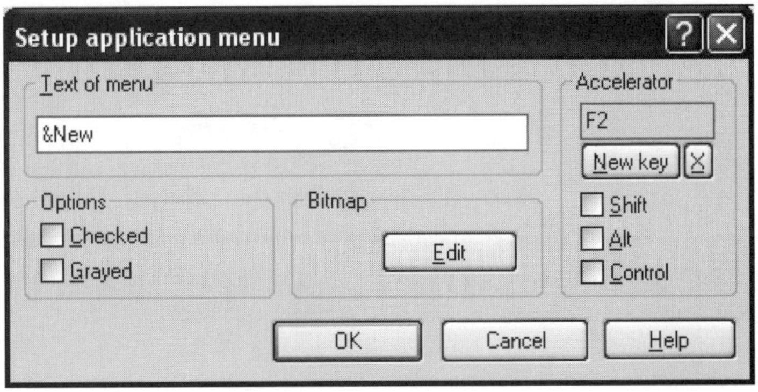

FIGURE 17.4   Editing a menu entry.

Text of Menu: Type in the text you want to appear in the menu system. By using an &, you are telling TGF2 that it should underline the next available letter in the menu; in this example, the "N" would be underlined. This is to tell the user that he can access this option using a shortcut key (a key combination configured under the Accelerator section).

Checked: This will place a tick next to the word in the menu, and is useful for options that can be switched on or off (e.g., in the default menu, the user can turn the music on and off).

Grayed: A tick in this box will gray out the option in the menu; when an item is grayed, it is effectively switched off and cannot be selected.

Bitmap: By clicking on the Edit button, you will enter the Picture Editor and be able to create a button for your menu option. This is to allow users to create XP-based menus, in which many have graphic images next to the menu text.

Accelerator: Allows you to configure shortcut keys to menu options, which are used in many types of games and applications to allow you to quickly access certain options. A default example would be that to quit a TGF2 game, you can use the Alt key and F4 keys together to exit the program.

Menu Walkthrough

We are now going to change the default menu—which currently has the three options File, Options, and Help—and add a fourth entry called Book. Under the book item, we will create a number of entries, including one item with an image, a separator line, and two menus on the right of another item. An example of what the menu will look like is shown in Figure 17.5.

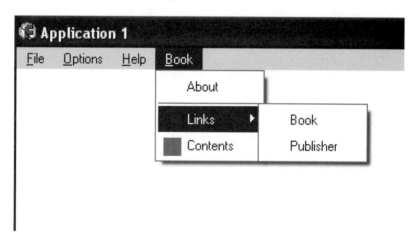

FIGURE 17.5 Reconfigured menu with some new options.

1. Start TGF2, and then click on the File | New option from the menu to create a new program file.

2. Double-click on the text "Frame 1" in the Workspace toolbar to open the Frame Editor.

3. Click on "Application 1" in the Workspace toolbar to bring up the Properties sheet. Within the Application Properties sheet, click on the Window tab to bring up options relating to the menu.

4. Under the section Menu, click on the Edit box to begin changing the configuration of the menu.

5. Use the scroll bar to scroll down until you see a blank space below the word "&About." Left double-click on the blank line, or single-click to highlight, and click on Insert an Item.

6. When the dialog box appears, type "&Book" in the Text of Menu edit box, and then click on the OK button. Click on the Push Left button to move the Book item to the left; this will make it into its own menu option rather than an entry under Help.

7. Scroll down again, double-click on the blank line under the &Book entry, type in the word "About," and then click on the OK button. Looking at the menu, you will notice that a new menu option has appeared. We want it to be an item under &Book, so ensure the About entry is highlighted, and then click on the Push Right button once to move it to the correct position.

8. Single-click on the blank line. Click on the Insert a Separator option to add a straight line under the About item.

9. Double-click on the blank line under the Separator item. Type in the text "Links" and click on the OK button.

10. Double-click on the blank line under the Links item, type in the text "Book," and then click on the OK button.

11. Double-click on the blank line under Book, type in the text "Publisher," and click on the OK button.

12. We now need to move both the Book and Publisher items to the right of the Links item. Select the Book line (which is just below the Links line) by single-clicking on it. Then, click on the Push Right button. Do the same for the Publisher item.

13. Double-click on the blank line under Publisher, type in the text "Contents," and then click on the Edit button in the Bitmap section. You will now enter the Picture Editor, select the Fill tool, and select a color. Fill the small square image with a single color, and then click on the OK button. Then, click the OK button again to return to the Menu Editor. Ensure Contents is highlighted, and then click on the Push Left button to place it in the correct sequence in the menu system.

14. Your menu is now complete, so click OK to save the menu configuration to TGF2 (you will still need to save the game file to ensure all changes are kept).

To use the menu you just created, you will need to use the Event Editor to access its options and react to the user selections.

Programming for the Menu

If you want to make changes to the default menu, you will need to create conditions and actions, so when a player selects a specific menu option, the game will react in a certain way. All menu configuration is done via the Event Editor and via event code. When adding a condition, from the dialog box you would choose the Special object (the object that looks like two computers connected to each other), and then from the pop-up menu, you would choose the Application menu to pick relevant conditions for what you want to be tested. In the following walkthrough, we are going to use the menu we just created, and create a condition that when the player selects Book | About, the game will display some text.

1. Start TGF2, and then click on the File | Open option from the menu. When the Open dialog box appears, browse to your CD-ROM drive and locate the file "Menu1," which is stored in the Menus folder. Choose this file, and then click on OK to open the file.
2. Double-click on the text "Frame 1" in the Workspace toolbar to open the Frame Editor. Click on the Event Editor button to begin programming the menu system.
3. Click on the "New Condition" text to open the New Condition dialog box. Right-click on the Special object, and from the pop-up menu, select Has an Option Been Selected? You will now see a dialog box as shown in Figure 17.6.
4. Click on the Click Here button to see the already created menu, and choose Book | About. You will now see an event that says "Menu option 'About' selected."
5. Move to the right of the event until you are directly under the Formatted Text, right-click, and choose Visibility, Make Object Reappear from the pop-up menu.

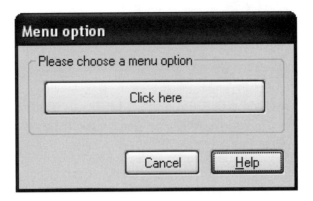

FIGURE 17.6 Menu option selector.

WEB BROWSER GAMES

Playing games over the Internet is great fun, but has a number of uses for someone who is making games for fun or as an independent developer.

- It's an easy and quick way to add additional content to your site to provide a reason for people to come back.
- You can use it as a marketing tool, to put your message across in a game.
- You can showcase your work.
- You can provide players with a way to see and play a single level of your game without needing to download a demo version of it.

To create a game for the Web, we will be using a special plug-in for TGF2 called Vitalize™, which allows games to be put into a Web browser and then displayed on a user's computer. The end user will need to install the Vitalize plug-in by downloading and running the executable file, or running the online installation program.

At the time of writing, Vitalize 4 isn't available, so additional commands and functions may have been implemented. Please consult the Clickteam Web site for any changes or updates to the information in this book. The plug-in for Vitalize can be found at www.clickteam.com.

Creating a Game for the Web

The first thing you need to do to be able to create a game on the Internet is to save the game in a format that can be uploaded to a Web site. This format is called CCN, and is a file that the plug-in program can recognize and read into a Web page. Once you have created the CCN file, you would then create an HTML (Web page) file that links to the file. You would then upload to your Web page and run it as a standard URL.

1. Start *TGF2*, and then click on the File | Open option from the menu. When the Open dialog box appears, browse to your CD-ROM drive and locate the file "web1," which is stored in the Plane folder. Choose this file, and then click OK to open the file.
2. Click on the application name, which in this case is application 1. Once you click on this, the Properties toolbar will display the Application settings as shown in Figure 17.7.

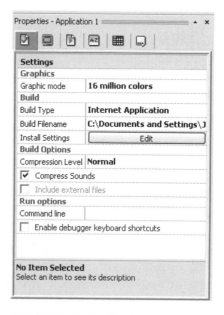

FIGURE 17.7 Application Properties configured for a Web file.

3. Click on the Build type, and select Internet Application.
4. On Build Filename, select the save location for the file, and then enter a filename for the CCN.
5. To create the special formatted file, you need to build the file. This makes TGF2 look at the currently running file and create it in a format Vitalize will understand. To build the file, go to the File menu and select File | Build

| Application. If you now go to where you entered the file location, you will find the built CCN file.

Creating a Web Page

Now that you have the CNN file, you will need to create a Web page with the file on it. You can do this by using any standard HTML editor such as MS Frontpage®, Macromedia® Dreamweaver®, or even Notepad if you know what you are doing, and then enter specific code to point to the created file.

ON THE CD An example of a CCN file running within a Web page is provided on the companion CD-ROM. The file is called "Vitalize.html" and is located in the Web folder. Open the HTML file, and you will see that you can play a game from within a Web browser.

1. Create an HTML file in your chosen Web design program.
2. Insert the Vitalize specific code in between the <body> and </body> tags of your HTML file, as detailed here:

```
<OBJECT ID=Vitalize28263 WIDTH=640 HEIGHT=480
CLASSID=CLSID:EB6D7E70-AAA9-40D9-BA05-F214089F2275
CODEBASE=http://www.clickteam.com/vitalize3/vitalize.cab#Version=3,5,11
7,0>
<PARAM NAME=URL VALUE=planeweb.ccn>
<PARAM NAME=TaskPriority VALUE=50>
<PARAM NAME=BackColor VALUE=0,0,0>
<PARAM NAME=ProgressBar VALUE=0,0,0,0>
<PARAM NAME=ProgressBarColor VALUE=0,0,0>
<PARAM NAME=ProgressBarBorderColor VALUE=0,0,0>
<EMBED type=application/x-cnc width=640 height=480
Pluginspage=http://www.clickteam.com/vitalize3/plugin.html
CheckVersion=3,5,117,0
TaskPriority=50
BackColor=0,0,0
ProgressBar=0,0,0,0
ProgressBarColor=0,0,0
ProgressBarBorderColor=0,0,0
src=planeweb.ccn
</EMBED>
</OBJECT>
```

Important values that will need to be amended as necessary are:

Width: The width of the plug-in.
Height: The height of the plug-in.

Codebase: Where the latest version of the Vitalize install program is located. If users visit the Web page and don't have Vitalize installed, it will allow the installation of the program so they can run it.

URL: The URL location and name of your file.

TaskPriority: How much processing time you want to allocate to the game; the number in the example is 50, but could have been 100 to signify all processing time.

BackColor: The color used for the background where the Vitalize plug-in is used (this is only shown when loading).

ProgressBar: The size and position of the loading bar to show the end user when the game will begin to run.

ProgressBarColor: The color assigned to the progress bar.

ProgressBarBorderColor: The color you want to assign to the border around the progress bar.

Visit www.clickteam.com for the latest details on this plug-in.

ICONS

When you run a game within an Application window, or look at the executable of any game you've created by browsing the folder in which it is stored, you will see a graphic icon. These icons are created to differentiate the game from others on your machine as shown in Figure 17.8. The image on the left in Figure 17.8 is the graphic image you will see if you search for the program using Windows Explorer; the icon image on the right can be seen in the top-left corner of the Application window. There is a default set of icons premade within TGF2 that can be changed to better represent your games.

To amend these icons:

1. In the Workspace Properties toolbar, click on the topmost object (icon) to reveal the Application Properties in the Properties tab.
2. Click on the About tab in the Properties toolbar.
3. Click on the line that represents Icon, and then click on the Edit box that appears.
4. The Picture Editor appears with four icons you can amend. An example of the icons used in the final version of "The Lab" is shown in Figure 17.9.

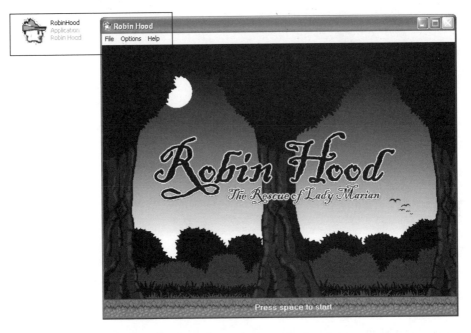

FIGURE 17.8   An example of two icons that are displayed. ©Jason Darby 2005. Reprinted with permission.

FIGURE 17.9   Example of the icons being amended.

Notice in Figure 17.9 that there are four icons. The larger icons represent the image that is displayed for the actual executable, and the smaller ones will be shown when running the game in an Application window.

 You might be wondering why there are two of each icon that needs to be changed. This is because the second set of icons is for lower resolution displays (256 colors). Although many PCs don't run at this low a resolution, some might, so the second set of icons ensures your games run on a wide variety of PC specifications.

ADVANCED GAMES

For those readers who completed the three main games "The Lab," "Amazing Fighter Pilot," and "Robin Hood," and want to take game making to the next level, we have included two more games for you to look at. These advanced games are called "Saturn Storm," and "Jack in the Forest," as shown in Figures 17.10 and 17.11. These files include the full source of a single level to open, dissect, and run. Both games have the basic structure of the four other games of a frame for the main menu, game and the Hi-Scores table, but use more complex programming code and graphic scrolling.

FIGURE 17.10 Side-scrolling shoot-'em-up "Saturn Storm".
Game developed by Teddysday Ltd.—reprinted with permission.

FIGURE 17.11   Side-scrolling platform game "Jack in the Forest".
Game developed by Teddysday Ltd.—reprinted with permission.

"Saturn Storm" and "Jack in the Forest" examples can be found in the
Advanced folder on the companion CD-ROM.

*When looking at the example files, you will notice that there doesn't seem to be
much code in the game frame; this is because the code is applied to specific objects
under Behaviors.*

SUMMARY

This chapter showed you how to add File menus into your programs, upload your
games to the Internet, and provided insight into more advanced features that you
can use within your own games. This should give you a good grasp of the types of
games TGF2 can make, and illustrate the power of the program. The following
chapters concentrate on what happens while you are developing your games, and
what happens after they are completed. You will learn how to find bugs, what to do
when the game is finished, and where to get help on any aspects of TGF2.

18   Bug Finding and Fixing

In This Chapter

- What Are Bugs?
- Why Find Them?
- Bug Fixing and Product Releases
- The Debugger
- Testing Run-through

In this chapter, we look at program problems and bugs, how to find them, and then fix them. No matter how hard you try, bugs will appear in any program you write, but it is very important to ensure that you minimize them before you distribute your game. We will also be looking at ways to find a bug in your program, and remove it (not always as easy as it sounds). Finally, we will go through the tools TGF2 provides to give you the best chance of squashing those nasty bugs—the debugger.

WHAT ARE BUGS?

Computers, and the software used to run them, are made by humans. Unfortunately, no matter how hard we try, we cannot prevent problems with incorrect code or design issues from happening. These issues can cause random crashes and data corruption at any time, and can be infuriating for the user of the PC that's having the problem. Programmers and hardware designers are human, and thus subject to error, and can unwittingly introduce bugs into programs. This will also be true when you are programming and making games in TGF2. TGF2 uses a special programming language, and bugs will be introduced because of assigning incorrect data from one object into another, or just wrong coding in the Event Editor. You, too, will probably introduce bugs into your software; the key is making sure you look for them and try to remove them where possible.

WHY FIND THEM?

A great piece of software can appear average or poor based on the frequency and location of the bugs in it. Recently, a few games reviewed in computer magazines were losing around 10–20% of the games rating (score) just because of bugs. The perception from customers is also the same; the more frequently the bugs appear, the lower they will rate the software. You have spent a lot of time developing your game, so you probably want it to be as good as it can be. Although the development of a product is difficult and complex, the last few months of game development are very risky for a TGF2 developer. Your product is nearly complete, and you are excited to try to get it online (or to your friends) as quickly as possible. The problem with this is that you might become less concerned about the product in the last days of development than when you first started out, especially if development has been long and difficult.

If you are just releasing games to your friends or online as freeware, you should still try to get rid of any bugs, as the negative feedback from users will probably make the entire project feel like a waste of your time. If you are making a game to sell online, you will definitely need to allow time to remove any bugs you know about.

BUG FIXING AND PRODUCT RELEASES

There are a number of areas in which you might consider fixing bugs, or need to ensure that all bugs have been removed. This can be broken up into a number of distinguishable phases. Although based on normal product releases, you should still follow this process even if your games are meant for family and friends only.

General Bug Fixing: When you are creating your game, you will also test to see if it works. This is just to confirm that you have completed that section of code and can move on to the next part of the program. You may, at this stage of development, come across a bug that stops this section working significantly enough for you to confirm that the functionality is available by removing the code issue. There may also be issues with the look and feel and just general stability. All of this will be done while you are programming the main part of the game, but you will not be going out of your way to find problems.

Alpha Version: When the product is in a suitable condition and much of the functionality has been implemented you can then say your product is at version Alpha. This means that it is still unstable, but many of the options work (although not all), and it has the general look and feel of the final product. The product may still have some major bugs and issues, but this is the first version considered suitable enough to show people the work in progress (even if you are a hobbyist creator). The Alpha is used to get feedback on how the product sticks together and if the interface works well. This is the final stage of development before the product will be locked down with regard to features and its look and feel. The main issue with development discussed previously is that you could continue to add new features and never actually release a product. The end of the Alpha stage is an indication that this is the beginning of the final program and its functionality.

Beta: At the end of the Alpha process, you may have feedback about how the product looks, and if the interface works well. After considering all the comments, making final decisions about the interface, and incorporating those changes in the product, you enter the Beta stage. The Beta stage is where the product is fully locked down with regard to functionality, look, and feel. This stage means that all that needs to be done is to remove any bugs within the program. You can give this version to your testers, who will then try to locate any problems within the game. Beta testers could be a group of friends, or anyone who downloads the game from your Web site and submits feedback.

Post Release: Once the product has been released, people will be using the game on configurations you may not have expected, or ways even the Beta testers didn't consider. There are generally bugs to be fixed once the product is available to a larger amount of people. These types of bugs need to be fixed as quickly as possibly, and you will need to upload a patch (using Clickteam's Patch Maker, for example), and upload a new full version. This is so any new users of your product don't have to download the game and then the patch (the more downloads people have to get may discourage them from trying the game at all).

Beta testers are an essential resource for finding bugs within your games. Developers who have been working on a product for a while will find it harder to find bugs, as they are used to the product. A new user tries things the developer might not consider, and can be a great asset for finding those bugs you know existed.

THE DEBUGGER

One of the new features in the latest release of TGF2 is the debugger. This new functionality allows developers to more easily search out program bugs within their games. The debugger is very much in line with code-based programming languages, and offers many features to make the developer's life much easier. Every program you make contains data information; for example, the current number of lives the player has, the location of the spaceship on the screen, and so forth. All this information is essential if you want to fix issues with your program. The new debugger allows you to access all these details so you can spend more time developing your programs rather than bug finding.

Starting the Debugger

To start the debugger, you will need to have a program running within TGF2. Once you have opened one of your games, if you run the frame or the entire game, the debugger will appear in the top-left corner, as shown in Figure 18.1 and Figure 18.2.

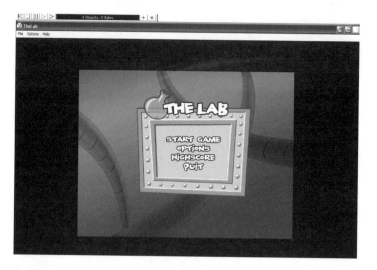

FIGURE 18.1 The debugger open and ready to use. ©Jason Darby 2005.
Reprinted with permission.

FIGURE 18.2 A close-up of the Debugger bar.

There are a number of buttons and functionality you can access:

■ If you click on the "+" icon on the right side of the Debugger bar, it will expand the amount of information available to you. All options and program data can be viewed. Within the entire program (each frame, object, etc.) is specific information, be it location on the screen, screen size, current counter values, and string details. The expanded debugger can be seen in Figure 18.3. To collapse it back, you need to click on the "–" sign that replaced the "+" sign when you clicked on Expand.

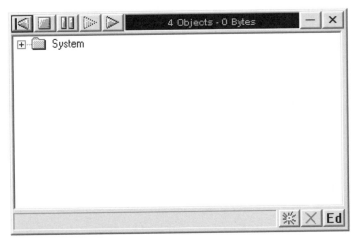

FIGURE 18.3 The debugger expanded to reveal more information.

■ The first button on the Debugger bar (the line with the left-pointing arrow) signifies that the program will start from the beginning of the frame once clicked. This is very useful if you are trying to track a bug and want to watch what is being changed (something we will detail shortly); you can repeat the process until you find the problem.

ON THE CD

■ There is an example of how the Go to Start of Frame button works on the companion CD-ROM. The example is called "debugger1"; open this file in TGF2 to see how it works.

■ The square icon on the Debugger bar is the Stop button. This stops the frame and program from running, and closes the running game and the debugger.

- The third icon is the Pause button, which will pause your program (i.e., nothing will happen on the game's playfield) until you press Play to start it back up. This will allow you to get to a specific point in the program and then check the result of the current data being stored by TGF2.
- The fourth icon from the left looks like a grayed-out right-pointing arrow. This is the Next Step button, which allows you to step through you game code one line at a time. To use this function, you will need to pause the program first using the Pause button mentioned previously. This is a very useful option if you want to slowly see what changes are made to your program.
- The fifth icon is the Play button; once you have paused the program, you would use this to start it back at real time (playing at normal speed).
- The display in the middle of the Debugger bar shows two bits of useful information: how many objects are being used in the current frame, and the amount of bytes for the total memory used by the application.
- The default information shown within the expanded debugger is for the basic application level. What this means is that if you created a blank game, this information is always present (top-level details are separate from anything you might add, such as game objects you might have placed in your game). To see what information is contained within the expanded Debugger box, see Figure 18.4.

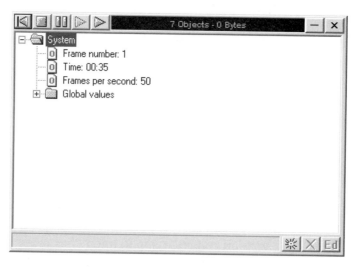

FIGURE 18.4 Basic information stored in the debugger.

- Expanding the System folder will give you all the standard game information. *Frame number* is the current frame running within the game. *Time* is the actual time the frame has been running (very important to remember that the time is reset between frames). You also have another expandable folder, which allows you to see all of the global values used within the program. At the bottom of the expanded debugger are three more buttons that you can use to add and remove additional items. The first icon is to add additional items, the second is to delete any items (if you only have system to begin with, it will delete that group), and the third is an "Ed" button for when you want to edit specific data entries.

Although the time in each frame is reset in the System folder, you can create an object that saves the amount of time the entire application has been running, which you can then add to the debugger and view it.

Adding Items to the Debugger

ON THE CD You now want to add an item to the debugger so you can watch it and see what happens to it when your game is running. Open the game "The Lab" on the companion CD-ROM. You'll find it in the folder \debugger, with the filename "debugadd."

1. Run the game by pressing the Run Application button on the toolbar. This will start the game and open the debugger. Click on the Start Game button within the game to move to frame 2.
2. Click on the Add Object to Debugger button, which will open the dialog box. Expand the Other Objects folder to reveal what objects you will need to add so you can watch it. An example of this dialog is as shown in Figure 18.5.

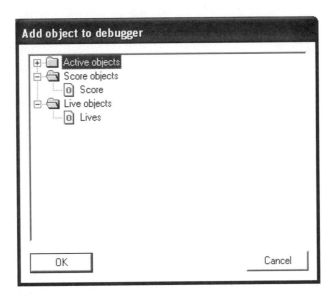

FIGURE 18.5   Click on the "+" signs to see what you can add to the debugger.

3. We want to watch the score, the number of lives, and see how they change when playing the game. Click on the Score object and click on OK. You will then need to add the score using the same process.

4. Begin to play the game, and notice that the score changes every time you hit a block. The number of live objects will also reduce every time the ball goes out of the play area on the right side of the screen.

It is important to note that for each frame, you will need to set up the objects you want to watch. Once you move frames, the debugger resets the items within its list to just system. This is because each frame will have different objects allocated to them, so it needs to do this to refresh the list.

TESTING RUN-THROUGH

■ To ensure that you fully understand the debugger and the power it has, the following is a short run-through of a program that doesn't have a bug, but some configuration has been forgotten. This will allow you to see what a great feature the debugger is, and how it can fix bugs in your code, and code you may have forgotten to implement.

1. Start TGF2.

2. Click on the menu option File and then Open to load a TGF2 file into the program.

3. Browse the companion CD-ROM for the debugger folder (on the root of the CD), locate a file called "debugtest," and double-click on it so it loads into TGF2.

4. Click the Run Application to make TGF2 start the game with the debugger.

5. Click on the "+" sign on the Debugger bar to expand the view. Click on the game's "Start Game" text, which will take us to the second frame where the game will start.

6. If you expand the System option within the debugger, you will see that the game is on frame 2, the time is incrementing upward, and the frames per second is changing rapidly. This shows that the game is currently running, and is awaiting a key press to launch the ball.

7. Click on the Pause button within the debugger bar to pause the program. This will mean that you cannot make the ball move, as the code has effectively stopped running until you press Play again.

8. Click the Add Object to Debugger button to bring up the dialog box. You will see three items; expand the score objects. Once you have done this,

highlight the Score object and click OK. Click on the Add button again, and do the same for the Live object (expand the Live object, highlight it, and then click on OK).

9. Notice that the score is at 0, which is not a problem, as the game hasn't started yet. The player hasn't begun to destroy any of the blocks on the playfield, and so has no score. You may also notice that the Lives object is currently set to 0. This would be set at the start of the game to whatever number is appropriate for your game; in "The Lab", the number of lives starts at 3. If you were to play the game and the bat misses the ball, you will find that you don't lose a life (as you don't have any anyway), and that the lives graphic doesn't show up on the game screen.

10. This is a problem, and the great thing about the debugger is that we can actually edit the data while the game is paused. This allows us to test the game with different data results without needing to come out, reprogram, and then start the debugging process again. Click on the Number of Lives object in the Debugger dialog box and you will see that the Ed button is no longer grayed out.

11. Click on the Ed button, which will bring up the Edit dialog box. Type in the number "3," which is the number of lives the player has at game startup.

12. Immediately, the program is updated with the new results, and the Number of Lives graphic now has three little circles in it (representing each life).

13. If you now start the game and try to lose a life, the game plays correctly, so you will need to close the game and debugger and set the number of lives in the Initial # of Lives to 3 (this is located in the Runtime Options Properties tab).

14. Although this is a very simple example, hopefully it proved how powerful and easy the debugger is to use. You can now in one screen, look for a bug, see if you can rectify it, and monitor the results.

SUMMARY

Although bug fixing may be one of the last things you do in the development of your game (and one of the last things on your mind), its importance cannot be overstated. Ensure that you leave enough time between the end phases of your product and its release to get rid of any bugs that might be hiding. You won't be thanked if the program runs smoothly, but you will certainly receive many complaints if there are serious bugs in your game. If you are selling your own games online, a customer who has purchased or tried one game from you that worked badly is unlikely to come back and download another, so quality and minimizing bugs are essential. If you want to make many games and want to increase your user base, it's very important that the user perception of your products remains positive.

19 Product Creation Afterthoughts

In This Chapter

- Installers
- Making an Install Program
- Upgrades with Patch Maker
- Making a Patch Program
- Trial Periods and Demos
- Distribution Methods
- Publishing
- Marketing
- Taking People's Money
- Copyright Issues

You've finished writing your game, so now what? In this chapter, we look at what to do with your completed project, and what potential issues and pitfalls might be waiting for you as you attempt to get it distributed. First, we will look at how you can package your game into a professional-looking installation program, and then how to keep it up to date once you have found bugs in it. If you intend to place the game on the Internet and perhaps even sell it, we will look at ways to get people to notice and use your program so you can make money from it.

INSTALLERS

To make your program look more professional, it is recommended that you place it within an installation file. The installation file is a single executable that installs your game to a specific directory and adds menus and desktop icons. All professional game companies use an installer to place their product onto a user desktop, so if you want to look professional, there is no alternative. You might think that an installer is going to cost a lot of money and be complicated to use. We chose Install Creator, because it is free to use (the unregistered version has an end screen promoting the Clickteam Web site), very powerful, and makes it easy to create a basic installation program. If you then decide to begin selling your creations, you can upgrade to the standard or professional versions for a reasonable fee.

ON THE CD

The companion CD-ROM includes a free version of Install Creator and a demo version of Install Creator Pro for you to try.

Installer Requirements

There are two installation requirements, one for building the installer and the other for what type of configuration the installation file can run on (the person installing the game).

For Install Creator and Install Creator Pro:

■ Windows 95 OSR-2 / 98 / Me / NT 4 / 2000 / XP / or later, with Internet Explorer 4 or later installed
■ 32 MB RAM
■ Hard disk with 4 MB of free disk space

For the install programs created with Install Creator or Install Creator Pro:

■ Windows 95 / 98 / Me / NT 4 / 2000 / XP / or later
■ 32 MB RAM

Installing Install Creator

Before we begin making our first installer, we must first install the program Install Creator. Locate the file icinst.exe, which can be found in the demos folder (using Explorer), or on the CD-ROM included with this book (under the Demos menu

ON THE CD

option), and then click on the Install button. If you are unsure of any of the installation options, you can find an installation video of how to install all the products mentioned here under the Videos menu option.

Double-click the file incinst.exe to begin the installation. If you are running Windows XP Service Pack 2, you may get a security warning about running an executable file, an example of which is shown in Figure 19.1. Click on Run to continue the installation.

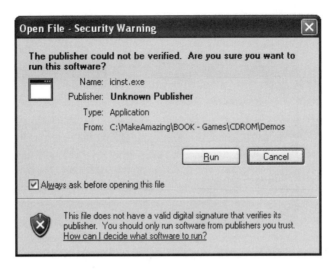

FIGURE 19.1   Windows XP SP2 Security dialog box.

1. On the product Welcome screen, click on the Next button to continue the installation.
2. Read the product details on the information screen, and then click on the Next button.
3. You will then be asked to select a version of Install Creator to install, either unregistered or registered. If you haven't purchased a license for Install Creator at this time and want to use the freeware version, select Unregistered (the unregistered version is free to use for commercial installations, but places a Clickteam page at the end of all installations). If you have purchased Install Creator, make sure you have your serial key ready. Make your selection, and then click on Next.
4. Read the license agreement, select "I Agree with the above terms and conditions," and then select Next.
5. If you selected the Registered version of Install Creator, you must now enter the serial code you were given at purchase; otherwise, move on to step 6.
6. You will now be presented with a possible installation path for the install files. The install is only a few megabytes, so if possible, leave it at the default option %systemdrive%\Program Files\Install Creator. If you want to change this, select the folder selector and choose a different folder.
7. If you went with the default option, a message box will appear, stating, "The destination directory doesn't exist. Do you want it to be created?" Select the Yes option to continue.
8. The installation files will then be copied to your computer.

9. The final Installation Complete dialog screen appears (shown in Figure 19.2).

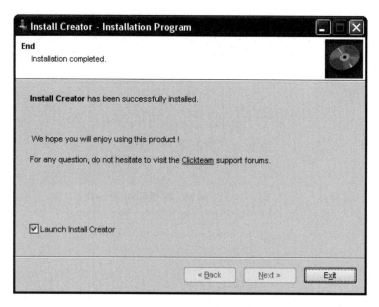

FIGURE 19.2 The Installation Complete dialog.

MAKING AN INSTALL PROGRAM

When you run Install Creator, you will be given the option to use the wizard, which is a quick and easy way to put your installer together. Until you have had more experience using the installer, it is a great way to make simple installation programs. We are going to use Install Creator to put our first created game, "The Lab", into an installer using the wizard.

1. Start Install Creator.
2. You will be presented with the Install Creator program and the Welcome screen as shown in Figure 19.3.
3. Click on Next on the Welcome screen to continue with the wizard, which will start the process of guiding you to making your own installer.
4. The Directory selection dialog box will then appear (as shown in Figure 19.4); click on the Browse button to move to the correct folder where you saved "The Lab." Untick the Include Sub-Directories box. Then, click on Next to continue with the build.

FIGURE 19.3   The starting screen for Install Creator.

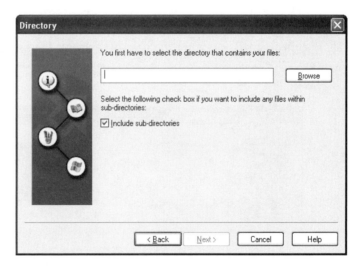

FIGURE 19.4   The selection of files and folders to be used in the installer.

5. You will now be presented with setting up the install program's title screen. Select the language (we are selecting English, but you might have a different language), and then type in the program name (in this case, "The Lab"). You can see what the install screen looks like by pressing the Preview button. An example of this screen can be seen in Figure 19.5. Once you are happy with how it looks, press the Next button to continue with the wizard.

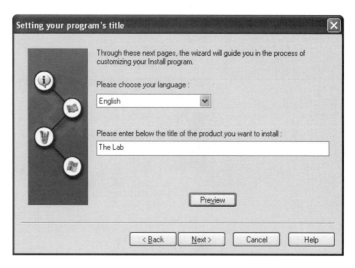

FIGURE 19.5 Title screen name dialog.

6. Install Creator allows you to have a dialog-based install (in a small window), or a full-screen format. In our installer for this example, we are going to choose small, but you can click on each and then select preview to give you an idea of what it will look like. An example of the installer selection is shown in Figure 19.6.

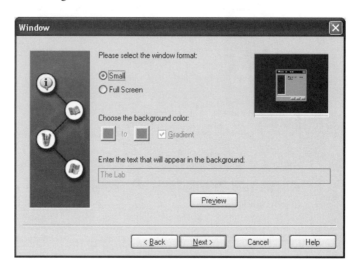

FIGURE 19.6 The installer selection.

7. Next, we need to select the template that will affect the look and feel of the installer. Leave the defaults, but click on Preview again to give you an idea of what you can change. You have three template options: Classic with bitmap, Classic without bitmap, and default. See Figure 19.7 to see the Default dialog selection.

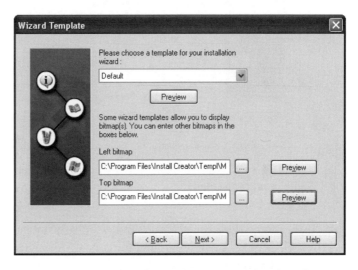

FIGURE 19.7   The default template is currently selected.

8. You have the option of adding an Information screen, which will appear when the user is installing the game. Type whatever you want in this screen, and it will appear when the user is installing the game. This is a great place to add more information about the product or about your Web site (you can add a *www* address to direct people to your site). Click on Next to continue.

9. If you have any license agreement information to enter, you can put it in the License dialog box. Normally, you would enter information about making backup copies and only installing on one machine. Enter some information, or click on Next to continue.

10. The Installation Directory screen (as shown in Figure 19.8) allows you to place the install files in a directory of your choice. The default option is #Program Files#/The Lab. Leave it as a default, as most programs get installed into the Program Files directory (the users can change it on installation if they want to). You can test the installer by pressing the Preview button. We do not need to make any other changes to the registry or an INI file now, so click on Next to continue with the wizard.

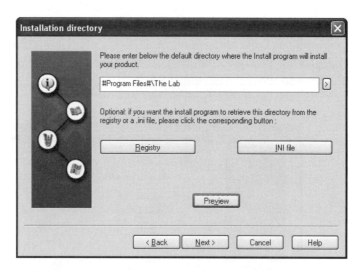

FIGURE 19.8 You can point it to the directory in which you want the product installed.

11. Next is the Shell screen (Figure 19.9), which is where you specify menu and desktop icons. For the Start menu icon, click on Browse, and locate the lab.exe file. With the corresponding icon file, you can point it to the icon and it will use that (if you have a separate icon file, you can point to that instead). As you have made your own icon within TGF2, it's easier to use that. Tick the Add Desktop Shortcut selection box, and then point the shortcut to your executable file. This will add the icon you made for your program, and put it on the Windows desktop. Click on the Next button to continue with the Installation Program wizard.

12. You now have the option of adding documentation to the installer so the user can read any last-minute readme files or any other text-based information. You can also specify that the program launches your game (or something else) once the install has completed. You would click on the browse buttons to select the relevant files. For this installation, we are going to leave it blank (as shown in Figure 19.10), and then click Next to continue.

13. You are now given the option to include an uninstall program with your game. This means that users can uninstall the program once they have finished with it. It is recommended to have the option to uninstall a program, as you are likely to upset users if they have to manually remove the files from the system. Leave the options at default, and then click on Next.

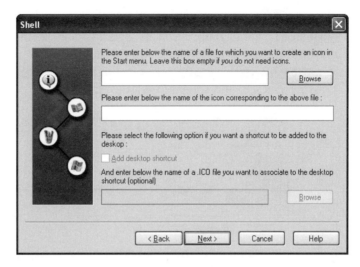

FIGURE 19.9   Example of the Shell dialog box.

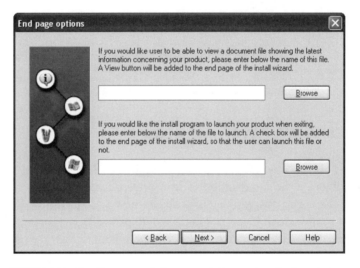

FIGURE 19.10   If you want documentation to be displayed at the end of install, it can be done here.

14. You will now be presented with the last screen in the wizard, aptly named the End dialog box. This is an information screen letting you know that it will begin to build the installation file (into an executable). Click on Next, and then specify the location where you want it to create the installer. The installer will be built, and all you need to do to install the game onto your machine is locate the file and run it.

15. You will notice if you run the file that because you are using the free version of Install Creator, a simple advert for Clickteam appears at the end. This is a small price to pay for an excellent installer, although you can remove it by purchasing the registered or professional versions. An example of the End screen is shown in Figure 19.11.

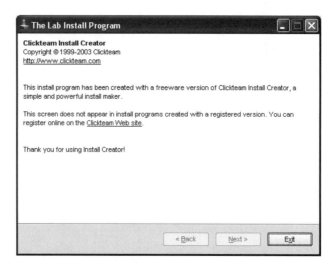

FIGURE 19.11 The advert is shown on all programs made with the free installer.

UPGRADES WITH PATCH MAKER

What do you do once your product has been released and suddenly you find there is a bug in it, or you decide to add more content? You certainly don't want to upload the entire program again with the new additions to it, as your users will not want to download it again. This is where product patches come into play, and this is where Clickteam's Patch Maker can help you.

There is a free version of Patch Maker for you to try out on the companion CD-ROM.

ON THE CD

Patch Maker Requirements

There are two requirements, one for building the patches, and the other for what type of configuration the patch can be run on (the person installing the patch).

For Patch Maker:

- Windows 95 OSR-2 / 98 / Me / NT 4 / 2000 / XP / or later, with Internet Explorer 4 or later installed
- 32 MB RAM
- Hard disk with 4 MB of free disk space
  For patches made with Patch Maker:
- Windows 95 / 98 / Me / NT 4 / 2000 / XP / or later 32 MB RAM

Installing Patch Maker

Double-click the PMUS12rf.exe file to begin the installation.

1. If you are running Windows XP Service Pack 2, you will receive a security warning; click on Run to continue with the installation.
2. On the product Welcome screen, click on the Next button to continue.
3. Read the product details on the information screen, and then click on the Next button.
4. You will then be asked to select a version of Patch Maker to install, either unregistered or registered. If you haven't purchased a license for Patch Maker at this time and want to use the freeware version, select Unregistered (the unregistered version is free to use for commercial installations, but places a Clickteam page at the end of all patches). If you have purchased Patch Maker, make sure you have your serial key ready. Make your selection, and then click on Next.
5. If you have selected the Registered version of Patch Maker, you must now enter the serial code you were given at purchase. Otherwise, move on to step 6.
6. You will now be presented with a possible installation path for the install files. The install is only a few megabytes, so if possible, leave it at the default option %systemdrive%\Program Files\Patch Maker. If you want to change this, select the Folder selector and choose a different folder to install into.
7. If you went with the default option, a message box will appear stating, "The destination directory doesn't exist. Do you want it to be created?" Select the Yes option to continue.
8. The installation files will then be copied to your computer.
9. The final Installation Complete dialog screen appears (shown in Figure 19.12).

MAKING A PATCH PROGRAM

To make a patch of one of your programs, you will need a folder containing the old installation, and another folder containing all of the new files (executables, external

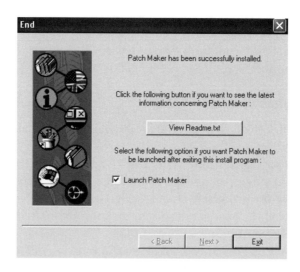

FIGURE 19.12 The end of the installation.

ON THE CD

graphic files, etc.). To help you create a test patch, there are two folders on the companion CD-ROM that you can use while you go through the process of making a patch. On the CD-ROM, you will find a folder called "PatchMakertest," and within this folder are two folders called "New Build" and "Old Build." You can use this to give you an example of how to build your own patch.

1. Start Clickteam's Patch Maker either from the desktop icon or from Start | Programs | Patch Maker. The Patch Maker screen will appear as shown in Figure 19.13. We will be using the wizard to build our patch, as it is relatively easy and quick to do. You can quit at any stage, and use the menus to make the patch manually if you want.

2. Once you have clicked on Next, you will be presented with the Directories dialog box as shown in Figure 19.14. From here, select the folders for your old version (old build, in this case) and the new version (new build). Untick the Include Subdirectories tick box (which you would use if your patches had subfolders; in this case, we don't.) Then, click on Next to continue with the patch wizard.

3. Choose the language of the Patch (in our case, English) and then enter the name of the Patch, which will be "The Lab v1.1." You can click on Preview if you want to see what the main patch screen will look like. When you are happy with what you see, click on Next and then enter any product-based

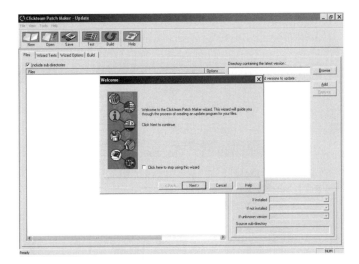

FIGURE 19.13   The Patch Maker Startup screen.

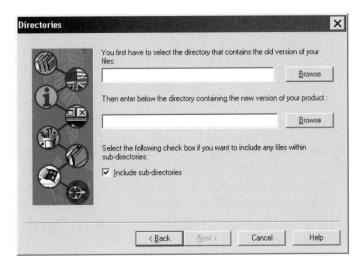

FIGURE 19.14   Selection of old and new directory.

specific information into the Information dialog screen. This is a good place to enter any information about what the patch fixes, and provide a link to your Web site for further details. Once you are ready to continue, click on the Next button.

4. Now you have the option to specify if you want to have the program take up the entire screen, or just a small dialog box in the middle (as shown in Figure 19.15). If you are not sure which one you might like best, click on

the radio buttons and then click on Preview to see how it will look to the user. For this patch, we are going to select Small. After doing so, you will notice that the text has been grayed out, because it is only used on the top left of the screen for the full-screen selection. Click Next, and you will be given the option to enter a bitmap image to display on the left-hand side of the window. We are not going to select that option, so click on Next to continue.

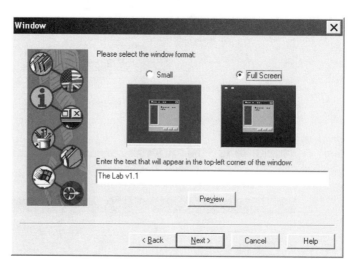

FIGURE 19.15 Window Screen Size Selection dialog.

5. Now we need to specify the location of the files we intend to update (on the target platform). You will remember when making the installer for "The Lab," you had to specify a default path for it—#Program Files#\The Lab (as shown in Figure 19.16). When you are making patches in the future, it is recommended to write the installation path to the registry or an INI file so you can retrieve it later without having to worry if the user has installed it in a different location. Click on the Next button to proceed, and the End screen will appear. Click on Finish to complete the Patch Build wizard, and then save the patch file executable to a folder.

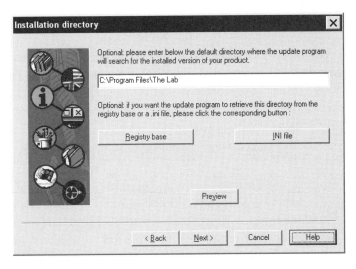

FIGURE 19.16 Installation update path.

TRIAL PERIODS AND DEMOS

It is very important to allow people to try your product before they purchase. No one will buy a software product these days unless they get to see what it looks like and what features it contains. There are a couple of ways to do this:

■ Time Limited (most features, but limited to 30-, 60-, or 90-day use)
■ Demo version (no save functionality and restricted functionality)

How you time limit your program or create a demo version of your game is not within the scope of this book or TGF2. The time-limited functionality is part of an advanced feature of the MMF professional version. We can create a demo version of our product using TGF2 and Install Maker unregistered version using the tools we already have. Once you have created your game, make another version of it (saving it as another file), and then take out the levels of the game leaving only a basic template. Add an extra frame at the end of the single/couple of levels saying how to upgrade to the full version with instructions on how to buy and information on what they will get in the full product. Build it as an executable; then, if using the unregistered version, package the program in its own installer and then distribute. The benefit of upgrading to the Professional version of Install Maker is that you can have a single install file with both the full and demo versions included in it, so you only need to distribute one file. When users want to purchase the full version, they can just reinstall from the same file from which they installed the demo version.

DISTRIBUTION METHODS

If you intend to distribute and publish your game yourself, there are a number of options available to you that will depend on your budget. Taking into account a number of other factors including cost, postage, product size/packaging, and the location of customers will ultimately help you decide which option is the best route for you to take.

Floppy Disks

Floppy disks are very cheap these days, although most games companies have stopped using them for product distribution in favor of other media such as CD-ROMs and the Internet. Floppies have been included here for sake of completeness, and its inclusion is by no means a recommendation. There is no need to distribute using floppy disks these days, and they are not very useful to the budding developer due to the small amount of space available on them. Floppy disks also have a nasty habit of being easily corruptible, which can be a problem if you are sending them via the postal system and they are being shipping internationally; the customer would have to wait even longer for a replacement. If your product spans multiple disks, the copying, labeling, and cost of overall production will certainly start to look less than favorable.

CD-ROM and DVD-ROM

CD-ROM was a great format replacement for the floppy disk; not only could it contain around 600–720 MB of data, it also became a cheap media for distributing larger programs. Windows 95 was released on 29 floppy disks, so if one disk were faulty, it would prevent the entire installation. As more and more computers had CD-ROM drives fitted, the cost of media and duplication dropped considerably, meaning that hobbyists had a cheap format they could pick up and run with. You have two main options when considering distribution by CD/DVD. The first is writable media that you can purchase from most computer-based stores; the second is to get it professionally glass mastered and printed. If you intend to keep distribution on a small scale because of finances and less overall risk, CDR is a good place to start. You will need to consider labels and a good CD-Writing package to ensure compatibility on your users' machines. Don't be too concerned that the software is not on a professionally printed CD; you can get very good results from an ink-jet printer and CDR labels. You can also keep costs low by purchasing in bulk (100 CDRs); although it sounds like a lot, if you also use them to keep backups of your project, you will soon use them up. As software changes so quickly these days (patches and updates), some companies (even one or two well-known ones) are starting to send software out on CDR. This reduces the overall cost, as they don't need to throw away large numbers of old disks that have been replaced by a new version (they just copy some more when they need to send them out). Therefore, when a new version is released, they just replace the version when they make more. DVD writers are slowly taking over as a replacement format for CDR, but unfortunately, there are two formats fighting to be the chosen standard: + (plus) and – (minus). This adds to the complexity of sending out software, as some users have one version, some have the other, and some have dual drives that can read both.

The only time you will need to have your software professionally glass mastered and created in standard CD format is if you intend to get the product into stores. If someone else is distributing the product for you, this won't be a concern. However, if you're doing this yourself, it's something you are going to have to organize. The first stage of this is to provide a CD-ROM version of your software already built on a CDR to a duplication company (with any auto-run options, folders, etc.). You will also need to provide them with any art for the CD-ROM and any packaging (if any) you intend to create with it. There is usually a charge for creating the glass master (the master disk they use to duplicate), there will be a charge for each CD-ROM, and you will need to have about 1000 created before the price starts to reduce and become more reasonable. As already mentioned, unless you are getting it placed in stores, there is no current reason to go for glass mastering and professional printing. It will be more costly, and if you cannot sell the items, you will have a lot of stock left that you cannot do anything with. You will also be stuck with an outdated version if you have to update your program later.

The Internet

The Internet is a great way to distribute your own software. Many Web sites will provide links to your site or your files; most are free, and a few have a fee involved. One of the best-known download sites is *www.download.com*. Download.com charges a small amount per year (around $79) to create a link to your software. The service also provides an idea of how many people have downloaded your software, and how they have rated it. If you are serious about people downloading your software, this is a great place to start. You also have the option of free HTTP hosting with Download.com. You could also put the file onto your own Web site for people to download. The main issue you have with putting the files on your own site is that most Web site hosting has a bandwidth limit, so always check this before you start placing files on your site to be downloaded. If you have a small download limit, uploading your latest creation might make you go over your bandwidth. This could mean unexpected costs, or your site may be switched off by the ISP until the bandwidth reduces.

Check www.download.com for the current charges. Always check your download limits with your hosting site before beginning any advertising of your product.

PUBLISHING

There are two models for publishing: publishing your game yourself via your Web site or getting it into stores, or getting someone else to publish the product for you. Publishing yourself means that you would potentially make more money per item sold, but has more risks and costs associated with it. While getting someone else to publish your product takes away many of the issues concerning printing and packaging, you will be paid less per item sold, but also have the potential for selling more. There are various benefits and pitfalls to both, which we cover here.

Self-Publishing

One of your biggest decisions is whether you are going to publish the product yourself, which could cost a substantial amount of money to get it up and running. Some of the things to look at include:

- Marketing will be very important (this will be discussed shortly), but you will need to ensure that you try to get your product known; otherwise, you won't get anyone visiting your site and purchasing your game.
- A good-looking and professional Web site is of paramount importance if you are going to convince visitors that they are buying from a proper company. If the site looks good, this will reduce any fears a customer will have about buying from you.
- Multiple options for payment are essential if you want customers to buy. Many customers are worried about credit card fraud, and buying from Web sites they haven't purchased from before. By offering multiple payment methods, you reduce this concern, as they will be able to pay with something other than a credit card.
- Consider the options of sending out media to customers or investing in Install Creator Professional, which will save you the effort of shipping files out to customers, but will increase your file download bandwidth. It is very important to take into account the effort and costs involved in CD-ROM duplication or automatic file download. Using Install Creator Professional would allow you to put a demo and full version within one executable. Once customers have purchased, you will only need to send them a serial key to unlock the product when reinstalling it. The effort required then on your part will be to email them

their serial key, much easier than duplicating software and posting it to potentially another country.

■ If you want to sell in stores, you need to consider the type of packaging that is standard within those stores (some stores will not display items that do not meet their own shelf standards), professional box art, and ensuring you have a product barcode. Remember, you may need to give extensive discounts before (and if) those shops will even consider taking your product.

Self-publishing is a lot of work, but the rewards are potentially much greater for you in the long term. Try to be realistic, and don't put all your efforts into one area only. By spreading the risk, you have a greater chance of success, so make sure you have backup plans if your product isn't picked up by any stores, or you don't sell as many online as you expected. The main benefit of selling your product online only to begin with is that you don't have to get any professional media printed or boxes, so if it isn't successful, you are not left with 1000s of boxes you cannot sell.

Finding a Publisher

If you don't feel that you can self publish your product, the other option is to find a company that will do it for you. This is not as simple as it sounds, and your product will need to look and play great to have the option of being picked up by a publisher. You may find that it will only be picked up if it's sold as a budget title, or for much less than you expected price wise. Try to be realistic; most games have a team of people working on them for over two years, and you cannot compete with a product with that kind of budget or staff levels. If you feel that your product is at the same level, then you are ready to look for a publisher. If not, you can then begin to see what areas you need to improve. Some ideas on what you need to do before and while you are finding a publisher include:

■ A great way to get an idea of how good your product will be received by a publisher is to release a demo and see what comments you get back. Not all comments will be helpful or constructive, but you should be able to get a consensus.

■ Go to the local PC games stores to see what types of products are being sold, and their prices. This will give you a good indication of what level your product can be pitched at to the publishers.

■ Make a list of all the publishers that are producing similar titles and those that might be interested in your project. Call them and try to arrange a meeting to show the product; they may ask you to send them a copy of the product to look at before any meeting.

■ If you are invited to go and discuss publishing the product, ensure you have a presentation ready that illustrates the benefits of your game (levels, target audience, bonus options, etc.). Ensure your presentation is well thought-out, and consider what questions they might ask about your product so you are prepared.

■ Stay calm and act professional. If they decide they do not like your product or don't think it's suitable, accept their decision, and use it to your advantage in the next meeting you have with another company. The publisher has more to lose if they intend to publish your product, and so may want to really take your product apart; make sure you are ready for this.

■ If you get acceptance of your product for a publishing deal, ensure you read the contract carefully and consult a lawyer where needed. There may be some points in the contract that could be misunderstood; if this is the case, make sure you get clarification before signing, as this may cause you more problems later. It is better to walk away from a poor contract if they are not willing to change, than it is to try to argue with them once it is all signed and legal.

■ Make sure you fully understand any sublicensing options that may be in the contract. This is very important, as you might suddenly find your product being sold in another country without your knowledge because of a sublicensing deal within your contract. You will also get less money, as the company publishing your product will get a bigger share of any profits from the sublicensing (where you could have potentially gone direct and realized a bigger percentage).

■ Don't over hype your product within your own mind; it is very easy to think your product is better than it really is. Try to be realistic and understand how good your game is (making game comparisons as suggested earlier will make this much clearer). Doing so will make you consider what you can and cannot negotiate on the contract, and get it signed much quicker.

MARKETING

Your budget will determine what marketing you will be able to do. There are many different options available to you, which can be explored further. Where possible, select a few different ways and then monitor the rate of success. That way, you can continue to do marketing where it works best, which in turn will be more profitable.

Magazine adverts: advertisements vary in size and cost, depending on how successful the publication is (how many issues it sells). With regard to computer game adverts in the associated magazines, you are looking at around $2000 for a full-page advert, with the price reducing with the more ads you want to place. Of course, the cost of this is out of the general public's price range, but if you are considering this route, you will need at least three to six months of adverts before you see a return on your investment. Many magazines have space in the back of the publication for smaller half-page or quarter-page adverts, which means that you can get part of a page for a cheaper price. This will allow you to see if it is worthwhile looking for a full page in the future, which would depend on the response you get back. If you are seriously looking at advertising in magazines, make a list of all possible publications with the costs and publication circulation numbers. This will allow you to get the best cost per circulation ratio possible, which is very important if you want to reach the maximum audience. One thing to remember is to only advertise in magazines that relate to your product (be it a game, application, etc.). Even if you are given a great discount on the advert, if it's not for your core market, you are unlikely to get any response.

Magazine CD-ROMs: By getting your demo game onto the CD-ROM of a computer magazine, you have the potential of selling direct to your customers without any impact of potentially limited bandwith. Many magazine sites have the option for you to upload or link to your product, so they can add it to the next CD-ROM they are creating. Other magazines will require you to phone them or send them an email link to your product. If your product is of an acceptable level, you should have no trouble getting your demo into a couple of magazines, but unless it is very good, it won't appear in more than one consecutive CD-ROM for that publication. The main reason for this is that the more popular the magazine, the more content they will have each month to fill the CD-ROM, so it's unlikely they will put it on more than one month's issue. Obviously, this is dependant on the magazine, and as there are quite a few, it's possible to rotate your product so you reach a different audience each month. Ensure that within your product and the installation file, you provide details on where to find your Web site (URL) so people know where to get more information on your game.

Google Ad Words®: If you want to drive traffic to your Web site, you can use Google Ad words. This is a system that, when someone enters a term on the Internet, lists your product or Web site on the page. Once users click on the link, Google will then charge you a specific amount. Ad Words is a great way to drive traffic to your site for a small cost, and allows you to enter the total amount you want to spend, so you can manage your budget easily.

Banner Ads: If spending money isn't an option, setting up a Banner Ad system could be a way to get traffic to your site for free. There are a number of free banner advert sites available on the Internet; you can find them by typing "banner ads" into any popular search engine. You will need to read the small print of each site to see which one offers you the best options, but generally, all you need to do is add the site's specific banner code to your Web site, and for each group of visitors you will get a banner credit. This credit will increase, and then you can use it to display your own banners on other Web sites (this is all done automatically). When users then click on your banner, they are taken immediately to your site.

Discount codes: To find out if different advertising techniques have been successful, it is very important to ensure your funds are directed at the most cost-effective marketing possible. A good way to track marketing is to set up discount codes on your products based on a campaign. You will then know how many people have purchased based on an advert or demo on a CD-ROM. If you have a limited budget, it is essential to know what works with your marketing, as you will not be able to continue to spend money in all areas.

TAKING PEOPLE'S MONEY

If you are looking at making money from your creations and intend to distribute your products via your own Web site, you will need to consider the options for taking people's money. Without some common form of payment, you probably won't make any money from your latest creation any time soon. There are a number of ways to take payment, each with its own positive and negative points.

Paypal®

Paypal is one of the biggest (if not the biggest) payment providers available today. It became a very popular payment method due to the auction Web site eBay®. Users needed a method of paying for items quickly, safely, and easily, and Paypal stepped up and made this possible. You can purchase many things with Paypal these days, and it's available in multiple countries and currencies. Taking payment is a fairly simple process involving registering for a business account with Paypal at *www.paypal.com.* There is no initial charge for using Paypal, and only a percentage per transaction (which depends on what amount you are charging the customer). The great thing about Paypal is that you can quickly start receiving payments for your programs, and keep track of who has purchased them. A large number of people have already registered for this service all over the world, thereby creating a userbase of people who can pay. Money paid is put straight into your Paypal account, so an external bank account with the same name is needed to withdraw any credits you may have received. It's advisable to have this already created before setting up your Paypal account.

Please consult the Paypal Web site for the exact charges.

NOTE

Checks

Checks are generally fine if they are from the same country in which you reside (the currency is the same). However, things get a little more complicated if customers are sending them from a different country. You may be charged a handling fee from the bank for handling a check from a different country, which can be quite expensive (especially if the product you are selling isn't very expensive). Always consider this, and ask for alternative methods of payment if this is going to be the case. Take standard precautions concerning checks, waiting for them to clear with the bank before sending any software or license key (a check from another country may take longer to clear than one from your own).

Cash

Unless you are selling in a market stall or store, you shouldn't be taking cash. Always advise customers not to pay via the postal service using, cash as there are too many risks and no way to track the money. They cannot prove you didn't receive it, and you cannot prove they sent it, so stay clear of this method of payment and ensure none of your customers tries to pay with this method. It is recommended that you put a message on your Web site stating that payment in cash is not advised, and you cannot be held responsible for any money lost within the postal service.

Credit Card

Credit card payment is now becoming a popular and common form of transaction on the Internet. A number of credit card payment systems can get you up and running (visit your local bank, as they will most likely have a system that can be used). A well-known international credit card transaction company is Worldpay, at *www.worldpay.com*.

You must follow a number of procedures before you are accepted to be able to take credit card transactions (these may be different for each company). For example, you might need an official Web site, payment and returns information Web pages, and a business bank account. The process can take a few weeks to get up and running, so consider this when releasing a game (it will be no good if the game is available before people have an option to pay for it). With some systems, there will be a yearly fee and a fee per transaction, so understand what you are signing up for with regard to payments. The main downside to credit cards is the fraud aspect, where someone may use a stolen card to purchase a product or license key from you. The credit card companies will take certain precautions, but you may be expected to assume some responsibility for ensuring the transactions are legitimate. If you accept a payment from a stolen card, you may be expected to pay money back to the card company, which means you'll lose both goods and money. Ensure you check what the arrangements are concerning credit card fraud when you take out your payment system.

Bank Transfer

Unless you are selling to other organizations, you are unlikely to get many bank transfers. They are easy to set up, and once you have a business account, the bank can provide you with the necessary details someone would need to give to their bank to get money transferred. It is a fairly straightforward process, and bank charges are minimal.

COPYRIGHT ISSUES

Copyright is an important area to consider for any retro or hobbyist game makers. Are you making a fan game (a game based on a TV show or celebrity), or a remake of a classic title you played some years ago? If you are considering making any game for which someone might retain copyright, you need to take care. Some developers come on to the game-making forum saying they are going to make a game about a favorite computer character, and then someone else mentions that they could get sued. An argument then erupts between the two parties that they will or won't get into trouble for making it. This is always a difficult discussion to have, as there is no right or wrong answer. If unsure, you should always consult a lawyer regarding your rights. The best advice from developers on the forums is to contact the owners of the copyright and see if they mind you making a fan game. If they do, it's best to do something else instead. Some users believe they won't get into trouble, thinking that a large corporation won't go after a hobbyist developer who is going to share a game with a few friends and place it on the Internet. There have been cases of small fan games and Web sites being shut down by a large company trying to protect its investments. Some won't mind if you are only making a free game and not looking at making money with it, but again, it's subjective and depends on the company involved. If copyright is a concern, there is no reason why you cannot make a game with a similar concept but with your own graphics, levels, and ideas, as it will be much more worthwhile in the end. Some people consider fan games as missing the point of game creation, and that producing one shows a lack of creativity. The one great thing about trying to replicate a concept from another game is that you are learning gameplay methods that are used in games that are sold to the general public. You will, at the very least, understand how it has been put together, and hopefully come up with something better and more interesting for your own products.

Always consult a lawyer about copyright law if you are unsure about your rights.

SUMMARY

You will hopefully now have some ideas on how to package, market, and sell your creations. Products like TGF2 are never going to compete with the *Half-Life*-type products. However, in the successful budget and independent games market where there are many niche products, you can make a success of it. Making games can be a lot of work, but also very rewarding and not necessarily from the financial point of view.

20 Getting Help

In This Chapter

- Who Needs Help?
- TGF2 Help
- Useful Web Sites

WHO NEEDS HELP?

Whom can you turn to if you are really stuck and don't have a friend who can help with your problem? There are many resources, both within the products covered in this book and on the Internet that you can use to speed up your development, and ensure you don't spend too much time trying to fix a difficult problem. This book is dedicated to making games quickly, so we want to make steady progress, not get bogged down in trivial issues.

TGF2 HELP

There are a number of ways to access help from within the program, and this should be your first choice for getting support. Many problems you will face when you first start using a product can be fixed by using the product's built-in support features, which will be faster than waiting for a response from any online forums.

Help Files

All products have some form of help file, be it an HTML document or Microsoft Help formatted program. The good news is that TGF2 comes with an extensive help facility, which also includes the usual title, word, and search functionality of any modern help file.

To access the Help system:

1. Start TGF2, and then go to the menu bar at the top of the screen.
2. Select the Help option.
3. Select the Contents option. The Help system will now load.

The great thing about the help system is that you can search for keywords, titles, or previous results. This is very handy when you are looking for something specific.

Help About

The Help About option is something you will only use when contacting Clickteam's support staff or using their online forums. The Help About option displays information about the current program and the level of patches currently installed. Always mention the product and version number in any correspondence to ensure a faster response to your problem. The Help About option can be accessed from the menu system.

1. Start TGF2, and then go to the menu bar at the top of the screen.
2. Select the Help option.
3. Select the About The Games Factory 2 option. The About box will now load.

An example of the About box is shown in Figure 20.1. You will need to make a note of the build number, as this is what you will be asked for on the forums.

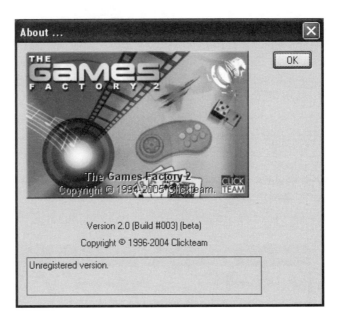

FIGURE 20.1   The product's Help About dialog box.

Tutorial

The Tutorial option (which can be accessed from the Menu system, Help, Tutorial) loads a help file that gives you an example game to create. If you feel like you need a bit more basic understanding of how to use the product, the tutorial is a great way to improve your skills quickly and easily. It is recommended that you look at how this tutorial is put together from the story and programming point of view. You will learn a lot from looking at other games, as it will help you understand the things that are required to make them interesting.

Examples

TGF2 comes with a number of game examples for you to try, which also allow you to explore the code in more detail. If you are stuck with a specific concept or game type, look at the examples to see if makes it easier for you to implement in your own game. This is a very good way to find out how a specific game type is made, but if you have problems, copy the code bit by bit into a new game and see what it does.

Keyboard Shortcuts

Keyboard shortcuts allow you to use certain key combinations versus finding items within the menu system. Within TGF2 is a default set of shortcut commands, which you can amend them to suit your own requirements. Over time, you may find that you are duplicating certain menu combinations when you are developing your games, so by setting up your own keyboard shortcuts, you will be able to work faster and more efficiently. The other option you have is not to change the defaults, but make a list of all the important key combinations you use for future reference.

To view the default keyboard preferences:

1. Start TGF2, and then go to the menu bar at the top of the screen.
2. Select the Tools option.
3. Select the Keyboard Shortcuts option.

The Keyboard Shortcuts dialog box will then load, as shown in Figure 20.2.

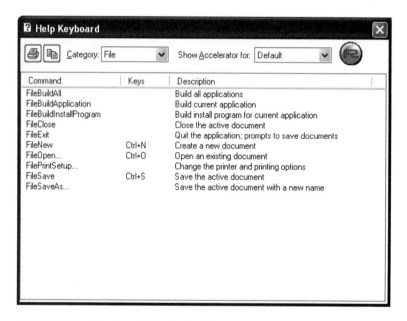

FIGURE 20.2   Keyboard Shortcuts dialog.

If you want to configure the keyboard shortcuts so you can assign you own commands, you will need to go into the Toolbar Customize option. To access this, right-click on any blank space on the TGF2 toolbar. A pop-up menu will appear; se-lect Customize to bring up the Customize Configuration dialog box. From here, we can customize the look and feel of TGF2, but we only want to amend the keyboard shortcuts, so click on the Keyboard tab. You should now have a dialog box similar to that in Figure 20.3.

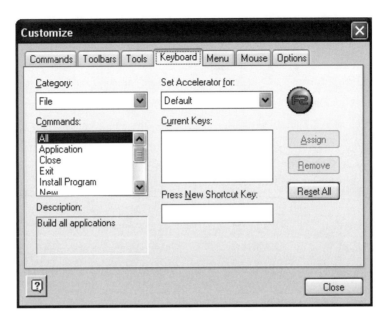

FIGURE 20.3 Customize Keyboard options.

Select the category and command you want to amend, and it will show the current key assigned. You will then need to click on the Remove button to remove this assignment. Press the left mouse key so the cursor is situated in the Press New Shortcut Key, and then press the key combination you want to use. If the key combination you press is already assigned to another command, text will appear below the Press New Shortcut Key box stating the command with which it is associated. Try a different combination. If you still want to assign a combination that is already in use, you will need to change the original to something else before assigning it to the one you want. You also will see a description for every command, which let's you know what each shortcut key does. If you make a mistake or decide that you want to go back to the original settings, click on the Reset All button. Some default key combinations are listed in Table 20.1.

TABLE 20.1 Common Key Combinations

Action	Key Combination	Details
Copy	Ctrl+C	Copy the selection and put it on the Clipboard
Cut	Ctrl+X	Cut the selection and put it on the Clipboard
Delete	Delete	Delete the selected object →

322 Making Amazing Games in Minutes

Action	Key Combination	Details
Enlarge canvas	Ctrl+W	Enlarge the canvas of the picture
Events Editor	Ctrl+E	Open the Event Editor window
Events List Editor	Ctrl+L	Open the Event List window
Find	Ctrl+F	Find the specified text
Frame Editor	Ctrl+M	Open the Frame Editor window
Help	Shift+F1	Display help for clicked-on buttons, menus, and windows
New	Ctrl+N	Create a new document
Open	Ctrl+O	Open an existing document
Paste	Ctrl+V	Insert Clipboard contents
Play	F5	Play the current frame from the current position
Print	Ctrl+P	Print the active document
Redo	Ctrl+Y	Redo the previously undone action
Run Application	F8	Run the current application
Run Frame	F7	Run the current frame
Save	Ctrl+S	Save the active document
Select All	Ctrl+A	Select the entire document
Storyboard Editor	Ctrl+B	Open the Storyboard window
Undo	Ctrl+Z	Undo the last action
Zoom in	F2	Zoom the current window inward
Zoom out	F3	Zoom the current window outward
Zoom to fit	F4	Set the zoom factor of the current window to obtain a complete display

Patches and Service Packs

It is always recommended that you install the latest patches, as this makes sure that if you are getting problems, it's not something that has already been fixed in a later release. You will also find that people are more willing to help you with your problem if you have installed the most up-to-date version, as they will ask you to update before offering advice. Patches usually include fixes to bugs, and sometimes new features, so it's to your benefit to keep up to date. If you are in the middle of development of a game, you should consider waiting a few days or even a couple of weeks before applying a new patch. Although unlikely, it is possible that this could cause you problems with the program you are already working on, and could have catastrophic results. Before applying the patch, make sure you have backed up any programs you're making, so if you need to, you can roll back to a previous release without losing any code.

USEFUL WEB SITES

If you are looking for product information and support, the Internet will be your best friend. You can find instant results to your problems, and be able to located helpful material and downloads such as tutorials/game examples.

The following is a quick round up of useful sites.

Support and Game Sites

Make Amazing Games

To accompany this book, a special Web site has been created (Figure 20.4) to give you the latest information on the book and game creation. Make Amazing contains links to any updated TGF2 demo files, and has some of the CD-ROM files available to download.

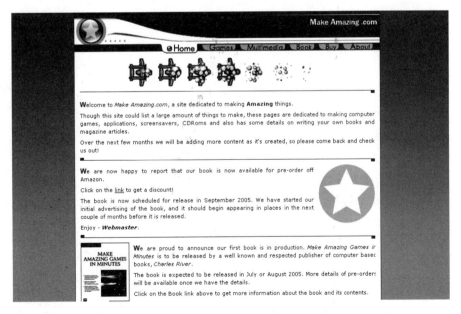

FIGURE 20.4 The Web site that accompanies this book, *www.makeamazing.com*.

Clickteam

This is the home of TGF2 and its more powerful brother, Multimedia Fusion 2 (as shown in Figure 20.5). From here, you can download demo versions of other products you might need, or read articles and information about the products. It is recommended that you register on both the mailing list and the forums. This will mean that you can keep up to date on developments as they happen, and have the ability to post questions on any problems you might have during the development process. Users on the forum are generally very efficient and helpful, which usually means you will get a response within 24 hours, if not sooner. As with all forums, it is best to read the FAQ before posting, as there are rules to follow to ensure that things go according to plan.

FIGURE 20.5 Clickteam's Web site, *www.clickteam.com.* ©Clickteam. Reprinted with permission.

The Knowledge Base

If you are stuck on a specific concept or how to use an extension object, and you still cannot figure it out after looking at the product's help files, the Knowledge Base is the place to go (Figure 20.6). The KB is a list of user-created articles on subjects ranging from creating a screensaver to making a database connection. The site is growing all of the time, and this author has a number of articles there.

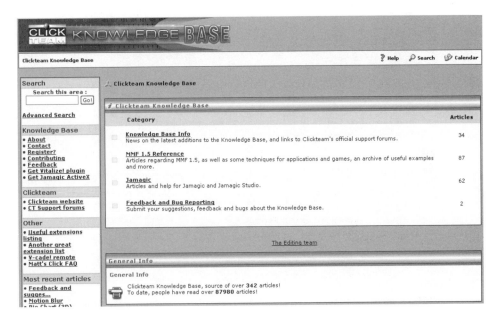

FIGURE 20.6   Knowledge Base Web site. *www.clickteam.info/kb/start/.* ©Daniel Burke & Clickteam. Reprinted with permission.

Extension List

Earlier in the book, we discussed the benefits of using extension objects within our games to add a lot more power and functionality to anything you are going to create. Therefore, what better than to have a site that lists all the current extensions available for TGF2 and those that aren't currently compatible? This is what the Extension List Web site does, and it can come in handy if you are looking for something specific to use in your program (shown in Figure 20.7).

The V-Cade

The V-Cade is a service providing a Web-server-based high-score delivery and tracking system to game developers using Clickteam's *TGF2* or Multimedia Fusion 2 (Figure 20.8). You can sign up with a developer account and then upload your game within minutes. This means that online Internet game players can then run and play your game within a normal browser. The other great thing about this system is that any game uploaded can then be linked to from any Web site. Consequently, if you have a credit linking to your Web site from your game, you can get extra visitors and traffic to your home page.

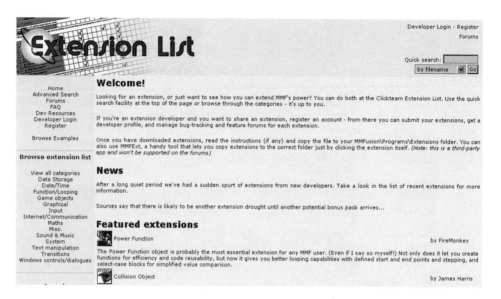

FIGURE 20.7 Extension List Web site. *www.clickteam.info/extensions/.* ©Chris Branch & Clickteam. Reprinted with persmission.

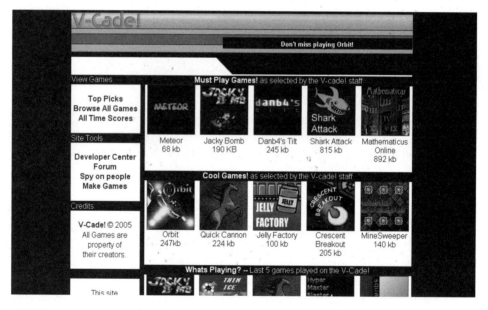

FIGURE 20.8 The V-Cade Web site. *www.vitalizeme.com/.* ©Jeff Vance & Clickteam. Reprinted with permission.

The Daily Click

A user of the original Games Factory loved the program so much he decided to make his own "Community" Web site (Figure 20.9). The site is aimed at teenage users, but still provides some very useful information and downloads in a newspaper-style format. The site is generally well moderated and is a great place to hang out if you want to check out what other users are creating with the products. Sometimes, the users who post here amaze other users with their game ideas and graphic skills—certainly a site to visit now and again to see what is happening.

FIGURE 20.9 The Daily Click Web site. ©Daily Click. Reprinted with permission.

Click Convention

Every year, a group of dedicated developers gets together and shows what they have been working on (Figure 20.10). There have been four conventions so far—three near London in the UK, and one in Paris, France. Users have traveled from all around the world to come to this user event, from countries such as Australia, the United States, and parts of Europe. Check out the Web site for when the next event will happen and what is going to be shown. Clickteam staff and developers have also been present at these events, showing off the latest developments and product betas. You can find out what is in development and what exciting new products you might be using in the future. You will also get to meet like-minded individuals who are interested in making games, so it's a great place to make new friends and even get people to help you answer those difficult development questions. If the event is too far for you to travel to, keep an eye on the Web site, as information and photos of the event are posted there.

FIGURE 20.10 Click Convention Web site. *www.clickconvention.com.*

Retro Web Sites

Retro Remakes

One of the most popular retro Web sites currently available is this site (Figure 20.11). Many game developers make remakes of games for the PC platform and then upload them so you can download and play. Retro Remakes also holds a yearly competition that brings in even more games to their database, which means that you can enter to win thousands of dollars in prizes. You might not be familiar with some of the games mentioned, but it still is a very useful Web site if you want to get the look and feel of retro games.

Ovine by Design

A favorite Web site for the hobbyist game creator is Ovine.net (Figure 20.12). Ovine is a small game-making team that designs games and remakes in their spare time. They seem to be able to make games at a phenomenal rate, and there is usually something new every month or two. Use this Web site to see how things should be done, and it's a great Web site to get some ideas. The thing that sets these people apart from many of the others on the Internet is that they contact the original authors of the programs to see if it is okay to remake them. Many developers just go ahead and make them anyway, so it's refreshing to see developers go out of their way to get permission.

FIGURE 20.11   Retro Remakes Web site. *www.retroremakes.com/.* ©RetroRemakes.com. Reprinted with permission.

Retro Gamer Magazine

Many magazines now realize that retro is back in fashion and have small sections within their issues, but one UK publisher decided to go all the way and make their own magazine, called *Retro Gamer* (Figure 20.13). The magazine started with a bi-monthly release, and due to the success of the first issue (which is no longer available, but can fetch up to $80 on eBay), they reduced the time between issue dates. The magazine is now a monthly release and has a wide range of articles and details about games from the past, so if you're looking for inspiration or ideas, try to get a copy of this magazine. Although it is an UK magazine, international delivery is available with additional cost for postage.

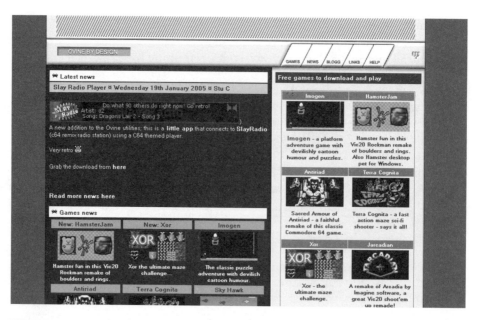

FIGURE 20.12   Ovine by Design Web site. *www.ovine.net*. ©Ovine by design. Reprinted with permission.

FIGURE 20.13   Retro Gamer Web site. *www.livepublishing.co.uk/retro*. ©Live Publishing. Reprinted with persmission.

Other Sites

Ejay

www.ejay.com

Want to make your own music for your games, but don't have a musical bone in your body? What if you cannot play an instrument or just don't know where to start? Ejay is a very popular music creator, and best of all, the songs you create with it are royalty free. Containing around 4000 royalty-free samples, Ejay lets you combine them to make musical scores using a simple yet very effective graphical interface. You can then save your masterpiece into a standard format, which you can then import into TGF2. Although some of the tunes can sound similar, Ejay does allow you to download more samples or import your own so you can make them unique.

Gamasutra

http://gamasutra.com/

Gamasutra is one of the leading game developer news Web sites, with jobs, articles, and whitepapers. If you register with the site, you can also post your résumé, look for jobs in the games industry, and find more detailed information about the concepts and technology used in the day-to-day development of games. If you are new to the games industry or just looking for more information, this is a good Web site to visit. The site also lists a calendar of events of conferences and exhibitions, so you can find out if there are any in your area.

Macromedia Captivate®

www.macromedia.com/software/captivate/

If you want to make videos of your software, demos, or just something to promote them, Captivate is an excellent product to try. Captivate records mouse movements and screen actions into a file (executable or Flash file), which you can then configure as a trailer, training tool, or interactive presentation.

Turbo Squid

www.turbosquid.com/

If you are great at game design but not very artistic, you have a problem if you are the only person involved in your game creation. Over the last few years, a number of Web sites have appeared to offer music, graphical, and product help—and Turbo Squid is one of the best. Prices for models, images, and music vary, but there is a large collection, so you should be able to find something you can use.

SUMMARY

There are many user sites available for TGF2 and MMF2, and you should take some time to search for them on the Internet and see which ones you like best. Not all sites will suit your taste and needs, but you might be surprised at what you can find. Make sure you take some time when you purchase any product to read the help files and try the tutorials so you can get into making games quicker. Above all, have fun making games.

About the CD-ROM

The companion CD-ROM contains everything you need to make all of the games discussed in this book. Additional applications needed for the "distribution and packaging" chapters are also included. You will need a computer that can run Windows 95 or better with a CD-ROM drive, a sound card, and a mouse.

DEMOS

The Games Factory (*www.clickteam.com*)

The filename for this application is TGF2SETUP.EXE and is located in the Demos folder.

Minimum System Requirements:

- Windows 95 with IE 4.0+ / Windows 98 / Windows NT4 SP3+ / 2000 / XPZ Pentium
- 32 MB with Windows 9x, 64 Mb with Windows NT, 128 Mb with 2000 and XP.
- CD-ROM drive
- Graphic card with 8 MB+ memory
- 50-100 MB Free Hard disk space
  Recommended:
- Windows 98 or Windows 2000 / XP
- Pentium 4
- Direct X 9.0
- 64 MB RAM with Windows 98, or 256 MB RAM with Windows 2000 / XP
- CD-ROM
- 3D accelerated graphic card with 32+ MB memory

- Sound card
- 100 - 200 MB free hard disk space

Install Creator (*www.clickteam.com*)

Install Creator is located in the Demos folder and the file name is ICINST.EXE.

- Windows 95 OSR-2 / 98 / ME / NT4 / 2000 / XP / or above, with Internet Explorer 4 or above installed
- 32 MB RAM
- Hard disk with 4 MB of free disk space
  For the install programs created with Install Creator
- Windows 95 / 98 / ME / NT4 / 2000 / XP / or above
- 16 MB RAM

Patch Maker (*www.clickteam.com*)

Patch Maker is located in the Demos folder and the filename is PMUS12rf.exe. The system requirements for Patch Maker are the same as for Install Creator.

FOLDERS

There are a number of folders on the CD-ROM that contain important files for use within this book, as well as additional information the reader will find useful.

Color Figures: Contains color versions of every Figure in the book.

Fullsource: The full source code to every game discussed in this book so you can take a look at completed versions.

Game1: Files for the game The Lab.

Game2: Files for the game Amazing Fighter Pilot.

Game3: Files for the game Robin Hood.

Retro: Files for the game Alien Invaders.

Demos: Location of the demo files that you can install.

GameExe: Final built versions of each of the games in this book.

Index